VOLUME 432
JULY 1977

THE ANNALS

of The American Academy *of* Political
and Social Science

RICHARD D. LAMBERT, *Editor*

ALAN W. HESTON, *Assistant Editor*

AFRICA IN TRANSITION

77-2179

Special Editor of This Volume

MARVIN E. WOLFGANG

President
American Academy of Political and Social Science
Professor of Sociology
University of Pennsylvania
Philadelphia, Pennsylvania

PHILADELPHIA

Library of Congress Card Number 77-000183

The articles appearing in The Annals are indexed in the *Reader's Guide to Periodical Literature,* the *Book Review Index,* the *Public Affairs Information Service Bulletin, Social Sciences Index,* and *Current Contents: Behavioral, Social, Management Sciences* and *Combined Retrospective Index Sets.* They are also abstracted and indexed in *ABC Pol Sci, Historical Abstracts, United States Political Science Documents, Abstracts for Social Workers, International Political Science Abstracts* and/or *America: History and Life.*

International Standard Book Numbers (ISBN)

ISBN 0-87761-217-x, vol. 432, 1977; paper—$4.00
ISBN 0-87761-216-1, vol. 432, 1977; cloth—$5.00

Issued bimonthly by The American Academy of Political and Social Science at 3937 Chestnut St., Philadelphia, Pennsylvania 19104. Cost per year: $15.00 paperbound; $20.00 clothbound. Add $1.50 to above rates for membership outside U.S.A. Second-class postage paid at Philadelphia and at additional mailing offices.

Claims for undelivered copies must be made within the month following the regular month of publication. The publisher will supply missing copies when losses have been sustained in transit and when the reserve stock will permit.

Editorial and Business Offices, 3937 Chestnut Street, Philadelphia, Pennsylvania 19104.

CONTENTS

BOOK DEPARTMENT PAGE

INTERNATIONAL RELATIONS AND POLITICS

AFRICA, ASIA, AND LATIN AMERICA

EUROPE

UNITED STATES

SOCIOLOGY

ECONOMICS

PREFACE

Last year was the Bicentennial of the United States, and the Academy celebrated by having a special Bicentennial conference on the Constitution. We called that conference "The Revolution, the Constitution, and America's Third Century." In conformity with our alternating domestic and international themes for our annual meetings, this year we have taken as our topic "Africa in Transition."

Every society, all life, is in a state of transition. Nothing, or relatively little, is stable. We move from birth to death, from being young to old, and if there is any merit in accepting the theory that society has an organic parallelism to the human, there is a birth and decay of civilizations. There are changes, evolutions, and revolutions that occur.

It is true that all societies are in some state of transition, but we have used African transition as our theme because there are tremendously dramatic changes occurring in that massive continent. There is movement from colonialism to independence; there is movement of populations from rural to urban communities, civil societies, to civilization. There is a transition in almost all social institutions of humanity in Africa: the family, education, criminal justice systems, economic and political systems. Africa today represents more of a state of radical and dramatic transition than any other continent in the world. This is why we feel justified in speaking about African transition as our theme.

There is turbulence in the shifting of political systems; there are totalitarian and democratic regimes. There are monumental economic changes occurring with increasing productivity in some places and amazing excessive importation of goods in others. There are educational changes; there is uprooting of families; there is an increase in crime; there are transitions of the elites, the intelligentsia, and the workers. Tribal groups are being reformed as local political entities. Food and population distributions are significantly altered as previously colonial-ruled groups become self-determiners of their fate.

The blacks have emerged as a racial group, pure and mixed, as significant members of the human race in a world of men and the world of politics. Cuba, Russia, and China vie with Israel, the United States, and Western Europe for allegiances and alliances in that continent. Dominance is replaced by persuasion, political hegemony is substituted by economic bartering. Africa has said adieu to white supremacy and is now entering the arena of economic and political tradeoffs for its own advantage. No longer the home of the white hunter, the upper class safaris, Africa is black resurrection demanding to be recognized for its pluralism and its search for unification.

There have been many significant developments on many fronts in Africa. They are placed before us almost every day in the press. There are important comments commanding world attention that are being made regularly by our representative to the United Nations. Referring recently to Nigeria's effort to mediate between Zaire and Angola to resolve the problem caused by the Katangan invasion, Mr. Andrew Young made a dramatic statement: "I say, let the Africans settle it. Our best policy is to encourage the Africans themselves to settle it."

It is clearly impossible for the Academy to cover all aspects of African transition. What we have done is to provide speakers and papers on a few important selected features. I hope the members and readers of this issue agree that our selection has been effective. We begin with population problems, move to agriculture, urban problems, crime, African unity, cultural transitions, and the role of China.

One of the more interesting comments about Africa appeared recently in the *New York Times* (April 6, 1977) by C. L. Sulzberger. "Today," he said,

the whites govern 87 percent of that hugh land [South Africa]. The plan now is to reduce that proportion only by a patchwork quilt of black "homelands" incapable of surviving alone. The obvious goal to work for is a set of "defensible borders" for South Africa, which concentrate the white minority in a far smaller area and relinquish what remains to black rule.

Statements of this sort are dramatic, especially in contrast to what was being said officially only five or ten years ago. Thus it is that our annual meeting was particularly enhanced by having as our principal speaker an authority on the United States' relations to Southern Africa, Mr. William Schaufele, Assistant Secretary of State for African Affairs.

In 1964 the annual meeting of the Academy was devoted to the topic "Africa in Motion." For anyone who wishes to make a comparison between the July 1964 issue and this one, clear differences in the political, economic, and general social conditions in Africa can be observed. Africa today is not simply beginning to stir, it is truly changing its identity and its relations with the rest of the world.

MARVIN E. WOLFGANG

ANNALS, AAPSS, **432**, July 1977

Trends and Prospects of Population in Tropical Africa

By ETIENNE VAN DE WALLE

ABSTRACT: Despite the uncertainty of the available statistics, it can be said that Tropical Africa remains the region of the world with the highest fertility and mortality. Population growth is substantial, and it often takes place in vulnerable ecosystems that are not suited to large populations. The Sahel and its problems of irregular rainfall illustrate the unsuitability of much of the continent for anything but bare survival. Relocation of population, some of it to cities, is inevitable; but intensified agriculture holds the key to the well-being of the increased number of people.

Etienne van de Walle is Director of the Population Studies Center and Chairman of the Graduate Group in Demography at the University of Pennsylvania. He has an LL.D. and a Ph.D. degree in demography from the University of Louvain. His work includes (with W. Brass et al.) The Demography of Tropical, Africa, The Female Population of France in the 19th Century, and articles on historical demography and the population of Africa.

1

OUR knowledge of African populations remains full of uncertainties. Not only are the official statistics pitifully inadequate; the diversity of local and regional situations is so great that almost nothing significant can be said that would apply to "the population of Africa." The present remarks will be restricted to continental, Tropical Africa, excluding the North African region and the Republic of South Africa. Even after these exclusions, the contrasts are so large as to defy generalizations: contrasts between savannah and forest, plains and highlands, rich coastal regions and drought-stricken Sahel, rural and urban areas, and, within rural Africa, between cash crop areas, resettlement schemes and subsistence agriculture where the main resource may be in seasonal migration. Each of these categories encompasses fascinating differentials in population characteristics and trends, on which too little information exists. Superimposed on the natural and economic regions are the ethnic and linguistic groupings. And finally, the diversity of administrative traditions inherited from colonial systems results in statistical by-products of different types, which further complicates the task of the analyst.

It has often been said that colonial empires imposed national boundaries that made little sense. In demographic terms, the fragmentation of Africa is best illustrated by estimates of population size.[1] Even leaving out minuscule island territories, there were, in 1974, 8 countries with less than 1 million inhabitants and 17 more with less than 5 million. There were only 7 countries (out of 40) with more than 10 million inhabitants.

There remained, moreover, considerable doubt concerning the exact size of many countries' populations. It is not uncommon that a census will enumerate 20 or 30 percent more people than was expected —either because the previous estimate was grossly inaccurate or because the census itself was inflated. The three giants in Tropical Africa— Nigeria with its official 61 million, Ethiopia with 27, and Zaire with 24—may well actually have markedly different totals. The political interests at stake in determining regional populations for Nigeria were such that overenumeration appears to have resulted, and the cause of accurate measurement may be jeopardized for some time in that country. In Zaire, which witnessed rather considerable economic and political upheaval, the population is reputed to have almost doubled in 20 years—a rather unlikely result derived from administrative estimates with untrustworthy bases. Finally, a real census has never been taken in Ethiopia. And similar problems exist in smaller countries as well.

The uncertainty is not limited to population size or distribution. There is no vital registration system in the area under review that even remotely approaches completeness. Estimates of fertility, mortality, and population growth are based on a combination of more or less reliable surveys taken at different dates, on indirect procedures and analytical techniques based on census results, and on models. The complexities of measurement, the rich reality of situations which underlies the differentials, have made Africa into an interesting demographic laboratory—however frus-

1. These data for 1974 are taken from the United Nations' *Demographic Yearbook*, 1974.

trating at times for those in search of precise answers and accurate facts.

POPULATION GROWTH

If we must generalize, it is safe enough to say that sub-Saharan Africa is the world region with the highest and least rapidly changing levels of fertility and mortality. The death rate remains particularly high. With a few exceptions, the continent has not seen the spectacular progress of public health that has brought the expectation of life in many countries of Asia and Latin America close to the European and North American levels. Although the level of mortality is particularly difficult to evaluate in Africa, most estimates place expectation of life at birth at 40 years or less compared to 70 years or more in Western countries. National and international agencies have campaigned against certain of the infectious diseases and in some instances have achieved spectacular successes. Thus, smallpox seems very close to eradication. But the main killer, malaria, is still at large.

The diseases that account for a majority of all deaths (as they did in Europe prior to its public health revolution) are childhood diseases and intestinal and pulmonary complications, which depend in part on hygiene and diet and cannot be prevented without substantial changes in the way of life and the infrastructure. There are also some diseases, such as sleeping sickness and river blindness, which render large tracks of land unfit for human habitation. Morbidity contributes to poor physical performance, and the blessings of health and long life bring with them substantial economic benefits. This is fully acknow-

ledged by all governments, and the death rate should continue to decrease in the future. It will require great efforts and cost to increase the capabilities of public health services, to train and equip medical personnel, to make the environment more hospitable and maintain peace and order, and, above all, to curb unhealthy practices and poor nutrition.

A paradox of public health is that substantial portions of Central Africa seem to be affected by pathologically low fertility—possibly because of venereal diseases—among populations that greatly value high reproduction. In Gabon, the Cameroons, in parts of Zaire, and elsewhere it is possible that health campaigns will result in higher fertility. Even so, the birth rate in Tropical Africa remains uncommonly high, typically in the high forties (births per 1,000 persons— as a reference, the birth rate in the United States is now close to 15 births per 1,000). Nowhere is fertility regulated to any large extent by the conscious desire of couples, although there are various social mechanisms, such as marriage customs and intercourse taboos, that tend to cause rather large differentials in fertility from one group to another. Family-planning programs have made little headway in general. There are well attended clinics here and there in the urban areas, and some governments have demonstrated interest in reducing the national rate of growth and alleviating the burden of multiple pregnancies and large families for the health of mothers and children. In general, however, family-planning programs are a subject of low priority. In a recent list of government positions on population growth and family planning, only four

Tropical African countries were said to have official policies to reduce the population growth rate: Botswana, Ghana, Kenya, and Mauritius. Eleven other countries had expressed official support of family-planning activities "for other than demographic reasons," that is, mostly for reasons of health or as a human right. Some countries in this category were, nevertheless, basically pronatalist and in favor of population growth. The other countries in the region had no stated position or were prohibiting the dissemination of family-planning services and information.[2]

With the slowly declining mortality and the persistently high fertility, the prospects of population growth are considerable. States are committed to reducing the death rate, and even if they unqualifiedly had decided to strive to reduce the birth rate, the dynamics of population are such that African nations have no real policy choice concerning their growth in the near future. The rate of natural increase has been estimated at 2.8 percent by United Nations statisticians, and this is enough to double the population by the beginning of the next century. Many African politicians and social scientists claim that the continent is underpopulated. The test of this proposition is in the future, as the great increases in number will have to find their place either in the modernizing economies (where unemployment threatens) or in the over-burdened subsistence agriculture.

It is often assumed today that the pressure of numbers on limited resources leads inevitably to catas-trophe. The Malthusian view is that human populations are adjusted to the fixed amount of resources available to them; imbalance resulting from natural increase is called over-population, and it soon leads to starvation and high mortality. I shall argue here that the reality is more complex. But recent events appear on the surface to have confirmed the views of the doomsday prophets. The drought in Sahelian Africa was seen by many as a typical Malthusian crisis brought about by increasing numbers and a forewarning of larger problems in the future. Large loss of life is represented as nature's mechanism for bringing the population back to the capacity of the land. A careful look at the Sahel's drought, however, leads to very different conclusions. What will follow is borrowed from the most thorough discussion of the drought and its demographic implications by the best specialist of African population, John C. Caldwell.[3] At the time of the drought, Caldwell devoted several research trips to the stricken area.

THE SAHEL DROUGHT

The term Sahel refers to a strip of dry grassland, some 200 miles wide, that provides a transition between the Sahara desert and the thicker vegetation cover toward the south. It is an area of fierce sunlight and spare rainfall, where man scrapes a living with exceptional difficulty even under normal climatic conditions. The main activity is nomadic pastoralism. In the early 1970s, the monsoon rains failed several years in a row; this culminated in a

2. Dorothy Nortman and Ellen Hofstatter, *Population and Family Planning Programs: A Factbook*. Reports on Population/Family Planning, The Population Council, 1976.

3. John C. Caldwell, *the Sahelian Drought and Its Demographic Implications*, Overseas Liaison Committee, American Council on Education, paper no. 8, December 1975.

massive disruption of living conditions in 1972 and 1973. Since then, rainfall seems to have returned to normal. The Sahel countries are Senegal, Mauritania, Mali, Upper Volta, Niger, and Chad, although the largest part of the population of these countries lives outside of the Sahel proper. The zone affected by the drought was not limited to the Sahel, but distress was felt far and wide in a belt of shifting cultivation stretching to the south and to the east into the Sudan and Ethiopia, where the provinces of Wollo and Tigre were much affected.

Even when the rains come at their appointed time with the customary abundance (which in other parts of the world would be sparcity) the region sustains some of the lowest levels of living reached anywhere. Senegal and Mauritania, thanks respectively to good cash crops and mineral wealth, have raised incomes and enjoy reasonable prospects of economic development. But the landlocked countries on the verge of the desert have a per capita income under $100. The population is almost exclusively engaged in subsistence production. They live much as their ancestors did, and have little prospect of rapidly improving their lot, except by migrating to better climes and changing the traditional way of life. Through skillful adaptation to an extraordinarily difficult environment, survival has been possible, but not prosperity by our standards. Modern technology has no obvious solutions to substitute for the nomadic life of herdsmen who follow their cattle where the grass grows. The ecology of the region is fragile, so that overgrazing or shifting cultivation without sufficient fallow would lead to permanent damage to the land. Drought is a recurrent feature of the area,

even though this generation seems to have benefited from a bountiful (by their standards) climatic spell. Oral traditions recount the far graver drought of 1913, with its appalling losses of human life and large-scale destruction of the herds.

Population growth in the area has probably been slow but sustained since at least the beginning of the century; there may have been an acceleration since the Second World War due to the decline of mortality. Caldwell estimates the expectation of life "in a normal year" at under 35 years, infant mortality under one year at above 250 deaths per 1,000 births, and the crude death rate at above 40 deaths per 1,000 persons. With a birth rate at 45 (births per 1,000 persons), this would leave one-half of a percent growth per year.[4] The Sahel is an area of very low overall population density, and the number of its inhabitants may reach 2.5 million. Of course many more people were affected by the drought as well. The Sahel countries number 25 million.

One of the most surprising features of the recent crisis is that it does not seem to have resulted in exceptional loss of life or even to greatly increased malnutrition. This may sound almost shocking to the readers of newspaper stories in the United States. It should be remembered, perhaps, that these stories—and the pictures that accompanied them—originated mostly in the refugee camps of the south rather than in the Sahel region itself. Refugee camps were collecting the most destitute of the nomads and were exposing them, often for the first time, to contagious diseases from which the low densities of their usual environment had protected

4. Ibid., p. 9.

them. Caldwell concludes that the available evidence indicates no measurable increase of mortality. The conclusion is partly due to the inadequacy of our instruments of measure, in the absence of a reliable statistical system. Normal mortality is already high, although impossible to evaluate with precision; for lack of a baseline, exceptional mortality cannot be estimated. "The figures in the newspaper headlines were figments of the imagination, and many apparently serious reports were little better."[5]

The point should not be misunderstood. The drought was immensely distressing; it caused pain and sickness; it broke up households and herds; and it forced many to sell treasured articles. But it did not halt population growth. It is doubtful whether deaths in the Sahelian countries during the 1970–74 period numbered more than a quarter of a million above what would otherwise have occurred. This number would have been sufficient to have raised the death rate by 2½ points or perhaps to have lowered the rate of natural increase by one-sixth, from possibly 1½ to 1¼ percent per annum.[6]

To a demographer, it is hardly surprising that reliable statistics could not be collected on the demographic consequences of such an overwhelmingly visible cataclysm, because statistics are a luxury that only developed countries can afford. It comes as a surprise, however, that other disciplines were also unable to measure the extent of the phenomenon and its true human dimensions. Several nutritional and medical survey teams were at work in the Sahel in 1973, and their findings are so unexpected that they deserve to be quoted at length. These findings refer to both

the nomadic and the sedentary population of the provinces in Upper Volta and Mali that were most affected by the drought in July and August of 1973, that is, during the period when the least food was available (even in normal times, these are the months of the "hungry season" just before the new crops become available).

The British medical team in northern Upper Volta reported that the nutritional levels found there were similar to those found at different times and places elsewhere in tropical Africa [Seaman, Holt, Rivers and Murlis, 1973, p. 777], while the American group in Mali observed, "Villages visited in the Nioro and Nava area (both declared disaster areas by the Malian government) showed insignificant rates of undernutrition among the child population" [Center for Disease Control, 1973, p. 28].[7]

The tests for malnutrition were of the kind that can be rapidly administered to large numbers of people. For instance, the teams from the Atlanta Center for Disease Control examined 3,500 children and computed for each the ratio of weight to height—the so-called Stuart-Meredith Standard. They found on that basis that 7 percent of the sedentary children and 17 percent of the nomad children were severely malnourished. The corresponding results in Upper Volta, for sedentaries and nomads, were 9 and 10 percent, respectively. Such proportions, of course, would be appalling in the United States; but they are not remarkable in an area of constant hardship and abysmally low expectation of life. The outward signs of malnutrition are often the result of infectious diseases. Children are the most vulnerable group, and the symptoms

5. Ibid., p. 26.
6. Ibid., p. 48.

7. Ibid., p. 11.

were greatly reduced at older ages. In observing the phenomenon at first hand, Caldwell "became convinced that the drought publicity hid the vital truth. . . . The real lesson was not how easily man succumbed to the drought, but how tenacious he was in managing his survival."[8]

The affected area had periodically known such conditions for many millenia, and adaptive mechanisms are built into the mode of life. Pastoral nomadism itself is a technique designed to extract a living from the inhospitable environment. Edible plants and wild animals, including insects, are known for their food value, even though they are little used in normal times. The cattle themselves, around which the life of the nomads revolves, constitute a moving supply of food. Meat and dairy products normally serve as trade items to obtain cash, and they are exchanged for grain from the sedentary farmers. The coastal cities and the cash crop areas in the south, where cattle cannot thrive because of the sleeping sickness, get much of their meat from the Sahel nomads. In case of famine, however, they will eat their animals themselves. This is a last resort, because the old way of life must disappear if the survival of the herds is jeopardized.

Nomadism involves low densities, large territories, and constant movement. The normal adaptation to the drought was but an extension of the usual behavior of the nomads. The herd is constantly on the move, in search of grass. Even when the monsoon has failed overall, there is tremendous variability in local conditions. Local showers occur, and the cattle move on in search of microclimates where the rainfall has been better and the water holes have not dried up. In the process, the range of migration increases. The herds go further and further south, through areas which sleeping sickness usually renders unsafe for the cattle— but the tsetse fly itself cannot live without a certain humidity. The nomads push on, until they reach areas where the herd can graze. If most of the cattle had died and been eaten in the process, they continue until they reach the cities. "In late 1973, a large Malian Tuareg group of men, women and children arrived in Ibadan in Southern Nigeria and camped (and traded) around Mapo Hall on the top of Mapo Hill, the traditional center of the city."[9]

An additional factor differentiates the present from the past and alleviates the potential human losses to famine and malnutrition. This is the increased effectiveness of states and the reaction of the international community to human suffering. Outside relief arrived surprisingly late in places, because it had taken time to gain awareness of the emergency; but the reaction was vigorous after the world had been alerted to the drought. By 1973, the food was pouring in. Road systems, trucks, airlifts all played their part. This would have been utterly inconceivable during the drought of 1913 which, although more severe, was not heard of outside of the region. Famines, as always, are caused by a lack or a disruption of transportation, not by a shortage of food on the world market.

The refugee camps focused some of the horror of the existing conditions, and press agency photographers had a field day picturing pathetic children and emaciated mothers. But the camps were the centers where the relief was dis-

8. Ibid., p. 26.

9. Ibid., p. 27.

tributed. They attracted the most needy, and the most destitute migrants were left behind in the camps as the nomads moved on.

Mostly they were the targets of migration chosen deliberately by nomads as offering the best option available. If they had not been established there would undoubtedly have been more death and greater misery, but the greater majority of those who chose to stay in the camps would otherwise have continued south. Indeed by the time they had reached the camps the harshest areas were already behind them. In many cases the men and older boys did continue south (or had already gone there) leaving the women, young children and people in the camps.[10]

As Caldwell puts it: "The major demographic response to the drought had not been death but migration."[11] Some of the moves were temporary, and their function was to provide an adjustment to recurrent problems. Some were durable, but inspired by an old logic, an old flexibility. In much of sub-Saharan Africa, the men move out during the dry season and come back when the planting season starts. The purpose is double: to relieve food supplies at home by "eating away"; and to use the period of seasonal unemployment to secure cash and goods unavailable at home. In areas of shifting cultivation, too, the attachment to one home or one piece of land, which is such an important part of the cultural legacy of the West, does not elicit the same response. Most significant for the future, perhaps, is that migratory movements may become irreversible. Caldwell observes that many of the streams of migration that arose from the drought were increasingly directed toward the towns and that

a large number of refugees were settling in a new life, perhaps permanently. "Nomads, like food gatherers and hunters in other parts of the world, are often happier, if forced, to take the leap from their kind of life to urban employment than to farming, which is a far more specialized way of life with a mystique all of its own."[12] Thus, for example, Tuaregs appeared on the employment market of the large coastal cities as an aftermath of the drought; they were appreciated as night watchmen because of their reputation as fierce warriors from the desert.

THE PROSPECTS

In the twentieth century, whether we like it or not, the prospects for nomadic pastoralism are not good. The ancestral way of life, at its best, afforded only the most primitive living conditions. Increases in the number of people and of heads of cattle, as a result of the gains of modern medicine and veterinary science, may have led to overgrazing and new encroachments of the desert on what used to be pastoral land. Despite efforts at irrigating and stabilizing agriculture, it is unlikely that the dry savannah lands of Africa will ever successfully accommodate large densities.

The lesson of the Sahel, however, is not that overpopulation threatens to cause a return to some Malthusian equilibrium through the death of the excessive numbers. Mortality is not a condition that is produced automatically by the unsatisfactory functioning of an economic or an ecological system. It is caused by exogenous accidents—by unfavorable climatic spells, the disorganization of trans-

10. Ibid., p. 28.
11. Ibid., p. 13.

12. Ibid., p. 29.

portation and civil services in warfare, the prevalence of disease. And it is relieved by external factors — organization and transportation, migration to more favorably endowed regions, the improvement of the medical delivery system.

Historically, economic development has always gone together with a great deal of population growth; overpopulation is a term that is largely synonymous with economic stagnation, and its cure is investment and intensive labor. The population of Tropical Africa is growing, and has been doing so for some time. The main question raised by this growth is not whether it will stop soon—the answer to that would be that the numbers will increase greatly before fertility declines and natural increase stabilizes. The main question is how the population will be accommodated and what the social costs of the changes brought about by growth will be.

Elsewhere in the world, development has implied vast relocations of people whose way of life, however idealized it has been by their descendants, was harsh and exhausting. Communication has broken the isolates open, and the competition of less severe, better-rewarded lifestyles led to the abandonment of rural areas where people had once led a rustic, self-reliant life. In Africa, too, a continent characterized by the severity of the physical environment and the isolation of cultures inherent in the enormous distances, the improvement of communications and the unequal development of certain regions is leading to enormous shifts of population. Africa is in the midst of an urban revolution; the expansion of the cities' population has been spectacular in recent years, in large part because of the pressure of population in the rural areas.

Though social and economic developments in the towns have been considerable the revolution in urban growth has not been complemented by a comparable revolution in economic development. As a result economic and social resources are under pressure and an industrial revolution of sufficient proportions to be able to meet further increased demand on these resources is unlikely in the foreseeable future. There is an urgent need to at least reduce the rate of urban growth through some reduction in the rate and volume of movement from the rural areas.[13]

This implies rural development rather than the haphazard accumulation of population that has occurred on the land. Growth is not only destructive of former social relations and institutional arrangements, it is also a threat to the fragile ecosystems of the tropics. The old adaptations to the environment, based on long fallows and shifting land use and on labor saving, extensive methods of cultivation, were not designed for populations that double their numbers every 25 years. In spite of the low densities, the unmodified cultivation systems of many regions of Africa may be approaching the limit where land deteriorates and loss of fertility sets in. In the West, the economic take-off of the last two centuries was accompanied by a large demand for labor and massive rural depopulation. The challenge of population growth in Africa will have to be met, not by large-scale capital investment in industrial equipment and urban facilities along the Western model, but by smallholder agriculture.

13. R. Mansell Prothero, "Population Mobility and Rural-Urban Systems in Contemporary Africa," working paper no. 30, African Population Mobility Project, 1976, p. 13.

* * *

QUESTIONS AND ANSWERS

Q: You concentrated on the nomadic tribes in the Sahel region, which are part of a chain of differentiated agriculture economies from nomadism to shifting cultivation, transhuman cultivation, and then the small and large holder agriculture. Would you make the same kinds of rough generalizations about the more settled, more densely populated agriculture regions of Africa? Is the same kind of adaptability to economic tragedy also evident in other areas?

A (van de Walle): The traditional adaptation mechanism to population in Africa has been shortening the fallow period. If the local cultivation system was such that fallow would last for 10 to 20 years before people came back to a piece of land, it obviously would be an enormous reservoir of available land. If you restrict the fallow period too much without supplementing the nutrition of the land by adding fertilizers, then there is the danger that the land is going to lose its texture and deteriorate. The mechanism that has often worked is using crops that were tolerant of poor land. One of these crops is casaba. It has been spreading over many parts of Africa. It is tolerant of very poor land, but once again there is a cost. The hypothesis suggested by Esther Boserup, who wrote on the effects of population growth on the social system, is that the density of population will lead to a more intensive use of cultivation. This occurs at the cost of investing more human labor on the land. The African

population has been very reluctant to lend itself to this kind of agriculture.

Q: Here in the United States, we are victims of chemical pollution in food. My ignorance about Africa gives me the feeling that those people are not victimized by manufacturers who seek a profit at the expense of the health of the people. Would you comment on that?

A (van de Walle): First of all I want to resist the temptation to believe that Africa is a vast green continent. As far as the pollution of food, I believe that the problems are different. The vast majority of the people do not have the luxury of the United States to worry about the quality of their food. I remember once when I was in one major African city, there was a DDT truck going through the streets, surrounded by an enormous white cloud. Of course, this was a direct threat to the health of these people, but the local support was so overwhelming for DDT and the elimination of flies and mosquitoes that there were hundreds of children running behind the truck cheering it on.

Q: Are we in the United States today consuming food which ought to be eaten by some of the people in Africa?

A (van de Walle): The answer to that is that there is very little trade in food occurring, at least in grain. Of course deficient food is hard to narrow down. If coffee is food, then we are importing food from Africa. There is some export of food to the coastal areas and the big cities, but in general it is not a very substantial amount. Most of the cultures can be supported at this time by their own agriculture.

Smallholder Agriculture in Africa Constraints and Potential

By K. G. V. KRISHNA

ABSTRACT: Peasant farming is the backbone of the African rural economy. In the predominantly agrarian societies of Africa, smallholder farming plays a major role in producing food for both rural and urban populations and in providing incomes, employment, and export earnings. However, these farmers have received a disproportionately small amount of available developmental resources. Few people in Africa live in wholly subsistence economies. Peasant farmers are steadily increasing their share of marketed output and, in the process have belied the myth that rural societies are stagnant. Extending effective support to widely dispersed farming populations requires financial and manpower resources on a scale which few African countries can afford. Few technical packages exist, extension services are scanty, and marketing and credit services are deficient. These are formidable problems the resolution of which will take much time, effort, and resources. But the potential for improvement is so considerable, and the social implications so immense, the national agricultural policies should articulate the needs of smallholders far better than they have so far. Given proven and comprehensible technical packages and advice, and attractive prices for their products, peasant farmers have shown a capacity to increase their contribution to the economy in a quick and efficient manner.

K. G. V. Krishna has been a World Bank Staff member since 1966 and is presently Deputy Division Chief of General Agriculture, Eastern Africa Projects Department. From 1956–66 he was a Lecturer at the University College, Nairobi, Kenya, and prior to that he served as Visiting Lecturer at Syracuse University, in the Department of Economics, and Lecturer at Gai Hind University College, Bombay, India.

SMALLHOLDER or peasant farming is the backbone of the African rural economy. It concerns the manner in which about 280 million people in sub-Saharan rural Africa, 50–55 million families, earn their living from year to year. The overwhelming majority of these people (about 85–90 percent of the total population of this area) are peasant farmers. Their activities—crop production and livestock herding—play a major role in feeding the rural and urban populations, acting as the main source of employment and earnings, and providing the principal basis of exports and often of government revenues as well. Because of the quiet and unobtrusive way in which these activities take place from year to year, the role of peasant farmers is seldom the focus of much attention and their activities are more or less taken for granted. What is even less apparent is that the very significant contribution of peasant farmers to the economy often takes place within a framework of primitive techniques, low levels of productivity, and much uncertainty concerning production levels attained from one crop season to the other. More than anything else, this situation reflects the fact that the majority of the rural population has tended to receive only a meager share of the resources available for development and that it has largely been ignored in the plans and programs which are periodically formulated in their capitals.

Contrary to popular belief, there are no wholly subsistence economies in Africa in the sense of people leading self-contained lives. In fact, living in a wholly subsistence economy has, for many years, been neither feasible nor practical in most countries since the breakdown of complete isolation and the steadily growing requirement to pay taxes. Having been forced initially to participate in the market economy at least to a small extent, peasant farmers have actively sought to enlarge their role both as consumers and producers, often encountering much frustration in the latter role. In fact, given the difficulties in participating actively in producing for the market, what is surprising is the extent of progress already achieved in this regard. In the few situations where governments actively sought to encourage smallholder production—either for political or socio-economic reasons—through a combination of incentives and support services, there has been an amazing degree of responsiveness from the latter, thereby belying the myth that rural societies are stagnant and fatalistic or devoid of ambition and initiative. It has been a hard struggle, however, since there continues to be much skepticism, and some ignorance, among governmental authorities with regard to the potential role of smallholder agriculture.

PAST POLICIES

The colonial period

Past policies with regard to smallholder agriculture have tended to be influenced by the number of considerations depending on whether they were formulated within the framework of colonial governments or the independent governments which succeeded them. During the colonial period, policies tended to vary as between situations where there was an active attempt to introduce expatriate capital and enterprise to develop the economies and those where the focus was on promoting market-oriented production, but strictly within the framework of traditional peasant agriculture. Policies varied further depending on whether overseas settler-farmers were to be encouraged and assisted in developing modern agriculture or whether overseas initiative would be limited to plantation companies. Where a settler element was involved, as in the highlands of Kenya, not only did it entail concessions and privileges to settlers out of proportion to their number, but it became apparent before long that there was a clear dichotomy between the role envisaged for the settlers and the potential role of traditional peasant agriculture.

This dichotomy is most vividly brought out in the experience of Kenya which had an active and influential settler community that, despite its small numbers, succeeded within a relatively short period in becoming the major source of market-oriented production, whether for exports or for the domestic market. During the period 1950–1960 for example, the large-farm sector, comprised of settler-farmers and the plantation companies, accounted for as much as 90 percent of the total marketed output. Not only were traditional farmers hopelessly ill-equipped to share in producing for the growing market, but also there were no government policies at the time which were consciously aimed at enlarging opportunities for the traditional sector comprised of millions of African peasant farmers. On the contrary, where some smallholders displayed initiative in producing cash crops —notably tea and coffee—which had been monopolized by settler-farmers, the latter put enough pressure on the government to seek a restriction of prohibition on such production, on the ground that the products of peasant farmers could

not satisfy and maintain quality standards of the export and, on occasions, even the domestic markets. The imposition of such restrictions seriously jeopardized and delayed the development of smallholder production. It was not until the late 1950s that this policy was modified and an attempt was made to promote a policy for the advancement of African smallholders in cash crop production. This policy, which was elaborated in the "Plan for the Advancement of Africans in Cash Farming" (Swynnerton Plan), began in and became a widely known success story. The plan cleared the way for significant smallholder—African—participation in market-oriented production. The share of such production which was as low as 10 percent in 1950 rose to about 30 percent in 1962, the last year before the independence of Kenya.

In some African countries where there was no expatriate settler-farmer element, overseas-based plantation companies were quite prominent. These companies, which were drawn principally from the former metropolitan powers— France, Belgium, United Kingdom —created the first modernized agricultural sectors in these countries. Their production was based on a system of obtaining low-cost land from the governments, hiring low-cost labor which ostensibly was underemployed, and combining these with foreign investment and modern technology to produce crops principally, but not exclusively, for the export market. While these companies dominated the production of certain crops—rubber, tea, coffee, and palm oil—they were not generally averse to sharing production with smallholder farmers whom they, in fact, encouraged and assisted on occasions. Their role in exemplifying market-oriented production was an important factor in stimulating smallholder participation in the market economy.

Post-independence period

Since attaining independence, many African governments have endeavored to encourage and assist large-scale participation by their nationals in all types of economic activity. As the largest sector of most African economies, agriculture has naturally been the focus of much attention and has received a substantial allocation of finance and manpower. The thrust of government policies has been twofold. In the first place, where African economies had for many years been dominated by foreign entrepreneurs, there was an understandable desire to Africanize or nationalize various enterprises as an initial step in promoting domestic enterprise. Since agriculture was in most cases—except where expatriate settler-farmers or overseas plantation companies played an important role—in the hands of native African farmers, the need here was not so much nationalization as giving an impetus to the sector so that it would begin to undergo a transformation with beneficial effects on yields and output. This was done through a combination of measures including improved and expanded extension, marketing and credit, and a better determination and improved delivery of suitable inputs. An important, although not spectacular, transformation has been achieved in the process.

Policies with regard to agricultural transformation or modernization have varied a lot among African countries. Three main types of policies may be identified in this regard. In the first place, there were those which were directed principally toward expanding the range and output of crops, but which did not reveal much preoccupation either with issues of a nationalistic nature or with considerations of equity. The main consideration behind this policy appears to have been to attain rapid progress in self-sufficiency in food or the expansion and diversification of export crops. Whether the enterprise which engineered progress was local or foreign or whether the government was actively involved or not was irrelevant for this policy.

The second policy emphasizes the importance of assigning a growing role to nationals but did not exclude a continuing role for foreign enterprise, particularly if it already existed and had performed an important role. The objective appears to have been the creation of conditions under which the participation of nationals would be phased in smoothly and in an orderly fashion while the role of non-nationals would be phased out in an equally smooth, nondisruptive manner. In both the above cases, there was no particular emphasis on expanding the role of smallholders, but only on helping them in whatever way was found feasible to participate in the market economy.

The third policy clearly aimed at the earliest possible assumption by nationals of responsibility for both food and cash crop production on the clear further assumption that large companies, large individual entrepreneurs, absentee landlords, and others who were not directly involved in agricultural activities would be speedily replaced by peasant farmers who would be the government's principal target groups.

It is perhaps premature to determine which among the three policies noted above has been the most or least successful. Moreover, any determination which is based on physical measures of progress may not stand the test of social factors, particularly the aspects relating to equity and income distribution. It is difficult to dispute the claim of the Ivory Coast that it has created the basis of an efficient agricultural system or of Kenya and Malawi that they have speedily opened up opportunities for African participation in production directed both to the domestic and export markets. It is equally difficult to prove that, despite their declared concern for smallholders, Tanzania or Somalia have really improved their lot. But these are short-term perspectives, and the experiences of the countries to date cannot be regarded as conclusive proof that any given policy has been particularly successful in raising levels of productivity and maximizing opportunities for raising living standards of large numbers of people.

LARGE-SCALE FARMING AFTER INDEPENDENCE

While the existence of large-scale farming in the pre-independence period of some African countries can be seen in retrospect in the context of expatriate companies or individual farmers, there is little rational explanation for its continuation—particularly of individual large-scale farming—in the post-independence period. Typically, many of these post-independence large farmers have been drawn from the ranks of government officials, professional politicians, and senior executives from private or parastatal organizations. Few, if any, have any legitimate claims to own land. The motivation is one of social prestige and

few have demonstrated their capability in farming. And yet, because of their influential position, they have managed to obtain for themselves a disproportionate share of the available resources, particularly credit and the agricultural services. However, because of their lack of direct involvement in agricultural operations (often resulting from their being absentee landlords), the productivity of land has suffered and has resulted in substantial economic waste, which is indefensible particularly in situations where the growing pressure of population on the soil has caused land hunger, shrinking opportunities in rural areas, and consequent exodus to the towns and cities.

THE CASE FOR AND AGAINST LARGE FARMING

In recent years, the case for and against large-scale farming has again become the subject of vigorous debate, although it should be recognized in the African context that nowhere is large farming the dominant mode of agriculture at present, nor is it likely to become dominant in the foreseeable future. Nevertheless, although large farming was either a straightforward adoption of an alien-inspired system which prevailed prior to independence or the result of the preeminent social and political position of the privileged few, some claims have been advanced in its favor. Among these are: (1) the responsiveness of large-scale farming to market opportunities, (2) its ability to keep up with, and take advantage of, improvements in farming technology, (3) the usual claims relating to economies of scale, (4) its ability to withstand fluctuations in prices, particularly of items destined for export markets, and (5) its ability to provide leadership to smaller scale producers.

However, barring the role of large international companies, there is little evidence that large-scale private or individual farming has, in fact, met the above criteria or that it has at least a potentially critical role to play. On the contrary, and again excluding plantations companies, there is evidence that large-scale farming is wasteful in terms of capital investment and managerial skills, that because of its frequent dependence on mechanized farming it promotes a pattern of development which conflicts with the prevailing resource endowment—particularly the availability of labor—and that it acts as a drain often on scarce foreign exchange resources available to the governments. Each of these factors is of vital significance for many African countries in view of the acute scarcity of precisely those items which large farming demands in substantial quantities. Moreover, the development of farming which depends on varying degrees of mechanization would, if encouraged and actively assisted, hamper the growth of rural employment, thereby causing an urban drift. It makes demands on scarce capital and even scarcer foreign exchange and adds to the burden of growing recurrent expenditures, much of it in foreign exchange, for imports of spares, fuel, and technical services. The case for large-scale mechanized farming, which was already weak prior to the steep increase in fuel prices, has since become weaker still. Its continued encouragement would, therefore, be contrary to the overall economic interests of many African economies unless its advantages could be established clearly and conclusively.

PAST POLICY TOWARD SMALLHOLDER FARMING

Despite the many disadvantages of large farming and its unsuitability to the agro-social environment of Africa, this sector has continued to receive much encouragement, often at the cost of small farming. It is well known that when the production of crops is being undertaken in the large farming sector this very fact often militates against these crops being grown by smallholders on grounds such as scale economies or sophisticated management. But the point here is not that large farming has received too much attention, but that small farming has perhaps received too little. Given the fact that small farming is by far the dominant mode of farming in Africa and, hence, it is obviously important to improve its overall performance, why do agricultural policies in many countries fail to reflect an adequate concern for smallholders? And again, assuming that there is no lack of desire on the part of governments to assist smallholders, are there any major and indeed insuperable problems in assisting them? Has it been established beyond doubt that smallholders either cannot produce certain crops at all or only produce them at such high cost that it cannot be justified in terms of its benefits? And finally, has the actual performance of smallholder agriculture—with or without assistance from the governments—been such that only negative conclusions can be drawn from it, or are there cases where it has proved to be sufficiently imaginative and adaptable as to record significant achievements? These are important questions which should have an important bearing on the scope and thrust of future policies with regard to smallholder farming in the years to come.

SMALLHOLDER AGRICULTURE— SOME FALLACIES

Lack of initiative

Among the most persistent fallacies pertaining to smallholder farming is the one that, by and large, these people are unwilling and often unable to take advantage of new technical packages, agricultural services, and innovation generally. Apart from the fact that this is without foundation, it has in it the dangerous implication—often evidenced in government policies— that assistance provided to small farmers has justification more socially and politically than strictly economically, and hence that it represents only a desirable transfer from the more to the less privileged classes. It also assumes that small farming cannot be depended upon in the realization of objectives such as greater food self-sufficiency and expansion and diversification of agricultural exports and, by implication, that large farming constitutes the main element not only of stability in agriculture, but also of its orderly growth.

Although, as noted above, much of the better publicized and documented modernization and growth of African agriculture has taken place in the organized, large-scale sector, including the private plantations, there is much (relatively much more in overall terms) that has taken place in the smallholder sector. One need only recall the role of peasant farmers who produce cocoa in Nigeria and Ghana, coffee and cotton in Uganda, and tobacco and cotton in Tanzania— just a few of the dozens of examples which may be drawn from all over Africa—to demonstrate how well and how much these people have responded to opportunities provided to them. It is to be noted, however, widespread participation by smallholders generally occurred in situations where either the governments felt, for political or socio-economic reasons, that the activities concerned should be spearheaded by small farmers or there was no initiative on the part of individual large farmers —either expatriate or local—to undertake these activities. The absence of large farmers was a significant factor insofar as the governments were not only not distracted by the belief that quick increases in production could be accomplished by encouraging large farmers or by pressures emanating from them, but also geared their policies toward assisting the smallholders in whatever way they could. The result was that smallholders responded very well to the opportunities which became available to them. In the process, production for the market was expanded, cash incomes grew, the domestic economies as a whole were strengthened, and government revenues became more firmly based.

There were, however, other situations where smallholder participation in production for the market had been artificially held back for various reasons, the principal reason being the pressure of large growers, including plantation companies, who did not relish the prospect of opening the floodgates of competition from peasant farmers. The example which most vividly brings home this point is smallholder tea production in Kenya. It was not until the mid-1950s that the Kenya government, with financial and technical assistance from the British government, established a scheme for enabling smallholders to cultivate tea. From small beginnings the scheme expanded rapidly, so that by 1963, when the country became independent, smallholder tea was already well established. Since then there has been considerable progress with the result that today over 100,000 peasant farmers grow tea, each with an average of less than one acre of tea. The scheme which is being implemented by the Kenya Tea Development Authority has been a major source of cash earnings for participants and has brought about a number of supplementary benefits, including a significant contribution to export earnings and some wage employment. The quality of smallholder tea compares favorably with that of the estates. In retrospect, there is no doubt that, in the absence of a special effort and appropriate institutional arrangements, smallholders would not have made a successful entry into tea cultivation. Given the needed encouragement, smallholders demonstrated both their responsiveness to economic opportunity and their willingness to allocate their land and labor to a new and untried activity.

High cost of servicing small farmers

It is often claimed that it is difficult to assist large numbers of smallholders because of their widely scattered location, limited numbers of government personnel, lack of suitable institutions, poor governmental organization, and the shortage of funds. These are, of course, real problems, but they are by no means overwhelming. The danger is that these problems are often used as an excuse for the rather limited efforts to assist the rural population in breaking away from their isolation and participating in the market economy, with the result that the situation is perpetuated. None of the problems noted above is insoluble in the long run if there is a firm commitment on the part of governments and remedial measures are being taken. The delay in assisting smallholders often stems not from a lack of the answers to the problems in this regard but from the elaborate solutions worked out which, in the end, exceed both the financial and manpower resources available to governments.

A further factor which often limits the efforts of governments with regard to smallholder farming is the feeling that programs designed to assist them may not be cost effective, particularly by comparison with large farming. While this may be true in some cases, failure to assist those who may now be difficult and expensive to serve would result in their always being less cost effective and hence possibly never being worthy of support. In that event, two situations could result. The first is that support to small farming may be motivated purely by political considerations, for example, by selecting an area which happens to be the constituency of an influential politician. The second is that, when schemes designed to assist smallholders are formulated, they may tend to be so overdesigned to make them foolproof that benefits accrue to only a small number of people. Some of the successful smallholder schemes are characterized by their rather limited impact in terms of the number of beneficiaries. While the success of these projects is no doubt commendable, it also serves as a reminder of the task yet to be undertaken in assisting those who have still not enjoyed the fruits of development.

The spill-over effect

The argument is sometimes advanced that the interest of smallholders is better served not by explicitly recognizing them as a target group, but by enabling them to benefit indirectly from schemes directed at those—mainly large-scale farmers—able and willing to take advantage of new opportunities. It is claimed that, as the latter break new ground, take risks, and open up markets, some opportunities will accrue to smallholders who could then be introduced into market-oriented production in a manner which minimizes risks. There are two problems with this reasoning. The first is that it implies that small farmers would be unable to make any headway except under the protective cover of the government. The second is that it makes them dependent on a spill-over effect, which may not materialize for a long time and sometimes never at all. Any assumption either that a spill-over effect would automatically occur or that its impact would be sufficient when it materialized is over-simplistic and often unrealistic.

SMALL FARMING—SOME REAL CONSTRAINTS

While the case for maximizing assistance to smallholder farming is both strong and urgent in all African countries, it is also true that much patient effort is required to prepare the ground well for this assistance to both maximize its impact and make it a steady and orderly process. What is needed is not a single dramatic gesture, but a series of modest and well-considered initiatives which reflect a long-term commitment on the part of authorities and which also recognize that there could well be initial setbacks. There is no doubt that programs aimed at providing massive assistance to smallholder agriculture face some real constraints. Some of these are examined below.

Technical packages

Perhaps the most important type of assistance to smallholders, but often not recognized as such, is the offer of technical packages which actually work under the agronomic and sociological conditions which the farmer confronts. It is both uneconomical and counterproductive to ask the farmer to use seed, fertilizers, or insecticides if these have not been previously tested. The small farmer cannot afford to let himself be used as a guinea pig. If what is offered to farmers fails to work, it will create a mistrust on their part and will seriously jeopardize programs intended to help them. It is most important, therefore, that the combination of inputs and agronomic practices which are recommended to him are proven in the specific areas where they are to be introduced, that the small farmers both comprehend the advantages of using them and specifically agree to do so, and that there is a prompt follow-up which will ensure that the farmers could obtain guidance and assistance when needed. It is particularly important that the emphasis should be on the improvement of what already exists rather than on the introduction of systems, inputs, and techniques which are wholly alien to the farmers. In any program, the fact should not be lost sight of that the land and labor available to smallholders is limited, that food production for their own needs constitutes an important claimant on land and labor, that most smallholders are without any kind of cushion which will enable them to take risks, and hence, that the groundwork be properly prepared before they are ushered into competitive production for the market.

Delivery systems

The second major constraint facing smallholder production in Africa is the absence or the existence only in a rudimentary form of systems to deliver support services for agriculture. For example, the benefits from the promotion of modern inputs in smallholder agriculture would be severely constrained if extension services are deficient. Moreover, the recommended inputs should be available at the right time and locations in order to foster a sustained interest in their use by smallholders. Similarly, the creation of efficient marketing is critical to ensure the prompt handling of marketable surpluses produced by farmers. There is nothing more damaging to the morale of small farmers than the failure on the part of authorities to ensure an efficient disposal of production increases. The provision of credit is the third vital link, extension and marketing being the other, in the process of rural transformation, and its absence seriously inhibits the participation of smallholders in market-oriented production. The improvement of the delivery system is therefore vital for the success of smallholder farming.

Government policies

The advancement of smallholder production is often handicapped either by the absence of government policies supportive of it or the existence of some policies which clearly militate against it. The most glaring example of the latter is the policy still pursued in many African countries with regard to the pricing of agricultural commodities, particularly food. In general, governments have tried to keep producer prices for food as low as possible, principally in order to safeguard urban consumers, who tend to be better organized and informed and hence carry more political weight. However, by pursuing a policy of paying low prices for rural products but, at the same time, not protecting the rural population against a steady increase in the prices of urban products, including those imported from abroad, governments are causing a deterioration in the terms of trade for the rural areas. It is becoming increasingly clear that small farmers not only resent this, but simply cannot afford to continue to participate in an exchange which is heavily weighted against them. The best evidence of this is the growing crisis in many countries over food supplies caused, among other factors, by the farmers' unwillingness either to produce marketable surpluses at prevailing official prices or to deliver surpluses to official agencies at these prices.

Accessibility of small farmers

Any major program which aims to assist peasant farmers should in the first place, be able to reach the intended groups effectively. This is largely but not exclusively a function of transport and communications. In many African countries, a significant proportion of the rural population simply cannot be reached through the existing transport links. Even routine administrative links are weak and undependable. Hence, even where a commitment to support rural development programs exists, progress is limited since there is often a need to start from scratch. In the circumstances, rural roads, farmer training centers, and generally a more effective governmental presence should all be regarded as essential parts of agricultural development programs.

Widely scattered peasant populations seriously restrict the ability of governments to provide effective assistance not only in fields such as health and education, but even for agriculture. It is the concern that the existing situation may forever prevent governmental assistance to the isolated and less privileged rural people that prompted the Tanzania government to regroup its rural population into Ujamaa villages. The actual implementation of the Ujamaa program has not been without snags—including wrong siting of villages with regard to soil types and water and the coercive measures employed by overenthusiastic officials—but it is highly probable that the basic objectives would prove to be sound and wholly defensible in the long run.

SMALLHOLDER AGRICULTURE— THE FUTURE

Despite the very many problems and constraints inherent in smallholder agriculture, it is indisputable that it should receive far more attention and specific supportive measures than in the past. The case for this is not only social and political but, equally important, economic. Smallholder agriculture is so basic to the economies of African countries that failure to raise its productivity would constitute a grave deficiency in the resource allocation process. While the support to smallholder agriculture is justified on grounds of equity, this is not the only or even the main justification. There is a strong economic justification for this assistance which is to be seen in its appropriateness to the pattern of resource endowment in most African countries.

A major review of the policies toward smallholder agriculture is needed in most African countries. The main theme of such a policy should regard peasant farmers as the major source of production and the major object of support. In the long run, the efficient development of this type of farming would also tend to be the most economically advantageous one.

Experience with assisting smallholders has been limited, but it has proved encouraging. Peasant farmers have displayed initiative and responded well to opportunities which came their way. Active support to these people constitutes not only the most efficient method of accomplishing broad-based progress, but also the best hope of ensuring social and political stability in most African countries.

*   *   *

QUESTIONS AND ANSWERS

Q: Last summer, I had the opportunity to spend about a week in Ghana, where I found a very serious food crisis. I was told that the chief reason for it was that there was such a large-scale migration of people, especially young people, to the city that they were simply not growing sufficient food. Yet Ghana was said to be fully capable of being self-sufficient. As a consequence they were importing a large part of their food from abroad and food was very expensive. What could be done about a situation like this? Is it possible to establish government policy which would get people back to the farm?

A (Krishna): The point that you made about Ghana applies to a number of other countries as well. One of the reasons people tend to move away from rural areas is that the opportunities for productive employment are narrowing and there is a growing feeling that a rural environment does not offer an adequate and dependable livelihood. I suggest that the principal reason for this is the very heavy distortion in government policies, particularly in regard to prices. The center of power in most African countries lies in the urban area where the people are closest to those who govern the country. The remote farmer living where he cannot be reached is often completely left out of the calculations of the administrators and planners. Policies are formulated to serve the requirements of those close at hand.

For this reason, governments in many countries have for a long time been pursuing policies which are detrimental to the rural population, which is the majority of the country's population. Once the relation between effort and reward becomes so distorted, the rural population simply has no opportunity in the rural environment and has to move to urban areas. It is a very shortsighted policy to allow this because larger urban populations simply make it more difficult for the government to pursue more realistic policies in regard to prices, and there is no single factor more important

in stabilizing and promoting agricultural development than producer prices.

———

Q: I have two questions. As you know there is one argument that the problem of hunger and malnutrition in Africa is to some extent caused by too much emphasis on cash crop agriculture. To what extent is the so-called integrated approach by the World Bank contributing to this trend or alleviating the problem? The second question has to do with the terms of trade. You made a point that trade terms seem to favor the urban population. There may be some exceptions to that. I am sure in your organization you have found some cases where trade terms favor the rural population. In those particular cases, what is the basic factor which explains this disparity?

A (Krishna): With regard to the first question, the main point I would like to make is that the problem is one of the major concerns of many governments and, through them, the institutions for which I work. The colonial regime stressed cash crops, particularly for the export market. Along with this production of cash crops occurred such developments as the build-up of a domestic transportation system. It is very obvious that the rather modest communications and transport networks that exist in these countries were intended originally to move exports from production centers to ports where they could be exported overseas.

Now it is also true that the emphasis on producing cash crops for exports has, to some extent, detracted from the need to provide adequate food for the domestic markets. This is reflected in many countries having to rely on imports from year to year to meet the needs of the population, principally the requirements of urban population. If you look at imports on a year-to-year basis, the domestic destinations for the imported food are all in the urban areas. This is inefficient and uneconomical, and, where it involves using up the scarce foreign exchange resources, it is quite dangerous for economic stability. There are, of course, bilateral auspices under which food is either provided free or at nominal cost. Our conviction is that, in the majority of cases, the food that is imported could have been produced at home with adequate incentives and perhaps at even less cost. So we are working with the governments to change the emphasis on food crops and cash crops not to minimize the importance of export crops, but to achieve a balance between food and cash crop production. If a country expands cash crop production, replacing food production, and then has to import food and pay for it in foreign exchange, the effective increase in export earnings is immediately neutralized. So it is not a very meaningful way to expand cash crops.

Regarding the second question on the relative terms of trade, the best manifestation of the terms of trade having moved in favor of the urban population is that urban consumers characteristically pay a price for the basic necessities which does not reflect the true economic cost, particularly in food items. In many of these countries, the government fixes the producer price, a government marketing organization buys it from the producer at that price and then transports it, warehouses it, and sells it to the urban consumer. So there are a number of points at which the true

economic costs can be hidden so that the urban consumer price can be substantially less than it might have been in a completely free market.

The best way of understanding what the economic price might have been is to look at food which does not pass through official channels to reach the urban consumers. There are occasions when the cost of such food is two to three times higher than the official price. If the producer price is raised to a meaningful level and there is an increase in production, the necessity of having to import food and subsidize consumer prices in the urban areas could be at least minimized if not eliminated.

———

Q: One of the main problems of modernizing agriculture in Africa, especially in the Sahara region, is irrigation. Could you give your view on the organization that would be necessary to bring smallholders together and modernize irrigation? Is it better to actually collectivize agriculture or is it more profitable to leave it free?

A (Krishna): With regard to water, quite obviously very much depends upon the sources. There is not very much one can do in an area of low rainfall except use rainwater when it occurs, perhaps one or two months during the year. The most obvious thing one could do is by very simple technology to build pockets to collect the scarce rainfall. At the same time, one could supplement this by a very thorough probing of the ground water resources available. An important variation to the ground water development program is control or disciplined utilization of ground water.

In Ethiopia the government has two wells in areas used predominantly by nomadic people. There are mobile pumps, which pump out the ground water from the two wells. After a period of time, when cattle and human beings have used the water, they must move on and the well is locked up. This enables the well to be recharged for the next season and also protects overgrazing in the area. Anybody who wants to use the well must become a registered user, and one of the disciplines imposed on them is that they must move to another area later.

Political Transition in Urban Africa

By SANDRA T. BARNES

ABSTRACT: Political change in Africa has not met the expectations of pre-independence analysts. Civil wars, military coups, and the demise of multi-party states weigh heavily on the performance of public authorities and the smooth functioning of the body politic. At the local level, political and demographic changes also exceed expectations. Administrators are unprepared to deal with the vast numbers of migrants who are attracted to the burgeoning cities. At the same time, agencies are constantly reorganized and bureaucratic continuity is minimal. The result is that residents are forced to meet political needs through their own efforts. To these ends there has been an increasing Africanization of the polity, as seen in the proliferation of traditional authority figures who adapt their roles as chiefs or patrons to the modern urban marketplace, and a proliferation of organizations and networks that serve as interest groups or dispute-settlement mechanisms in place of formal governmental institutions. Although unanticipated, these features can no longer be considered deviations from a prescribed norm. They are an organic part of the political process. Today they account for much of the stability and continuity that are to be found in Africa's urban political systems.

Sandra T. Barnes is Assistant Professor of Anthropology at the University of Pennsylvania. The case study described in this article is a product of a field study conducted in Nigeria in 1971–72 and 1975 designed to examine the social, economic, and political adjustments of migrants to Lagos—one of Africa's largest and most industrialized urban centers.

POLITICAL change in Africa has not gone according to plan. Scholars who examined the new nations as they came into being assumed that subsequent political transitions would follow three directions. Political systems would Westernize; national loyalties would supplant ethnic loyalties; mass participation in national affairs would increase. But these predictions have not been borne out.

As is usually true with predictions, the past 20 years in Africa have seen untidy events which spoiled the tidy unfolding of the future put forth by the prognosticators. The rapidity with which change would take place was underestimated. Civil wars, military coups, and the demise of multi-party states were unanticipated. And, as I argue here, the weight of historical tradition in shaping the modern political arena was misjudged. It is now clear that beneath the tumultuous events of the past two decades there has been a movement of political systems away from the goals introduced by colonial powers and more toward modern African ideas of how a nation should be ordered.

For example, mass participation can no longer be measured in relation to national events such as elections or campaigns, nor is it found in national organizations such as political parties. To establish parameters for the African political scene we must look to small-scale interaction, that level which is indeed the lifeblood of a polity. Here the evidence is that African modes of interaction persist. An urban chief may be as effective an arbiter as a court judge. A mosque may double as an ethnic association and thereby act as an interest group on behalf of its worshiper-members.

At the local level, political and demographic changes also vary from expectations. The urbanization process is accelerating to the extent that rural productivity is in jeopardy. Through no fault of their own, administrators are unable to expand their services quickly enough to deal with the vast numbers of migrants who are attracted to the burgeoning cities. Not only are facilities and amenities stretched beyond their limits, but also the structures of urban governmental agencies are constantly reorganized and continuity in civil service personnel is minimal. One outcome of these circumstances is that residents are forced to meet political needs through their own grass-roots efforts. Their success can be measured by a growing body of evidence that competition for scarce urban resources continues unabated yet largely outside the formal political institutions.[1] The answer to how this is achieved can be found in the actual direction political change has taken and not in the plans for how it should have changed. In reversing the prescribed directions for political development, the public has found outlets for political needs and some measure of continuity and security.

The point I wish to emphasize is that by retaining African institutions, customs, and values, by retaining and manipulating ethnic group ties, and by diverting participation away from national affairs, ordinary citizens in all but the most totalitarian regimes still retain viable outlets for political activities despite what one observer sees as a "shrinking political arena."[2]

1. The term "formal" is here restricted to statutory political institutions.
2. Nelson Kasfir, *The Shrinking Political Arena* (Berkeley: University of California Press, 1976).

There are two ways this is accomplished. First, there is an increasing Africanization of the polity,
as seen, for example, in the proliferation of traditional authority
figures who adapt their roles as
chiefs or patrons to the modern
urban marketplace, assisting residents to fulfill personal and political
needs. Second, there are a number
of "invisible," or secondary, organizations and networks, such as
landowner associations, secret societies, and even religious groups,
that serve, among other things,
as interest groups or dispute-settlement bodies and, therefore, must
be considered a functioning part
of the political process. The degree
to which each complements rather
than contradicts formal governmental institutions varies with each
urban setting. Similarly, the degree
to which polities are Africanized
or to which invisible groups fulfill
primary political needs varies markedly from place to place.

At this point, let me be clear about
what I mean by the terms "politics"
and "political process." Politics is
the way in which individuals cooperate and compete for power in
the form of resources—both human
and material. It is largely a public
affair and is concerned with decision-making that affects a community.[3] In urban centers, resources
consist of jobs, housing, land, education, contracts, social services, prestige, status, and so on. Competition
for these resources and decisions
as to who is to receive, control,
and distribute them together constitute the political process. Today,
despite wholesale proscriptions on

overt participation in some nations,
the political process continues unabated. It takes place largely outside the formal political arena and
is often subtly embedded within
the ongoing encounters and exchanges of the daily social routine.

To support this position, I describe the inner-workings of Mushin
—one of three suburban political
communities within greater metropolitan Lagos, Nigeria.[4] Mushin is
briefly compared to other urban centers where certain striking simi-
larities are to be found. From this
evidence it appears that the most
important political transition taking
place is that, while unique to each
city, an identifiably African political
culture is taking shape at the local
level.

THE POLITICAL COMMUNITY
OF MUSHIN

With the possible exception of
Kinshasa, Lagos is now the largest
metropolitan area of tropical Africa.
It is the capital of the Federal
Republic of Nigeria, the overseer of
the bulk of the nation's import and
export trade, and the site of the
largest industrial complex in West
Africa. The influx of migrants seeking employment opportunities in
these and other sectors has trebled
in recent years, so that recent estimates place the population in excess
of 3.5 million.[5] Thousands of new-
comers who arrive each week must
adjust to an environment that is
more technologically and bureau-
cratically oriented than can be found
elsewhere in Nigeria. The social
transformations they undergo can be
associated with Africa's industrial

3. See Paul Friedrich, "The Legitimacy of
a Cacique," in *Local-Level Politics*, ed. Marc
J. Swartz (Chicago: Aldine Publishing Company, 1968), p. 243, for a discussion of this
definition of politics.

4. The case study is based on field work
carried out in Mushin by the author in
1971–72 and again in 1975.
5. *Business Times*, 11 January 1977, p. 1.

revolution. In view of these factors, Lagos presents an ideal setting for examining the contemporary political process.

Until 1976 metropolitan Lagos consisted of four separate political communities. The municipality of Lagos was administered by a city council, and three adjoining suburban districts were each administered by a town or district council. Each of the councils was overseen separately by the Lagos state government, and therefore there were no administrative connections between the political communities nor overlap in local officeholders or other authority figures. Local leaders zealously protected their political boundaries, perpetually engaging in activities to retain their community's autonomy and its political solidarity. The sense of community solidarity did not extend beyond politics, however. None of the four communities had a separate economic or social life. In other words, place of occupation, kinship ties, and social interaction did, and continue to, transcend political boundaries.

The suburb of Mushin officially came into being in 1955. An agricultural area before the Second World War, it has taken only three decades to become Lagos' most heavily populated sector. Mushin houses 1.5 million residents—it is largely a residential area—in contrast to the 1.2 million who live in the municipality of Lagos and the nearly 1 million who are divided between the other two suburbs.[6] The bulk of its residents are migrants, the leaders of whom have shaped it into a viable political community largely through their own efforts.

In the course of its development, Mushin has experienced a number

6. Ibid, p. 1.

of changes in its political system. It has gone from a decentralized to a centralized polity. Its administrative authority has undergone frequent and fundamental reorganizational shifts in its 21-year life-span. There has been little long-term continuity in civil service personnel administering the council. Finally, it has been shifted between jurisdictional authorities, the consequences of which are that Mushin is the least physically developed sector with the least desirable living conditions in Lagos.[7] To be fully appreciated, these changes must be elaborated.

Before colonization in 1861, and unlike its neighboring city-state of Lagos, the area now known as Mushin was not politically centralized nor were its villages tributaries of a larger centralized kingdom. During the colonial period, it was overseen by a district officer who, in accordance with the principles of indirect rule, should have had, but in this case did not have, a preexisting structure through which to administer his territory, save a few lineage elders who acted as headmen of the villages that dotted the region. Thus it was not until postwar urbanization that political centralization took place. As a first step, the village elders united to form village group councils which, in turn, chose representatives to act as emissaries between residents and the colonial government. The representatives were a farsighted group of migrant settlers who envisioned the day when their new homes would be an integral part of the metropolitan area. It was they who petitioned government to create Mushin by carving it out of a

7. Akin L. Mabogunje, *Urbanization in Nigeria* (New York: Africana Publishing Corp., 1968), pp. 300–9.

much larger rural district and to give it a separate governing council.

INSTITUTIONAL CHANGE: 1955–1976

When Mushin came into being in 1955 it had two bodies: a policy-making board of elected councilors and a bureaucratic establishment of civil servants empowered to implement policy and administer local services. Elected councilors were, by and large, the same leaders who lobbied for the creation of the council. Each represented an emerging urban neighborhood that had been turned into an electoral ward, and each was to serve a three-year term. A senior civil servant was to oversee the establishment and provide administrative continuity. This council structure remained unchanged during its first five years.

Then a series of frequent shifts altered the representational character of the council. Dissatisfied with the performance of the council and perceiving an opportunity to turn it into a partisan stronghold, party politicians, who by 1960 dictated local government policy, dissolved the elected council and appointed committees of management whose primary attribute was party loyalty rather than representational skill. Thus began a new trend. During the tumultuous period from 1960 to 1965, when the dominant Western Region party, the Action Group, fragmented and was succeeded by various partisan coalitions, five appointed councils came and went in Mushin. Each new council represented a change in the balance of partisan power.

Other changes were instituted after the military coup of January 1966, again altering the basic structure of the council. For a three-and-one-half-year period, the council was run, not by a representational body, but by a sole administrator who served both as policy-maker and implementer. Sole administrators then ran the council for 6 other interim periods lasting from 1 to 18 months.

In its first 21 years, the council seesawed between elected boards, appointed boards, and a sole administratorship 16 times. There have been 10 policy-making boards. Three have been elected by residents, four have been appointed by the ministry of local government acting on the instructions of partisan leaders, and three have been appointed by military edict. Only two councils have served a full three-year term; the longevity of the others has been from one month to two years, with shorter periods being more the rule than the exception.

In 1976 another radical change was effected at the behest of the federal military government which toppled the Gowon regime in July of 1975. Mushin was divided into two new administrative authorities —Mushin East and Mushin West— each with an administrative establishment and a paid, elected representational board. Elections were held in December 1976 as part of Nigeria's nationwide reorganization of local government and its preparation for a return to civilian rule.[8]

During the same 20-year period, the bureaucratic arm of the council has been subject to frequent changes. There has been a lack of skilled civil service manpower and repeated personnel shifts, particularly at the highest levels. Turnover has been so great, in fact, that there is

8. Federal Republic of Nigeria, *Guidelines for Local Government Reform* (Kaduna: Government Printer, 1976).

little bureaucratic continuity and, therefore, little incentive to develop and follow through on administrative programs. Although the council has been upgraded and expanded from a district to a town council, its staff expansion has been minimal compared to that of the Lagos City council. For example, in 1974–75 there were about 6,250 employees in the Lagos city council compared to just under 500 in the Mushin town council, despite the latter's larger constituency.[9]

In its short life, Mushin has been removed from one jurisdictional authority and placed under another on several occasions. These changes have had profound effects on the development of the area. Notorious for being a shifting no man's land,[10] Mushin has often been neglected and ignored, for the reason that no higher authority has been willing to invest in an area that might at any time be removed from its control. The contrast between Mushin and Lagos City in annual local government expenditures is revealing in this regard. In 1967–68, for instance, the Lagos City council expended roughly $18 per inhabitant, against about $1.20 per inhabitant expended in Mushin.[11] By 1974–75, using latest population estimates, the Lagos City expenditure remained nearly the same, whereas the Mushin expenditure rose to

about $3.50 per resident.[12] From its earliest years, neglect has been apparent in almost every respect: in economic, administrative, and judicial services; in town planning; and in the provision of amenities and police protection.

THE RISE OF URBAN CHIEFS

The most dramatic response to this neglect and to the resultant need for self-help has been the creation of a chieftaincy system. Just as squatter settlements are noted for organizing their own internal governmental services, Mushin, while not a community of this type, has responded to community needs by adapting an old political model to a new setting. The chieftaincy system consists of a hierarchy of chiefs and their advisory councils. Almost all of Mushin's leaders are in some way involved in the chieftaincy system as title holders, council members, or advisors. The basic criteria for participation is that a man or woman own real estate in Mushin or that a woman be a local market leader.

Real estate is the foundation upon which Mushin's political community rests. Real estate ownership in Mushin defines full political citizenship. It provides an entrée into the chieftaincy system and other local-level political groups including the Mushin town council. It affords economic security, in that virtually all housing is designed to produce rental income. It is a symbol of high status, and it attracts the respect of kinsmen, friends, and neighbors. Because political, economic, and even social power is derived from real estate, it is Mushin's

9. See Mushin Town Council, "Draft Estimates, 1975–76," pp. 5–26, and Lagos City Council, "Draft Estimates, 1975–76," pp. 56–132, mimeograph.

10. Pius O. Sada, "The Metropolitan Region of Lagos: A Study of the Political Factor in Urban Geography" (Ph.D. diss., Indiana University, 1968), pp. 83–4.

11. Ishola Oluwa and S. I. Talabi, Report of the Tribunal of Inquiry into the Reorganization of Local Government Councils in Lagos State, Minority Report (Lagos, 1970), p. 67.

12. Mushin Town Council, "Draft Estimates," p. 2; Lagos City Council, "Draft Estimates," p. vii.

most sought after resource, the acquisition and protection of which adds to the needs of owners for community solidarity. The vested interest landowners have in their property, and hence in Mushin, has been one of the more compelling forces in the establishment of the chieftaincy system.

Once again, it is necessary to examine the past for the origins of the chieftaincy element in Mushin's polity. The beginning of the chieftaincy system is to be found in the autonomous villages of pre-urbanized Mushin and in the headmen who kept order within them. Building on this example, settlers of new urban neighborhoods chose new headmen to provide leadership and social order. Settlers in the old but urbanizing villages retained existing headmen as their leaders. Within each expanding neighborhood, landowners, but not their tenants, served as an advisory council to the headman. These units were strengthened by government authorities who used headmen as tax collectors and their landowner councils as communication links to the public. They served as natural training grounds for the leaders who later emerged as Mushin's prominent politicians.

The creation of the Mushin district council added greater strength to the neighborhoods, 30 of which became electoral wards from which the first council was chosen. Once formalized, the neighborhood wards were easily politicized by partisan organizations. And once politicized, the role of headman grew in importance. Without governmental authorization, but with support of the public, the titles of headmen were elevated to that of chief, and the new chiefs began meeting together in divisional councils. At

this point, the system began to form a hierarchy. Divisional councils selected one of their members to serve as a senior spokesman, and before a few months had passed these spokesmen were thought of as paramount chiefs, their councilmen as junior chiefs.

In time, the suburb of Mushin had seven paramount chiefs bearing the titles of olú, "king of the city," or Bálè, "chief of the town," and seven chieftaincy divisions. Olú were chosen either from the ranks of new landowning settlers or from those of the old village headmen. To date, the Mushin chieftaincy system has not centralized to the point that one of the seven olú has emerged as ọba, "crowned king." Although the olú were at one time encouraged to complete their hierarchy by naming one among themselves as king of Mushin, they have resisted, since there is no agreement as to who should be so honored.[13]

The rules and customs governing kingship in ancient Yoruba city-states have been adapted to the Mushin chieftaincy system. The new chiefs have taken it upon themselves to learn the necessary sacrifices and rituals of community renewal. They have exercised their roles by appointing sub-chiefs and by giving titles to local notables. They act as dispute settlers, as spokesmen for their publics to government authorities, and as ceremonial leaders in local markets and other public institutions. Because the chieftaincy system was a new, rather than an ancient body, colonial authorities refused to recog-

13. The official titles of Mushin's chiefs differ from their informal titles. Both in addressing and referring to paramount chiefs, residents prefer to use the most honored title, ọba.

nize the chiefs or give the *olú* official roles in the Mushin district council as they did elsewhere in local government areas where traditional chiefs had preceded colonial rule.

Soon after Nigeria's 1960 independence, however, the seven *olú* were officially recognized by the government. Later they were constituted as an advisory board to the Mushin town council, and eventually they were given representation in the Lagos State House of Obas and Chiefs. In 1975 the titles extended by the seven *olú* to sub-chiefs and notables were officially recognized by the government, and in this way 81 new junior chieftaincy titles came into being in Mushin.

Institutionalization of the chieftaincy system was, in this case, a 20-year process. Within two decades, landowning settlers had created neighborhood councils, village headmen had become chiefs, and, finally, chiefs had become kings.

FLUCTUATING POLITICAL ASSOCIATIONS

Besides the chieftaincy system, there are or have been a number of other political outlets in Mushin. None have produced more conflict than the partisan organizations which dominated Mushin from the late 1950s to 1966, when they were outlawed by military authorities. Yet parties played an important role in the community, and I shall return to them later.

Following the military takeover, secret organizations, such as Freemasons, Ogboni, and Reformed Ogboni, known collectively as "secret courts," began to expand their membership and activities. Secret courts offer social and political outlets for members in the form of contacts and networks for solving problems, securing resources, or settling disputes. They also offer symbolic rewards in that some secret courts bestow chieftaincy titles on prominent members whose standing in political circles is thereby enhanced. Bonds between secret court members are reinforced through the fictive use of the kinship term "brother" and by initiation oaths that oblige members to assist one another in advancing their personal and public goals.

Also following the military coup, two community welfare organizations emerged. Each represented one of two factions that earlier had been embedded within the local Action Group organization (but not the splinter party, NNDP). Members included most of Mushin's prominent leaders from political and religious spheres and from labor unions and marketing associations.

Other voluntary associations have come and gone. There have been no national ethnic unions since 1966, when they were banned. But at a narrower level, associations whose members are recruited on the basis of family, clan, village, or district are abundant. Finally, a number of religious organizations—Islamic, Christian, and Independent—offer participatory outlets. Like the secret courts, some Islamic brotherhoods and Independent churches confer chieftaincy titles on prominent members. Within larger religious bodies, small societies are often found whose members share the same ethnic or hometown background. As such, they act in lieu of ethnic voluntary associations fulfilling personal and political needs of members.[14]

14. Sandra T. Barnes, "Voluntary Associations in a Metropolis: The Case of Lagos,

Over time there has been a waxing and waning in the membership strength, in the intensity of activity, and even in the type of activity undertaken by these politically oriented groups. For instance, community welfare organizations became active during the three-and-one-half-year period the Mushin town council was overseen by a sole administrator. When a committee of management that included prominent local leaders replaced the sole administrator, the community welfare organizations lapsed into inactivity. Another example is that of the neighborhood landowner associations which fused into the Action Group party structure at the height of the political era, but which re-emerged as apolitical neighborhood associations when partisan politics were banned. These are only two of many similar examples, the net effect of which has been a relatively constant shift in participatory emphasis. When one organization has been unable to function effectively for its members, another has supplanted it. Most shifts in participatory emphasis are a response to the external forces that impinge upon the local arena.

The picture of instability and impermanence that emerges from this institutionally oriented examination raises a central question. Given the rapidity of change, combined with the fragility of an organization's life-span or its effectiveness, how is it that Mushin is not simply a geographically delimited administrative unit, but a viable and cohesive political community? Elected representatives may have a power base in the Mushin town council for this month or this year, but not the next. Partisan organizations have a brief life-span. Bureaucrats circulate so quickly that there is no time to develop a clientele or a long-term administrative policy. Voluntary associations appear and disappear. How, in this fragile atmosphere, is continuity maintained? How is a sense of political community sustained?

THE CONTINUITY OF LEADERSHIP

The solutions are to be found not in political institutions but in political roles. The leader is the key to continuity and community in Mushin. He or she is to be found in each neighborhood. He assumes the role of patron (the person who is perceived as the source of the real or symbolic commodities he purveys), middleman or go-between (the person who purveys commodities that are not his own),[15] official (the director or guide of a local group or activity), arbiter (the judge, dispute settler, or witness), or adviser (the guide in personal, familial, even psychological matters). Above all, the political leader is a landowner, a member of his neighborhood landowner association, and in a few cases a leader of an indigenous landowning lineage. Typically—though not in every case—he is an independent entrepreneur, capable of managing his own time and bear-

Nigeria," *African Studies Review*, vol. 18, no. 2 (1975), pp. 75–87; Sandra T. Barnes and Margaret Peil, "Voluntary Association Membership in Five West African Cities," *Urban Anthropology*, vol. 6, no. 1 (1977).

15. See Robert Paine, "A Theory of Patronage and Brokerage," in *Patrons and Brokers in the East Arctic*, ed. Robert Paine (Newfoundland: Newfoundland Social and Economic Papers No. 2, Institute of Social and Economic Research, Memorial University of Newfoundland, 1971), p. 8, for a recent discussion of patrons and middlemen.

ing the financial burdens that leadership entails: hospitality, loans, contributions, and caring for a large number of dependents.

Throughout the early years, Mushin's leaders acted in the stead of town planners and in lieu of police by hiring nightguards to watch over their neighborhoods. Even today Mushin's leaders lobby government to secure the most basic amenities and services, such as trash removal. Leaders know how to secure licenses, sanitation permits, market stalls, or loans. They can settle land disputes, give educational advice, or preside at rites of passage or other ceremonies.

Mushin's leaders are basically of two types: neighborhood leaders whose sphere of operation is relatively restricted to localized interactions; and a few principal politicians whose sphere encompasses all of Mushin and beyond. To be effective at either neighborhood or community levels, leaders must cultivate a large number of contacts and networks. To the extent that their finances permit, they must participate in as many political groups and activities as possible and they must hold membership in chieftaincy councils, voluntary associations, or secret courts. By virtue of the contacts they are able to develop, lower-level leaders become clients of more highly placed leaders and so on up the ladder to a few principals who act as an axis around which most of Mushin's political life revolves. Through their wide-ranging networks, leaders manipulate public opinion so as to nurture a sense of political solidarity. Likewise, they guard the boundaries of Mushin against attempts by outside leaders to gain political followings within it.

An essential strategy for Mushin's principal politicians is, in a word, to be flexible. The role of politician is legitimate in and of itself and can exist outside any formal structure. Most politicians, however, take on as many offices as possible. Conditions permitting, a politician may serve as a representative on the Mushin town council at the same time he plays a role in the chieftaincy system, leads a market or transport association, holds a title in a religious group or secret court, and so on. Hence there is a redundancy in leadership positions, that is, a system of overlapping political offices.

Redundancy allows Mushin's leaders to absorb the impact of rapid change. As the balance of power tilts, or as one outlet is closed, the leaders shift the focus of their activities from one sphere to another. Because clients and followers are tied to individuals and not institutions, the burden of adjustment falls on a few individuals rather than the mass. In this way, continuity can be achieved despite institutional flux.

Another essential element in the political game, and here I return to a point raised at the beginning of this essay, is invisibility. The capacity to manipulate contacts and secure resources without visibility is a useful strategy for leaders in a climate of unpredictable and radical change. Thus, when virtually all other political outlets were closed to the leaders of Mushin in 1966, they turned to their contacts within the secret courts or to the two newly created community welfare organizations, both of which operated with manifestly nonpolitical goals but latent political intentions.

STRENGTHS AND WEAKNESSES
WITHIN THE POLITY

Invisibility and flexibility are as important to groups as they are to individuals. When regimes change or conditions are otherwise inimical to the political process, interest groups, to survive, must be able to blend into a neutral background or to hide themselves behind protective screens. Secret courts are, by their very nature, able to cloak their political activities. Other, more open groups must adopt other strategies. The formation of ethnic voluntary associations under the protective umbrella of religious bodies is a case in point. A more vivid example of political survival in Mushin, however, is to be found in the chieftaincy system. As a result of its prominent role in partisan politics, the legitimacy of the chieftaincy system was eventually questioned by military government authorities and its continued existence threatened.[16] For two years, therefore, chiefs and their councils submerged their activities by meeting discretely and by operating under the organizational aegis of one, if not both, of the community welfare organizations. Later, in a more tranquil period, the chieftancy system was allowed to resume public activities on the understanding that in future it would not engage in partisan affairs.

Clearly there are weaknesses to be found in a system such as Mushin's. For example, a test of the community's viability came during the period between 1963 and 1965. At this time, Mushin's principal politicians were cut off from their conventional outlets and resources.

Briefly, we must turn to national politics and the actions of political parties in Nigeria to understand what occurred. By 1963, as I have indicated, both the chieftaincy system and the Mushin district council were virtually undifferentiated from the Action Group to the extent that the latter resembled a political machine. This funneling of personnel and power through a single conduit was effective so long as Mushin's prominent politicians held government offices or otherwise had a role to play in the party itself. When regional power was transferred to the Nigerian National Democratic party (NNDP), in which Mushin leaders had no representation, the political process was blocked. The transition from Action Group to NNDP had been too rapid and bitter a process for adjustments to be made. As is well known, this blockage triggered extensive civil disorder in Mushin that, in combination with other regional and national events, brought about the 1966 military coup and the end of the partisan era.[17] Only a few weeks after the military takeover, Mushin's old guard appeared publicly to call for unity and order. New organizations emerged, but more importantly, access to government and the resumption of the political process were made possible by the appointment of old guard politicians to panels to advise the new regime on how to reorganize local and regional government. In short, still another outlet was instituted, a new order was planned, but the same key leaders were involved.

In this case, we see that stability

16. Sandra T. Barnes, "Becoming a Lagosian" (Ph.D. diss., University of Wisconsin, Madison, 1974), p. 208.

17. K. W. J. Post and Michael Vickers, *Structure and Conflict in Nigeria, 1960–66* (Madison: University of Wisconsin Press, 1973), pp. 227–32.

rests upon the viability of a few individual powerbrokers and their ability to operate both inside and outside the formal governmental institutions. Moreover, it rests on the ability of interest groups to adapt what is often a blatantly fictive camouflage. So long as there are resources to tap and room to maneuver, the system can function relatively smoothly. Eliminate access to institutional resources and the ability of leaders to direct their clientele to sources of aid, and stability is undermined.

The Mushin system, on the other hand, has strengths which must not be overlooked. For example, upward mobility is possible so long as the tacit landowning requirements are met. Despite the continuing influence of established leaders, new talent is prepared to assert itself and can be trained. The existence of many institutions and networks ensures their steady recruitment, but first as clients of the leading politicians. For the population as a whole, the clientage system is able to absorb large numbers of residents from all walks of life. Above all, it provides residents with human links via which they can participate in the local political process. It provides them with personalized interaction in what may be an otherwise impersonal urban world.

Both clientage and chieftaincy provide participatory options that have historical and cultural continuity. The chieftaincy system is a modern version of a highly valued traditional institution. Hence Yoruba-speaking residents find in chieftaincy the type of satisfaction that is engendered when the ancient past legitimizes the present. In a constantly changing environment, chieftaincy is a secure political landmark. Clientage, too, offers all residents, no matter what their ethnic background, an opportunity to transact political business in the city in the familiar face-to-face mode of interaction to which they are socialized in their small communities of origin and on which relationships of trust are based.

DISCUSSION AND CONCLUSIONS

To conclude, let me return to the themes with which this essay began. Those who believed that Western political institutions would inevitably replace the survivals of past political structures felt that because older systems were held together by personal loyalties they were incapable of achieving the kind of bureaucratic impersonality and efficiency necessary in a modern state.[18] In Mushin, however, chieftaincy is not a dysfunctional survival, but an integral part of a vigorous political community. Mushin is not alone in this respect. The role of urban chiefs elsewhere is well documented. Throughout sub-Saharan Africa from Freetown[19] to Dar-es-Salaam[20] to Ouagadougou,[21] urban chiefs are relied upon by residents and governments alike to serve as authority figures, primarily within their own ethnic groups. Almost universally, they act as the interpreters of old values and the synthesizers of what is new and different. For many urbanites, there-

18. See Lloyd A. Fallers, *Bantu Bureaucracy* (Chicago: University of Chicago Press, 1965), pp. 19–20.

19. Michael P. Banton, *West African City: A Study of Tribal Life in Freetown* (London: Oxford University Press for International African Institute, 1957).

20. J. A. K. Leslie, *Survey of Dar-es-Salaam* (London: Oxford University Press, 1963).

21. Elliott P. Skinner, *African Urban Life: The Transformation of Ouagadougou* (Princeton, N.J.: Princeton University Press, 1974).

fore, chiefs serve as orientation points around which they can construct new lives.

Clientage, which is also firmly rooted in the political past, plays a key role in the contemporary urban polity, be it in Umuahia,[22] in Kumasi,[23] or in Dakar.[24] Clientage is more broad-based than the institution of chieftaincy because patrons often serve an ethnically heterogeneous clientele rather than a specific ethnic group. Much of the political participation in urban Africa, as a recent study stresses,[25] takes place outside the conventional political structures and within the sphere of patron-client interaction. The same is true of Mushin. In my own survey in 1972, an overwhelming majority of residents stated that to achieve their goals in the city they were, to varying degrees, dependent upon patrons or middlemen. Precisely because it is not institutionally anchored, yet because it offers political outlets for a wide sector of the populace, clientage offers stability at the local level despite the sweeping changes that occur at the national level.

Those who believed that ethnic identities must be supplanted by national loyalties have been confronted with new arguments. Ethnic group solidarity is a two-sided issue. On the one hand, there is the position that tolerance of ethnically organized political groups leads to civil conflict, the result of which is to reinforce cultural cleavages and inhibit a national homogenizing process.[26] On the other hand, it has been shown that failure to tolerate ethnically organized outlets for populations that are unprepared to restructure their social interaction in terms of national loyalties, is a cause of, rather than a cure for, civil conflict.[27] In other words, ethnic associations organized on a local rather than national basis may offer positive participatory benefits that outweigh other, more negative, effects. Argued either way, the evidence is the same: openly or otherwise, many groups in African cities recruit members on the basis of shared ethnic identity and not on the basis of an overarching national identity. Institutions, such as mosques or churches, that veil the ethnic group solidarities within them demonstrate the hard fact that heterogeneous cities, with their heterogeneous work places, multicultural residential areas, and other forms of pluralistic social interaction, have yet to produce homogeneous polities.

Finally, scholars assumed that mass participation in nationally focused political affairs must increase because it was essential to political and economic development[28] or because, in evolutionary terms, it was an essential attribute of a large-

22. W. J. and J. L. Hanna, "The Integrative Role of Africa's Middleplaces and Middlemen," *Civilisations*, vol. 17 (1967), pp. 12–27.

23. Enid Schildkrout, "Strangers and Local Government in Kumasi," *Journal of Modern African Studies*, vol. 8, no. 2 (1970), pp. 251–69.

24. Stephen Maack, personal communication, 1975.

25. Kasfir, *The Shrinking Political Arena*, p. 5–14.

26. Clifford Geertz, "The Integrative Revolution," in *The Interpretation of Cultures*, ed. Clifford Geertz (New York: Basic Books Inc., Publishers, 1973), p. 277.

27. Elliott P. Skinner, "Political Conflict and Revolution in an African Town," *American Anthropologist*, vol. 74, no. 5 (1972), p. 1216.

28. Frederick W. Frey, "Political Development, Power and Communications in Turkey," in *Communications and Political Development*, ed. Lucian W. Pye (Princeton, N.J.: Princeton University Press, 1963), p. 301.

scale society.[29] Today, on a national level, departicipation in partisan organizations, in campaigning, or in voting is the trend, and even the goal, of many regimes. The dramatic decrease in nationally oriented activities is well documented.[30] But this has been a misleading focus. Participation must be measured in different ways and on a different scale. The urban arena presents a different picture. In local-level politics we can see behind the struggles of national elites. We can see a broad cross-section of the citizenry competing for the more mundane resources of jobs, housing, or a secondary education. Despite the sweeping changes to which the masses are exposed in their public and private lives, the political process in all but the most totalitarian regimes continues in the neighborhoods and the suburban communities of Africa's teeming urban centers.

It must still be asked why these predictions for post-independence politics were so inaccurate. Aside from being unable to foresee the turbulence with which political change would take place, what was missing? For one, the opinions of African elites were improperly assessed. Recent writers point out that the elite preferred to discourage nationally oriented mass participation because it feared an unenlightened public might interfere with long-term development goals. "Benevolent elitism" it has been labeled.[31] A somewhat contradictory view is that earlier observers were too preoccupied with elite opinions and national politics and, therefore, failed to assess the vitality of local participation and the forms it could take.[32] As the Mushin case demonstrates, the rapidity of change reinforced in citizens the need for fixed reference points— patrons, middlemen, or chiefs—and for lasting relationships on which trust could be based. The fact that citizens unexpectedly chose reference points that symbolized a past political order indicated not only that there had been a scholarly inattention to local politics, but that there had also been an inattention to value systems of the common man and to the weight of historical precedent.

The political process is now and will be governed by African rules. It takes place beneath the surface in the quiet and unnoticed interactions of daily life. It is often veiled behind a screen of African tradition. If we are to understand today's political transition in urban Africa, we must accept the fact of political continuity.

29. Talcott Parsons, "Evolutionary Universals in Society," *American Sociological Review*, vol. 29 (1964), pp. 353–56.

30. Kasfir, *The Shrinking Political Arena*, pp. 227–68.

31. Marc H. Ross, *Grass Roots in an African City: Political Behavior in Nairobi* (Cambridge, Mass.: The M.I.T. Press, 1975), p. 127.

32. Margaret Peil, *Nigerian Politics: The People's View* (London: Cassell, 1976), pp. 3–4. Peil summarizes the preoccupation with elite politics, but notes one exception to the trend: Richard Sklar, *Nigerian Political Parties* (Princeton, N.J.: Princeton University Press, 1963), pp. 503–4.

* * *

QUESTIONS AND ANSWERS

Q: It is known that urbanization is taking place in Africa, more than anywhere else in the world. In your opinion, what is bad or good in the urbanization process, and what are the ways of correcting what is bad?

A (Barnes): I would say that the negative side of urbanization and urban development is the fact that far too many people have been taken away from rural areas. They are not producing enough food to support the urban populations. Another perhaps negative side to urbanization is the fact that, unlike Western nations where the urbanization process went hand in glove with the development of industrialization and more job opportunities urbanization throughout the Third World is not developing at the same rate as job opportunities. We have far too many people going to urban areas for the jobs available, which presents us with a massive unemployment problem. I think it has a deleterious effect on the psychological feelings of these people. Another perhaps negative aspect of the urbanization process is that there have been status aspirations engendered in the past, particularly during the colonial era, wherein people have been expected to fulfill their economic goals in urban rather than rural areas. I think these status aspirations are being dashed and I think urban areas are a crucible for disappointment.

On the positive side, there are perhaps better health care facilities in urban areas. There are much better educational facilities in urban areas, certainly in Nigeria. Much of Nigeria's development funds have gone into the cities, so there are amenities and services there which are very desirable.

As to how we can correct the problems, why not start with farm subsidies and raising prices for farm crops? I think equalizing the world economy is the solution for urban problems, to a large extent. Certainly there are others, but that is my major solution.

Q: In a very enlightening presentation, you mention the word "authority" once. However, your description had to do with a considerable amount of authority— not necessarily governmental authority, but individualized authority in the chieftan. If the military governments continue and history reasserts itself, is it likely that governments in the countries to which you refer will be less than democratic?

A (Barnes): There are many sub-questions embedded in that large question. Democratic in the sense that we know it, on the national level, perhaps not, but democracy has a much wider interpretation than we give it. One of the things that I was trying to say today was that democracy, at least the opportunity to participate, is certainly there, and I do not expect that to disappear except in the most extreme cases. We now see several of the most extreme cases, but I don't expect those to last long.

I think that one of the problems has been that we have viewed authority from the top down, rather than from the bottom up. This involves the question of legitimacy. Who do we recognize as legitimate? Quite obviously there are a number of authorities— both authorities who have statutory legitimacy and those who have historical legitimacy. I accept this diversified authority and expect it to either maintain itself or reassert itself in the foreseeable future.

Q: Did you find anything in Africa that is similar to our own so-called social security system, which is making the poor more poor and the rich more rich in the United States?

A (Barnes): You have a double question. There is a very strong social security system in Africa— the family. The family supports its members during their time of need.

Secondly, is there a disparity between rich and poor? Yes, but it does not result from the social security system—the family—but from the economic system. A senior civil servant salary in government in many nations in West Africa is 30 times as great as that of the lowest level employee. In the United States, you might find the disparity is 15 to 1.

Crime and Development in Africa

By LAMIN SESAY

ABSTRACT: By itself, development seems to have nothing to do with crime. But when considered as a dynamic process of change, development and deviant behavior become inseparable. As the move away from traditional society gains momentum, the traditional institutions and way of life give way to new ideas of social organization, behavior, and authority, and many see this change as an opportunity to discard old values. The situation is further complicated by the rapidity of change which leaves little time to adjust to development problems. Industrialization accompanied by population redistribution, dissipation of traditional forms of social control, social mobility and technological changes, and improved mass communication are some of the factors of development which tend to increase opportunities for deviant behavior. Poor housing, disorientation of family life, unemployment, rapid population growth, and special labor needs of some enterprises also are conducive to crime and delinquincy. There is a need for a determined effort to correct or remove the socio-economic imbalances that are known to be detrimental to development through systematic planning and programming.

Lamin Sesay has served as Social Affairs Officer in the Crime Prevention and Criminal Justice Section of the U.N. since 1965 and was the Head of Services for Juveniles in the Republic of Sierra Leone from 1960–65. He has represented Sierra Leone in several international and regional meetings on crime and social development, including the Third U.N. Congress in 1965. He was educated at the London School of Economics.

THE purpose of this paper, as indicated by the title, is to outline some of the relationships existing between crime and development in Africa. Taken by itself, development, as a concept, seems to have nothing to do with crime. But when considered as a dynamic process of change, development and deviant behavior become inseparable. The magnitude of crime in relation to the development process will depend, to a large extent, on the complexity of changes in the lives of the people concerned.

TRADITIONAL AFRICA

Historically, the peoples of Africa had known and enjoyed a comparatively tranquil and traditional existence, devoid of the complex trappings of modern society and all the anxieties and restlessness involved in modern living. However, the emergence from a colonial/traditional past has brought with it not only a desire but an obligation to modernize and to develop a capacity to keep abreast of technological, scientific, economic, and ideological developments in other parts of the world, as a necessary condition for equal partnership in a highly complex and competitive world community. The process of evolution in Africa has undergone many dramatic phases. For the majority of countries, the change of political status—from dependent to independent—came with very little preparation for the enormous task of nation building.

The countries of Africa may have many valuable and tangible assets and resources desirable and necessary for development, but lack the most precious of all, which is simply time. Planning for development is time-consuming and it is quite apparent that the rest of the world will not stand still to wait for Africa. The process of development may take one of two forms: (a) a process designed to cause certain measured improvements or changes in some already established aspects of a society, such as health, social security, or education; or (b) a process involving a radical change in the foundation of a society to create a new one.

Because of the time limitation and other factors, development in Africa, has invariably implied the creation of new societies. While conferring on people enormous material and other benefits, the new political, economic, and social systems have tended to generate many complex problems, which are exerting a profound impact on the ability of the new systems to maintain dynamism and sustain quality of growth.

As the move away from the traditional forms of society gathers momentum, the traditional institutional framework and the old concepts of life and behavior gradually give way to new ideas of social organization, behavior patterns, authority, and responses to stresses. Often, these new ideas and the corresponding opportunities created are grossly misunderstood and exaggerated, especially by the young. Many see in these new changes boundless opportunities to discard old values, social ties, and obligations to others, with the likelihood of succumbing to the temptation to satisfy needs and desires through illegitimate methods and means.

DEVELOPMENT AND CRIME

The problem of crime and development in Africa is not a recent concern of the international community. Notwithstanding the various theoretical contradictions surrounding the issue of crime and development, the United Nations has paid considerable attention to this subject for many years. The concern of the United Nations is based on the conviction that (a) development that does not lead eventually to a more equitable distribution of benefits is a questionable endeavor; (b) the human factor in development is the essential basis of higher productivity; and (c) the ultimate objective of development must be a better life for all the people, with increases in production considered merely as a means toward this end.[1]

Therefore, the United Nations crime prevention program has directed attention to the consideration of the facts and problems confronting all the countries of Africa at various stages of development, to provide information on national policies and programs concerned with the prevention and control of crime and delinquency, and to examine conditions in society that could be criminogenic. The basic idea is to explore ways and means of planning for development that could contain crime prevention elements, which would lead to the establishment of more wholesome societies.

As is the case in many developing nations, the expectations generated by the new political, economic, and social systems in the African countries are, indeed, very high. However, the prospects for the timely and equitable fulfillment of the expectations and goals to be attained during a given time span are often not only remote but obscure. Experience has shown that many development plans are far too

ambitious and their implementation often left to chance. Competing demands for the limited resources, particularly those relating to national security considerations, are a further setback to implementation. Implementation of development plans being partially or wholly based on external funding and expertise often causes such plans to remain on the drawing board indefinitely. The unpredictable nature of political changes also imposes its own constraints on the development process.

The situation is further complicated by the rapidity of change which leaves the countries with very little time to adjust to development problems such as those associated with rural/urban migration, shanty towns, unemployment, idle and poorly educated youth, demographic changes, and, last but not the least important, political instability. These are some of the inevitable side effects which may constitute major breeding conditions for crime and delinquency.

The drawbacks inherent in unbalanced economic and social development and their interrelationships with criminality have not remained unrecognized by the governments of the African countries. In its 1964–70 Development Plan, for example, the government of the Republic of Kenya observed:

The maintenance of law and order is the very first task of the Government in promoting economic and social development and its importance cannot be overemphasized. The experience of developing nations all over the world has shown that regardless of other policies adopted, failure to maintain order within the country is sufficient to slow, if not completely half, development.[2]

1. See United Nations International Review of Criminal Policy No. ST/SDA/SER.M/25. Sales No. E.68.IV.7. This issue of the Review was devoted to the theme of the prevention of crime and delinquency in the context of national development.

2. Republic of Kenya, Development Plan, 1964–1970 (Nairobi: Government Printer, 1964), p. 117.

The Kenyan Plan for 1970–74 repeats this theme. It calls for

. . . the maintenance of law and order, protection of life and property, prevention and detection of crime, apprehension of offenders and the enforcement of all laws and regulations [and explains that] all these functions have a direct bearing on economic and social development.[3]

The concern for orderly development that is clearly demonstrated in Kenya's development plans is also shown by other countries in the region, and references to crime in relation to economic and social development can be found in almost all development plans. However, the timely recognition of this phenomenon should not give rise to the impression that there is widespread criminality everywhere in Africa. It is true, to a degree, that there are still some countries in the African region where crime is not considered a serious development issue.

On the basis of available data and information on crime trends in Africa, it could be assumed that a relationship between crime and development does exist. Industrialization accompanied by population redistribution, dissipation of traditional forms of social control, social mobility and technological changes, and improved mass communication are some of the known factors in the dynamics of development which tend to increase the opportunities for deviant behavior.

Poor housing, disorientation of family life, unemployment, and underemployment are also factors considered to be conducive to crime and delinquency. Rapid population growth, whether from natural increase or massive immigration, also accentuates the pressures within the

3. Republic of Kenya, *Development Plan, 1970–1974* (Nairobi: Government Printer, 1969), p. 548.

changing society. The anonymous and shifting characteristics of life in the large urban areas and temporary settlements near industrial centers also tend to breed a variety of criminal subcultures. Inevitably, the accompanying changing values in the society and the weakening of traditional forms of authority and behavior, the absence or inadequacy of family life, and the failure of large numbers of young people to reach certain prescribed standards of educational or vocational achievement create serious problems of juvenile delinquency and other forms of deviant behavior.

Also, the special labor needs of some industrial and commercial enterprises create new sets of problems, often difficult to resolve. The labor practices of some enterprises, mining companies in particular, usually exclude dependents from the temporary shelters provided for workers in their respective areas of operation. Consequently, large numbers of bread winners are separated indefinitely or for long periods of time from their families. This practice often leads to a situation where children growing up not knowing their fathers drift away to the large urban areas. Likewise, the fathers who quit the mines seldom return to their original hometowns and often drift to the cities in search of better jobs. It is also not unusual for the abandoned spouses to seek refuge in the cities where they will probably join the swelling ranks of street walkers.

In some of the African countries, successful attempts have been made to establish viable workers' communities around industrial and mining operations, through a series of partnerships and cost-sharing arrangements between governments and the companies for housing, educational, sanitation, and health facilities. This gradual process of re-grouping family units, both primary and secondary, seems to be producing some positive results.

To some extent, the selective hiring of workers from the same tribal groupings for particular industries or operations, with arrangements for sharing the same company residential facilities, provides an element of social security. It is not unusual for the group or its individual members to provide for others who have fallen on bad times. Similarly, the unemployed youth or new arrivals can count on the goodwill of the extended family until jobs are secured for them. Such well organized groups have often been used as the nucleus of government-sponsored social-security oriented local cooperatives.

An attempt has been made to outline in both specific and general terms the phenomenon of crime as it relates to development in Africa. Essentially, the crime problems associated with such development are rather different from those being experienced by the developed world. While being relatively free from the more violent types of crime, the countries of Africa are experiencing an unusual pressure from the crimes relating to property and public funds. The crimes which seem to prevail in Africa demonstrate a basic insecurity associated with underdevelopment.

TREND OF CRIME

Without oversimplification, the trend of crime in Africa can be predicted and the underlying factors discerned with relative simplicity, at given stages of development. The general low levels of economic development, designated by some as poverty, the exposure of people to modern consumerism and the attendant high prices, inequitable income distribution, high rates of urban unemployment, and chronic rural underemployment have given rise to a life of petty larceny and graft.

Many large urban areas in some African countries are known to be virtually under a state of siege, and residents are forced by thieves to impose on themselves what is tantamount to a curfew. Public property, supplies, and technical equipment, imported at very high costs for development purposes, are also not spared the attention of the thieves. For example, it is reported that one country had to abandon an important agricultural project because thieves persistently stole all the batteries and tires from tractors and other vehicles and equipment.

More seriously, graft and other corrupt practices have not only succeeded in holding back development in some countries, but have forced many other countries into a state of virtual bankruptcy. The effects of these crimes on revenue collection and capital formation are devastating. In addition to undermining the confidence of new investors, corrupt practices are known to have driven many existing companies out of business. It seems doubtful, therefore, that any real development can take place in Africa under these conditions of insecurity of person and property and what is now generally regarded as widespread dishonesty or corruption.

The direct and indirect costs of crime represent a substantial share of national resources, and in the budgets of some countries the allocations for the maintenance of law and order far exceed the combined allocation for health and education.

The fear of more crime, especially crime against property, has made people more receptive to the presence of more policemen than teachers and doctors.

CONCLUSION

In conclusion, therefore, I should like to stress the need for a determined effort to correct or remove the socio-economic imbalances that are known to be detrimental to development. This could be achieved through systematic planning and programming derived from the social, economic, and cultural realities of the countries concerned. In that context, planning for crime prevention must also take place as an integral part of overall planning for social and economic development.

To ensure effective planning, proper provision must be made for the collection and utilization of comprehensive statistical and other data on trends. The universities and other specialized institutions should be given a special role in the areas of research and the training of personnel over the whole range of disciplines involved in crime prevention. Special efforts must also be made to create a greater awareness of crime and its relation to development among certain categories of officials whose functions are not directly related to activities in the social sector.

In that connection, I should like to mention briefly some of the technical assistance that the United Nations has been extending to the countries of the region, as a consequence of the concern of the organization about the deleterious effects of crime on development. Since the early sixties, the United Nations has given both material and substantive support to requesting governments to assist in the planning and implementation of crime prevention programs, in the context of national development objectives and priorities.

The type of assistance that the United Nations provides varies according to the particular circumstances and the nature of the problem, and may include short-term or long-term advisory services, ranging in duration from one month to three years. Technical assistance may also include a training component—fellowships—as well as books, documentation, and technical equipment.

In 1973, for example, the United Nations interregional advisers visited 38 African countries to render short-term advisory services to governments. This type of assistance is diagnostic and is intended to assist the requesting government in determining the nature and the scope of its problems. The expert, after considering all the elements of the problem, will usually render advice on appropriate remedial measures on the spot or recommend long-term United Nations assistance. Long-term advisory services normally involve the recruitment of a suitably qualified expert, in consultation with the government concerned, to render advisory services locally for a period of one to three years.

Additionally, the United Nations sponsors a series of interregional and regional seminars, symposia, conferences, and training courses designed to encourage and promote collaborative efforts in the planning of programs and policy formulation for crime prevention. Through these cross-cultural exchanges, the countries of Africa stand to benefit from the experiences and mistakes of other societies.

Specialized studies and investigation of selected aspects of crime in relation to development are also conducted by the major organs of the United Nations concerned with the problems of crime. The network of United Nations regional research and training institutes, as well as the central institute in Rome, provide additional technical support at both regional and local levels. The Cairo Regional Centre for Social and Criminological Research currently serves the needs of both the countries of Africa and the Middle East, until such a time when a regional institute for Africa, south of the Sahara, is established.

Finally, it could be reasonably assumed that with continued international cooperation, as exemplified by the United Nations, the battle against crime in developing Africa may someday be won or perhaps a lasting truce could be accomplished.

*   *   *

QUESTIONS AND ANSWERS

Q: Traditional African societies have crime, but I cannot see how one can divorce the criminal situation from present urban conditions in Africa. Don't you think that we should address ourselves to the very close relationship between law and custom? If you look at post-colonial Africa today, our legal systems are exact replicas of Western legal structures. Since we have completely different customs, how could we expect these public and legal structures to work for us when they are not even working for most Western countries?

A (Sesay): My first reaction is that the United Nations is not blaming urbanization for all crimes. In fact, what I have tried to do is simply to show whether there is a relationship between development and crime. Our mandate simply states that we examine the development process to see what type of problems might predispose people to commit crimes. My statement lists a number of conditions considered factors in the creation of criminal behavior. I have not attempted to single out urbanization. Rather, we have been concerned with examination of conditions in the process of urbanization that might have a bearing on crime. To take the other point that you mentioned about colonial laws, we have a comprehensive study on that problem. In fact, we have a questionnaire on this particular issue that was sent to governments. It is our belief that the old laws have been creating more problems than they have been solving. What the old laws were supposed to do is not consistent with the present interests of the countries. But how do you change a law? To change a law you have ethnic and religious considerations, and the government itself has the problem of resolving all these difficulties. You find groups in all countries which are hanging onto the old colonial laws because it is the only protection they can get in the dynamics of change in Africa. As people throw away the colonial laws, they are finding that there is no law. We tell them: You handle it. When you decide that you want new laws, we can help you. We send experts to the governments who want to change the laws. But it is entirely up to them to change it.

Q: All of the information that we have had about the increase in crime has been in connection with urban development in Africa. Is there a concomitant rise in criminal behavior in the rural communities? They must also have a picture of new goals that they expect to meet. They are either operating under the old tribal laws or much more influenced by the old colonial laws. Does this make a difference?

A: (Sesay): In rural areas there is crime, but not as defined as in urban areas. As you rightly pointed out, the traditional forms of control of justice still operate in some areas. The level of tolerance for different types of crimes in the rural area is still much higher than in urban areas. In the rural areas, crime especially relating to property is not that significant, whereas in urban areas, most things taken for granted in rural areas have a cash value attached to them. For example, if somebody takes a chicken in the village, it is no crime. In the city, this is a crime. Of course, the problem of urbanization is serious. The lack of development or growth in the traditional African sector is forcing the people into the cities.

Secondly, there is the negative effect of education. When a school is established in a village, 90 percent of the children enrolled wind up in the city. They look for better opportunities. Now most of the educational institutions in Africa have matured. Where in the past the number of schools could be counted on one hand, now they are in the hundreds. When the young people start coming out of school, there are no jobs. So you have this bulge in the cities. The young people must have something to do. There has to be some connection between the growth of cities and the increase in crime.

Q: You also have to have a redefinition of what is crime in an urban area. If you steal a chicken in your community, you fight it out, but if you steal a chicken in the city, you have committed a crime. That must be making a very difficult problem too.

A (Sesay): That is a very important part of the problem. In fact, we have been trying to encourage governments to remove certain crimes from the book. But of course here, again, you have to maintain a balance between logic and human rights. If stealing the chicken was removed from the books, somebody could steal my chicken and go free. All of this would have to be taken into consideration.

Q: There are scholarly studies directly related to crime development, modernization, or organization, such as the work done by David Bailey, University of Denver. One proposition that he has come up with is that the type of crime we are talking about in Africa may actually be a system of redistribution. In capitalistic conditions that are developing, it is difficult for redistribution to filter to the bottom. Do you see a correlation between the mode of development adopted and crime? If that is the situation, are we not actually talking about developmental alternatives here that may lead to crime as opposed to crime as a problem in itself?

A (Sesay): I think the approach I will take here is the U.N. approach.

Development itself does not cause crime. It depends on the type of development. The Eastern block will say we don't have any crime, because nobody owns anything. It is only in the capitalistic system that you have crime. When you examine facts, you find that there is crime everywhere. The problem in dealing with crime today is first that of defining what is crime. Now in urban development all that the United Nations can do is conduct worldwide studies, get responses from governments, and then present it to the members. It is up to them to decide which one of those examples to take. We don't say which is successful, because each individual experiment's success depends on the interpretation that it is given by those who practice the experiment. Deciding which society produces more crime depends upon the systems that are operating—whether the society is tolerant of the crimes or not. If one society is more tolerant, that means it will have fewer crimes recorded, whereas another which is less tolerant will have more crimes.

Q: In three Asian countries— Vietnam, Cambodia, and to a lesser extent China—there has been a forced effort to move the people out of the city into the countryside. Are there any African countries that have gone about moving people from the cities to the rural areas in a very big way, particularly some of the more revolutionary ones like Mozambique or Tanzania?

A (Sesay): One thing that I should first make clear, what is happening in China, Cambodia, or Vietnam, cannot be equated with the experi-

ence in the African countries. In Malawi, for instance, we have a huge project that is designed to get people out of the cities. This project is jointly supplemented by the World Health Organization, UNICEF, UNESCO, and the Food and Agricultural Organization. What they have done, on the request of the government, is to create new communities to revitalize the countryside. The government has purposely created rural academies, and the conditions are that if you benefit from all the communities' services, you must stay there. To the government and those financing it, this is a necessary condition. In African countries, if the government gives you a scholarship, after your studies you must work for the government for a set number of years. With this project you are moved from the city and the government creates the facilities for employment. They are working to develop rural industries. All the needs of the human being are taken care of in this joint project, but if you move out you can never find a job or housing in the urban area. It is a deliberate movement but not compulsory in the sense that large numbers of people are moved out of the cities indiscriminately.

Q: It's been fashionable in academic circles recently to think about crime as criminal systems that are subsystems of larger social systems and develop with them. This was the case in the United States with immigration and the emergence of organized crime. Have there been similar patterns of development of crime in Africa? If there have not, what is the inhibiting factor?

A (Sesay): This question could be answered yes or no. So far, there is none of the type of organized criminal behavior one finds in the more developed countries. Perhaps one can attribute this to the present forms of social organization. The type of crimes being committed are generally petty crimes against property. The only organizational element in this is what one calls the fencing. This can be considered organized crime, but it is still at the elementary level.

ANNALS, AAPSS, **432**, July 1977

Organization of African Unity and Decolonization: Present and Future Trends

By GODFREY L. BINAISA

ABSTRACT: Although colonialism is now buried in most parts of Africa, its ghost still haunts us in the unnecessarily large number of states. The drive for independence in Africa was first propounded by blacks in America in the philosophies of Pan-Africanism, African personality, and négritude in the early part of this century. Africans derived moral support from the Atlantic Charter and the weakening by WW II of the 2 European empires. The demise of the Indian Empire was the final nail in the coffin of British Imperialism. The most important meeting leading to the formation of the OAU was the Conference of Independent African States in April 1958. In the same year, an East African group (PAFMECA) was formed, and by 1963 membership included 18 countries. Between 1960–62, 23 states achieved independence. On May 25, 1963, the OAU charter was signed, uniting 47 independent black and Arab nations to promote solidarity among member states. One of the most important objectives of the OAU has been decolonization of Africa, but even after this is achieved, the OAU will still be united in facing the numerous problems of political, economic, and social development in Africa.

Godfrey L. Binaisa is currently seeking admission to the New York Bar, has a L. L. B. degree from Kings College, Univ. of London, and he is a Queens Council. He was called to the English Bar in 1956, had a private law practice in Uganda from 1956 to 62, was Attorney General of Uganda from 1962 to 67, returned to private practice in Uganda from 1967 to 73 and in London from 1974 to 75. He was twice president of Uganda Law Society and since 1971 a member of the International Commission of Jurists. His publications include Report on the Ugandan Trades Union Congress *and* Right to Leave and Right to Return to One's Own Country, *for the Symposium sponsored by the International Institute of Human Rights, Strausbourg, France, 1972.*

A CATALOGUE of political, economic, and social events from the colonial era to independence leading to the creation of the Organization of African Unity (OAU) would leave us with all text and no sermon. The ambit of this paper, therefore, will not entail the citation of all the Articles of the Charter of the OAU which can easily be found in many works on Africa. The Charter will, however, be referred to wherever the context permits; emphasis will be laid on the political events in Africa leading to independence of most of the African states in the 1960s and the eventual creation of the OAU in 1963. A survey of the achievements and failures, aspirations and hopes of the OAU will be attempted and conclusions will be drawn regarding the future.

The continent of Africa is in the shape of a big question mark, 4,700 miles at its widest point, 5,000 miles at its longest point, and 11,700,000 square miles in area. Its population is 300 million persons divided into 6,000 tribes and speaking well over 1,000 languages and dialects. Africa is more than three times the size of the United States.

COLONIZATION

Colonization of Africa dates back more than 10,000 years. Around 8000 B.C. migrations into Africa started by peoples of the Middle East and probably South West Asia. This wave of immigrants was later followed by Semitic peoples from the Sabean Kingdoms of Southern Arabia into East Africa around 1000 B.C.

The Phoenicians settled in North Africa around 850 B.C., to be followed by the Romans in 200 B.C., who were in turn followed by the Byzantine Empire builders. The Arabs entered Africa in a significant

way between A.D. 639 and A.D. 1400. They were mainly interested in the slave trade and established trading posts for the collection of slaves and African gold and ivory.

It was not until the tenth century that the Europeans took interest in Africa when they sailed round the cape of South Africa on their way to India. This relationship with the Europeans has continued to the present day and provides the story of the colonization of Africa in the perspective of modern times. It is a saga punctuated by stories of brutal cruelties, romantic idealism, dedicated evangelism, and concepts of empire building by European powers.

The year 1884 is a landmark in the modern colonization of Africa, because during that year at the Conference of Berlin, presided over by Prince Otto von Bismarck, the Chancellor of Germany, the European powers carved up Africa amongst themselves. The United States was the only non-European power that was invited to attend, although she did not claim any part of Africa. The inhabitants of Africa did not participate at any level in the deliberations of the conference. For the sake of prestige, raw materials, ready markets for manufactured goods, and, to a certain extent, missionary zeal to convert Africans to Christianity, the European powers proceeded to divide Africa amongst themselves.

The emperor of Germany declared that he also wanted a place in the sun and was given present-day Tanzania, Cameroon, Togo, and South West Africa, known also as Namibia. King Leopold of the Belgians wound up with a million square miles of the Congo River basin, not as a colony of Belgium but as his own private estate. He kept it as such until 1908 when it was taken over by Belgium as a colony. It is the present-day Democratic Republic of Zaire.

The Balkanization of the continent did not follow tribal or ethnic groupings of the inhabitants of the territories, their interests were not recognized and, in most cases, were completely ignored. This is why, today, we have so many independent African states, some of whom are hardly viable economic entities. With very few exceptions, many of these states cannot finance their development programs without some kind of artificial respiration in form of grants and credits of different kinds from their former colonial masters. This foreign fragmentation of Africa answers the usual criticism that Africa is not capable of uniting into one strong and unified country on the pattern of the United States or the USSR and Africans are prone to disunity and tribalism is stronger and more appealing to them than one strong nation. If the delegates to the Berlin Conference had addressed their minds to this problem, instead of acting like vultures over a carcass, they would not have used longitudes and latitudes as boundary lines among the African states they created.

Although colonialism as it was known in the nineteenth and first half of the twentieth century is now buried in most parts of Africa, with the exception of South Africa and Zimbabwe (Rhodesia), its ghost still haunts us in the unnecessarily large number of states which the OAU is trying to unite. The differences in the foreign cultures of the departed colonialists, added to the different indigenous cultures, only compounds the problem and frustrates the wishes of all African nationalists by making true unity a most tantalizing mirage.

CREATION OF THE OAU

Historical note

The drive for independence in Africa was first propounded by black people who were descendants of African slaves in the Americas, that is, the United States and the West-Indian islands. This movement was conceived in the philosophies of Pan-Africanism, the "African personality," and "négritude," and dates back to the early part of this century. Prominent personalities such as H. Sylvester Williams, a lawyer from Jamaica living in England, and Bishop Alexander Walters of the African Methodist Episcopal Zion Church convened the first Pan-African Congress, whose declared intention was to secure for all African races living in civilized countries their full rights and to promote their business interests. Later other movements in Europe and the United States were formed to promote the idea of Pan-Africanism. For example, Dr. W. E.B. DuBois, one of the founders of the National Association for the Advancement of Colored People (NAACP), articulated the concept of Negro rights in the NAACP journal, *Crisis*. Another prominent figure during this period was Marcus Garvey from Jamaica, who established a journal, *The Negro World*, and founded the Universal Negro Improvement Association (UNIA) to promote rights of Africans. The UNIA Declaration of Rights included the statement:

We believe in the freedom of Africa for the Negro people of the world, and by the principle of Europe for the Europeans, and Asia for the Asiatics, we also demand Africa for the Africans at home and abroad.[1]

1. A. F. Addona, The Organization of African Unity, pp. 42–3.

Several Pan-African congresses were convened, but no African delegates from the continent of Africa participated in these congresses until control of Pan-Africanism was taken over by Africans from the continent. These Africans derived moral support from the Atlantic Charter which was signed in 1941 by U.S. President Franklin D. Roosevelt and British Prime Minister Winston Churchill declaring: ". . . the rights of people to seek self-determination had to be respected and that they wished to see these sovereign rights to self-government restored." This statement was interpreted by Africans as a promise to them of independence and self-government.

Another boost came by way of the weakening by World War II of the two European empires: the British and the French who had vast African empires upon which the sun never set and wages never rose. Inspired by all these events, the African nationalists held the sixth Pan-African Congress in Charlton Town Hall, Manchester, England, from October 13–21, 1945. About 200 delegates attended from all parts of the world. Jomo Kenyatta, president of Kenya, the late Kwame Nkrumah of Ghana, and George Padmore were among the delegates. The next step was to convert the emerging concept of political independence into reality.[2]

Immediately after World War II, Britain, under a labor government led by Clement Attlee, granted independence to the big subcontinent of India, to India and Pakistan. The demise of the Indian Empire was the final nail in the coffin of British Imperialism. The Indian Empire had always been the backbone of the British overseas empire, its passing

away opened the floodgates of demands for self-government and independence by all subjects of Britain. The British West-African colony of the Gold Coast, now known as Ghana, under the able leadership of the late Kwana Nkoumah was the spearhead in this move and became the first black African former colony to become independent in March 1957. It was renamed Ghana after an ancient African Empire in the area. From now onward, the move to independence in black Africa was quick, and, by the late 1960s, most of the European colonies in black Africa were independent and had taken their seats in the U.N. as sovereign states.

The OAU

The most important meeting leading to the eventual formation of the OAU was the Conference of Independent African States held in Accra, Ghana, in April 1958. Only eight African states were independent. Ghana and Liberia were the only two black African states represented; the rest were Hamitic Semitic states: Ethiopia, UAR, Libya, Sudan, Morocco, and Tunisia. The conference proclaimed the unity of purpose and the right to independence of all African states not yet independent and the desirability of an African bloc at the U.N. All those principles which had motivated the formation of the earlier Pan-African congresses were enunciated and given a new meaning and content at that conference. From now onward, the road to the eventual creation of the OAU was clear for everybody to see. Kwame Nkrumah of Ghana realized the limitations of this conference because it was confined to independent states only. In December of the same year, he convened the

2. Ibid., p. 50.

first All-African People's Conference (AAPC) in Accra. This was a conference of all African nationalists from all dependent territories. It was attended by 300 delegates from 62 African nationalist organizations. The conference, among other things, passed resolutions calling for unity and independence and laid emphasis on the need to develop the concept of a United States of Africa.

In the same year, an East African regional group was formed known as Pan-African Freedom Movement of East and Central Africa (PAFMECA), later to be modified to include (South Africa) Azania (PAFMECSA). By 1963 the membership included the governments and leaders of 18 countries. Kwame Nkrumah did not support PAFMECSA on the ground that such regional groupings divided Africa into blocs.

At about the same time, other meetings were being held with emphasis on economics—these culminated in the establishment of the U.N. Economic Commission for Africa (UNECA) in Addis Ababa and the creation of the French Community. The purpose of the U.N. commission was to assist the emerging continent in economic, or functional, activities.

The French Community was an association of France and her six former African colonies on a cultural, economic, financial, and technical cooperation basis.

THE MERGER OF THE GROUPINGS

Between 1960 and 1962, 23 states achieved independence:

Brazzaville, Casablanca, and Monrovia. The Brazzaville—Senegal, Ivory Coast, Dahomey (Benin), Upper Volta, Neger, Central African Republic (Empire), Gabon, Chad, Malagasy, Cameroon, Mauritania,

Congo (Brazzaville)—created the Union of African and Malagasy States (UAM) in December 1960 under the doctrine of French heritage and assimilation; today known as Organisation Commune Africaine et Malagache (OCAM), the family added Congo Kiushasa (Zaire) and Rwanda. This was the moderate group. Emphasis was on functional unity through an economic commission.

The radical groups used the Algerian War and the Congo crisis to convene a conference in Casablanca, Morocco, in January 1961. Among them was Ghana, Mali, Guinea, Morocco, the UAR, the provisional government of Algeria, Libya, and, strangely enough, Ceylon. This was the radicals' answer to the Brazzaville bloc. Due to the divergent interests of the members—with UAR being only interested in using the conference to attack Israel and Zionism, Libya to support Algeria in her war of independence, Morocco to register her disapproval of the creation of Mauritania on land she claimed—to Guinea it was a reaction to France's abrupt abandonment of Guinea. In spite of all this, the most significant result was the enactment of the African Charter of Casablanca, which called for an African Consultative Assembly made up of representatives from every African state to meet periodically. It was subsequently agreed to convene a conference to resolve the different viewpoints in the way of African unity.

In Monrovia, Liberia, the conference was sponsored jointly by Ghana and Guinea for the radical Casablanca group, Ivory Coast and Cameroon for the Brazzaville group, and Liberia and Nigeria for the rest. The conference was never convened because of objections from Ghana.

However, invitations were sent out to attend a conference in Monrovia, Liberia, to discuss African cooperation and solidarity. Leaders from 20 African states attended—these became known as the Monrovia bloc.

Another attempt at reconciliation was made at a conference in Lagos, Nigeria, but the Casablanca group refused to attend. A majority attended from 21 states in Lagos on January 25–30, 1962. Agreement, in principle, was reached to a charter to create an inter-African and Malagasy Advisory Organization containing, in substance, the principles discussed at the Monrovia conference. the charter included provisions for a representative assembly, a council of ministers, and a general secretariat. It later became the basic document on which the OAU was created.[3]

THE ORGANIZATION OF AFRICAN UNITY

. . . [A] single African organization through which Africa's single voice may be heard, within which Africa's problems may be studied and resolved . . . which will facilitate acceptable solutions to disputes among Africans and promote the study and adoption of measures for common defense and programs for cooperation in the economic and social fields . . . to which we will all belong, based on principles to which we all subscribe . . . [and whose decisions] will take full account of all vital African considerations.[4]

President Kennedy's message to the OAU's first conference in Addis Ababa, May 1963:

Africa's continuing march towards independence, unity, and freedom—principles revered by the American people since the earliest days of our own nationhood—is a vital part of man's historic struggle for human dignity and self-realisation. This unprecedented gathering of Heads of State in Addis Ababa clearly attests your dedication to these principles, and provides a dogmatic illustration of African prominence in world affairs.

As you seek to achieve the dignity and freedom of the human individual and the rights of men, we share your desire that these objectives may be realised and safe-guarded for men everywhere. From your actions other nations may draw renewed inspirations to combine their search for improved ways to understand each other and to cooperate in peace.[5]

The radical and moderate positions were presented in speeches by the African leaders. President Nkrumah of Ghana summed up the radical position:

African unity is, above all, a political kingdom which can only be gained by political means. The social and economic development of Africa will come only within the political Kingdom, not the other way round.

The moderate position was embraced in a speech by the Nigerian Prime Minister Abubaker Tafawa Balewa:

Some of us have suggested that African unity should be achieved by political fusion of the different states in Africa; some of us feel that African unity could be achieved by taking practical steps in economic, educational, scientific, and cultural cooperation and by trying first to get the Africans to understand themselves before embarking on the more complicated and more difficult arrangement of political union. My country stands for the practical approach to the unity of the continent.[6]

---

3. Ibid., p. 73 ff.
4. Emperor Haile Selassie I at OAU Founding Conference, Addis Ababa, May 1963.

5. Proceedings of the Summit Conference of Independent African States, vol. 1, sec. 2 (Addis Ababa, May 1963).
6. Ibid., pp. 104–5.

The OAU charter was signed by the heads of state and governments on May 25, 1963. Sixty-three years after the first Pan-African meeting, the OAU was born, and May 25 is celebrated throughout Africa as "African Liberation Day." Diallo Telli, former Guinean Ambassador to the U.N., was appointed administrative secretary general.

Purpose

The OAU represents 47 independent black and Arab nations of Africa. It was established on May 23, 1963, for the purpose of promoting unity and solidarity among the member states. Among the aims are the eradication of all forms of colonialism on the African continent, the organization of efforts to improve the living standards of the inhabitants of the continent and to defend the sovereignty, territorial integrity, and independence of all the member states. It is significant to note that all the African states that form the OAU resolved at the Summit Conference in 1964 to maintain the boundaries which were left by European colonial powers who had colonized Africa.

Organization

The Organization of African Unity has its headquarters in Addis Ababa, the capital of Ethiopia. It is composed of an Assembly of Heads of State; a Council of Ministers; a General Secretariat; and a Secretary General who is elected by the Assembly of Heads of State—he is the chief executive for the administration and coordinator of all matters among member states and other international organizations; an arbitration commission, which seeks to settle disputes among members; and, in addition, there are several specialized commissions.

The policy of the organization is determined by the Assembly of Heads of State, which meets once a year. Although procedural questions are settled by a majority vote, policy resolutions require a two-thirds majority. Chairmanship of the Assembly of the Heads of State is rotated each year among the heads of state. By convention the chairmanship goes to the individual head of state who happens to be the host of the yearly Summit Conference. He keeps the post until the next Summit Conference. It has to be noted that this is merely an honorific title and has no executive functions attached to it. This is why President Idi Amin of Uganda held the position of chairman during the year Uganda played host to the Summit Conference in 1975–6.

Decolonization

The resolution on decolonization was one of the 10 important resolutions at the May 1963 Summit. The resolution suggested diplomatic action against colonial powers in Africa, such as Azania (South Africa), Zimbabwe (Rhodesia), and Portugal, by appropriate action in the U.N. and severance of diplomatic relations.

OAU, through the U.N., has forced Azania out of the U.N. Economic Commission for Africa, the Food and Agriculture Organization, the ILO— and even the Olympic games.

OAU has generated pressure on other countries to sever relations with Zimbabwe. A sanctions bureau has been established in the OAU to monitor implementation of economic boycott of Azania.

Liberation movements

Coordinating Committee—Algeria, Ethiopia, Guinea, Zaire, Nigeria, Senegal, Tanzania, and Uganda—with headquarters in Dar es-Salaam to harmonize assistance to liberation movements and for managing the Special Fund. Added members are Zambia and Somalia.

The Committee of Eleven, or the African Liberation Committee (ALC), was criticized by some member states for lack of effectiveness and ran into difficulty in obtaining funds. The ALC does no fighting and consists of representatives of governments.

Relationship among member states

The relations among member states of the Organization of African Unity have not always been very happy, because some states have given refuge to individuals or groups of individuals who have fled their states because of disputes between them and the government, and almost invariably these groups or individuals have tended to try to organize the overthrow of their own state. At the same time, it has to be remembered that even the so-called liberation movement may be used against the existing leadership in a particular African country and not only against colonial rule. To this must be added differences in ideology wherever these exist. Concern has been expressed more than once by some states about the effects on their economy of some states if they were to carry out the resolutions of the Organization of African Unity against imperialism and colonialism in their letter and spirit. Such concern was highlighted at the OAU Summit Conference in Cairo in 1964 by Prime Minister Dr. Hastings Banda of Malawi. He said:

While I feel strongly against Imperialism and Colonialism in any form; while I am just as anxious as anyone in this conference to help our brothers and sisters still under colonial rule in neighboring territories, Malawi's power, my own power, to help is limited and circumscribed by geographical position. . . . I want to make it quite clear here at this conference that the geographical position of Malawi makes it impossible for me and my country to sever all ties, diplomatic, economic and cultural, with a certain power [Portugal] now still controlling great portions of our continent. I cannot promise here that I and my country will be in a position to carry out to the letter any resolution which demands total severance of all relations, diplomatic, economic, and cultural, with that power.[7]

Efforts to implement the OAU resolution on decolonization continue on moral, political, and economic levels as well.

Problems of OAU

Three major problems facing the OAU were:

1. apartheid;
2. European minority governments; and
3. relations between OAU and U.N., World Bank and similar institutions.

There were also problems of Africans against Africans. Issues tended to divide rather than unite—for example, subversion, refugees, regional groups, liberation movements, radical and moderate blocs. After the creation of OAU what would be the future of regional groupings in Africa?

7. Ibid., pp. 140–41.

Nkrumah and radicals criticized regional groupings as vehicles of division. At a meeting of the OAU Council of Ministers in Dakar, Senegal, in August 1963, there were sharp divisions. Radicals wanted the OAU as the primary political group in Africa, demanding that regional groups, such as moderate Union of African and Malagasy (UAM) states—the Brazzaville bloc—should surrender their authority to the OAU. The Brazzaville group, in adamant opposition, urged that regional groups strengthened, not weakened, the OAU. A compromise solution was adopted recommending that regional groups be in keeping with the charter of the OAU.

UAM was later dissolved as a formal organization and was substituted by the Union of African and Malagasy Economic Cooperation known by the French name, Union Africaine et Magache de Coopération Economique (UAMCE).

At a meeting in Nouakchott, Mauritania, in February 1965, former members of UAM formed a smaller OAU—Organisation Commune Africaine et Malagache—with headquarters in Yaounde, Cameroon, for the purpose of cooperation and solidarity to repel subversion from Ghana.

Achievements

When one discusses unity in the world as we know it today, one is immediately faced with problems of unity not only in Africa but around the world as well. For instance, the unity of the once formidable United Kingdom is now in the balance, with tribalism in Scotland and Wales and sectarian disruption in Northern Ireland. The unity of Cyprus only recently crumbled, disengaging two strange bedfellows—the Turks on one hand, and the Greeks on the other. The unity of Canada is now seriously threatened by differences of language and culture between the English-speaking and the French-speaking Canadians. Spain has an almost endemic problem of Basque separatism. In Yugoslavia it remains to be seen whether Croatia, Serbia, and the rest will have an enduring unity after the demise of Marshall Tito. The European community is the most recent bold attempt to unite Western Europe, but it is also beset by the teething problems of a growing child.

Seen through the mirror of this wider spectrum, the fact that Africa, with something like 1,000 tribal languages and a similar number of cultures, upon which was superimposed the cultures and languages of the colonial powers, has managed to organize all these diverse peoples into one organization for the good of all is one of the greatest achievements in contemporary international politics. The most significant achievement of them all, however, has been the survival of the organization for more than 10 years in spite of external problems, internal tensions, and a myriad of other problems in the economic, social, and cultural areas.

In the international arena, the Organization of African Unity has achieved observer status as the Organization of American States and the Arab League as a coordinator for the United Nations on African affairs. It has to be remembered that the Organization of African Unity states at the United Nations are almost one-third of the total membership of that body. They, in addition, have two nonpermanent seats on the Security Council.

The other significant achievement

of the OAU has been to provide a forum for the leaders of Africa to come together, meet, and get to know one another—a thing that was denied them when they were all under various European colonial powers. It is well known that until now Africa has not been able to solve the important question of communications. If an African in Kenya in East Africa, wants to call a friend in Dakar, Senegal, on the West Coast, over the telephone, there is no direct telephone link between Nairobi and Dakar so the call has to go through London, relayed to Paris, and then to Dakar. This, therefore, brings into focus the desirability of the leaders meeting together once a year to talk and discuss matters of mutual interests.

Failures

As in all fields of human endeavor, the OAU has had its strains and stresses. The most glaring failure has been in the area of violations of human rights in member states of the organization. The OAU has failed as a body to stand up and be counted in defense of human rights among its members, while at the same time continuing to condemn the violations of the same human rights in the two European minority regimes of Zimbabwe and Azania. This kind of behavior has had a tendency to reduce the credibility of the OAU in the international community. Violations of human rights in Uganda, Equatorial Guinea, or the Central African Empire (formerly Republic) are of no less viciousness because they are being committed by governments that are under black African dictators. The OAU must be in a position to condemn its own member states and pass moral judgments in all such cases.

The future of OAU

The Emperor Haile Selassie I of Ethiopia, at the founding conference in May 1963, said:

Today, we look to the future calmly, confidently and courageously. We look to the vision of an Africa not merely free but united. In facing this challenge, we can take comfort and encouragement from the lessons of the past. We know that there are differences among us. Africans enjoy different cultures, distinctive values, special attributes. But we also know that unity can be and has been attained among men of the most disparate origins, that differences of race, of religion, of culture, of tradition, are no insuperable obstacle to the coming together of peoples. History teaches us that unity is strength and cautions us to submerge and overcome our differences in the quest for common goals, to strive, with all our combined strength, for the path to true African brotherhood and unity.[8]

DECOLONIZATION

As has already been pointed out earlier in this paper, the decolonization of Africa was one of the most important resolutions at the first Summit Conference of the OAU which adopted the charter. It was the considered opinion of all member states that the independence of some states in Africa would be meaningless unless such independence was linked with the total independence of the entire African continent. The Portuguese African empire, having collapsed suddenly two years ago, thus resulted in the independence of Guinea Bissau, Mozambique, and Angola. In the case of Guinea Bissau and Mozambique, power was transferred to the nationalist movements which had been

8. Ibid., p. 210.

waging a guerilla war of liberation for more than 10 years. In the case of Angola, however, there was no smooth handing over of power to a single nationalist movement. The country had three nationalist movements—that is to say FLN, led by Holden Roberto and supported by Zaire and the People's Republic of China and some Western powers; UNITA, led by Savimbi and supported by South Africa and the Western powers; and MPLA, led by Augustino Neto and supported by the Soviet Union and Cuba and a majority of African states.

Of the three former Portuguese colonies, Angola is the most important because of its richness in minerals, agricultural produce, oil, and many other products. At the same time, Angola is the cause of much concern to Western powers by having declared its intention to build a Marxist-Leninist state based on scientific socialism. Added to this is the presence of some 13,000 Cuban troops who assisted the MPLA to achieve victory in the short-lived civil war that ensued immediately after the Portuguese left.

In several cases in the past, the Soviet Union, due to her phenomenal ignorance and lack of experience in Africa, blundered wherever she tried to meddle in African affairs. Over the years, however, she seems to have learned a few lessons. In her intervention in the Angola civil war, she relied on Cuban troops who came from a tropical country with a population consisting of around 40 percent blacks. The Cubans speak Spanish, a language that has much in common with Portuguese. They mixed more easily and blended themselves in the Angolan society far better than any European would have done. Their

success was, to many Africans, not a surprise.

What was a surprise to the majority of African countries was the unholy alliance which FLN and UNITA made with the minority white regime of South Africa. The acceptance of assistance from South Africa by the leaders of these two nationalist groups amounted to a kiss of death and left the independent African countries no room to argue about ideology. The invasion of Angola by white troops from South Africa, after Angola had achieved independence, was an unwarranted affront to the entire continent. It was regarded as the thin end of the wedge to the establishment by South Africa of another Bantustan where they, the white South Africans, would wind up as the bosses to exploit the economic resources of Angola and once again subjugate the Africans of that country to the same indignities meted out to the South African blacks. Nigeria, as the emerging African superpower, took the lead in going to the rescue of Augustino Neto and his MPLA.

PRESENT TREND

The OAU has miraculously overcome most of the problems which might have killed it in its infancy, as was clearly shown by the mood of jubilation among the member states at the tenth anniversary of its foundation in Addis Ababa in 1973. Members surely had something to congratulate themselves for. Here was an organization which had survived both external pressures and internal tensions. However, with the Portuguese African Empire having been relegated to the annals of history, there now remains only three territories in

Africa which have yet to celebrate their liberation: Rhodesia, named after the British Imperialist, Sir Cecil Rhodes and known to Africans as Zimbabwe; South West Africa, also known as Namibia, former colony of Germany, given to South Africa to administer as a mandated territory, at the end of World War I; and the biggest and the most intractable of them all, the Republic of South Africa. The trend today among all member states of the OAU is to see to it that these three territories attain their freedom by securing majority rule for the black Africans living in them. Let us now examine them one by one for the sake of clarity.

Zimbabwe (Rhodesia)

Zimbabwe, with a population approaching 7 million Africans and 270,000 Europeans, is the last bastion of privilege to people of British stock outside the United Kingdom. Unlike the Republic of South Africa, the European population is essentially British. This is what prevented the British government from sending troops into Rhodesia to suppress the rebellion when the European minority government of that country unilaterally declared independence. The questions of "kith and kin" prevailed over an open act of rebellion, which, to all intents and purposes, amounted to treason. The other argument was that, in any event since 1923, Zimbabwe was independent in all respects but name, having been granted responsible self-government in that year and the European prime ministers of Rhodesia having been accepted as such by other prime ministers of the independent members of the British Commonwealth of nations.

There is no need to argue the point that that kind of reasoning cannot stand up to close scrutiny. It must be fully realized that, unlike what happened in many areas in Africa, European colonization of Zimbabwe was by conquest. The Europeans were aided in the process by their technology. They used rifles while their African adversaries had only spears. It was like fighting a modern war with rifles while your adversaries have rockets and nuclear weapons. Whatever peace prevailed after the European victory was an uneasy peace. The Europeans did not treat the Africans they defeated as gallant adversaries according to tenets of war, but proceeded to debase them and exploit them as being only fit for manual labor.

Today, with the availability of modern weapons to the Africans, the war started in earnest with the intention by the Africans to get back their own country. This explains the distinction between the struggle for civil rights in the United States by the black Americans and the situation in southern Africa. In the United States, the blacks are a minority, unlike the Africans of Zimbabwe, whose population exceeds that of the Europeans by 22 to 1. Further, in the United States the issues are centered on the demand by the blacks for the implementation of all civil rights statutes and the 14th Amendment to the U.S. Constitution to their full force and effect. This is very different from the demands and claims of the people of Zimbabwe to be masters in their own house and take full responsibility of the destiny of their country. The European population of Zimbabwe are Europeans, and nothing will ever change that.

One has only to look at similar

incidents in history to be convinced that foreign occupation always remains foreign however long it may be prolonged. The occupied people never lose their inalienable right to reclaim their country from whoever has been occupying it. This happened in Britain, which the Romans occupied for about 400 years. It was repeated in the case of the occupation of Spain by the Moors. Again, the occupation of Greece and neighboring countries by the Ottoman Turks is a more recent example. In all these cases, the owners succeeded when the opportunity presented itself to drive out the intruders and assert their independence and self-determination. It is, therefore, submitted that the European occupation of Zimbabwe is indefensible in this day and age. Ian Smith, the prime minister of Zimbabwe, and members of his cabinet are just a bunch of dinosaurs from a bygone age who are incapable of understanding that the world around them has changed. In the final analysis, the guerrilla war in Zimbabwe is an extension of the earlier battles the people of Zimbabwe waged unsuccessfully against the European colonialists.

The present trend is that the OAU is fully committed to assist the guerrillas in their just struggle for independence. The front line African presidents, that is, the presidents of the countries nearest Zimbabwe, Tanzania, Mozambique, Zambia, Botswana, and Angola, recently gave their full backing and support for the Patriotic Front, which is the alliance between Joshua Nkomo, the leader of Zimbabwe African Peoples Union (ZAPU), and Robert Mugabe, the leader of the militant wing of Zimbabwe African Nationalist Union (ZANU). Ian Smith has reacted against this move by indicating that he is not prepared to talk peace with the Patriotic Front, but would go ahead and negotiate a settlement with moderate African political leaders inside Zimbabwe, like Bishop Mazorewa and some traditional African chiefs who are paid officials of the government.

Such a move, once again, highlights a complete lack of understanding on the part of the European colonialists of the situation as it stands today. The Africans who are fighting are the most courageous, determined, and committed people, who realize that it is only by taking up arms that they will achieve their ultimate objective. They are the ones who are fighting and dying; they ought to be the ones with whom to come to a settlement, as is the practice in all warfare. No war has ever ended by merely talking peace with people who never took part in the fighting. The only explanation that comes to mind is that Ian Smith does not yet accept the fact that Africans are as human as any other people and that they deserve to be treated in the same way as Ian Smith would have treated European soldiers if they had been fighting against him. European supremacy is all pervasive in Zimbabwe, and would forever prevent men like Ian Smith from reaching any kind of acceptable settlement. As long as the African is considered by the Europeans to be an inferior species of mankind, the hope of a peaceful accord will never be achieved. The OAU fully understands this and is therefore committed to an armed struggle as the only way still open to the Africans.

Azania (South Africa)

As already indicated above, Azania and Zimbabwe together with Namibia (South West Africa) are the only countries still under European minority governments in Africa. The term "European" is being used advisedly, because that is what the European population in the region regard themselves to be.

The history of Azania is littered with violence ever since that country was conquered by Europeans. Violence is a golden thread that is always to be seen throughout the web of past and present Azania. Not a day passes without some kind of violence related to the unhappy political situation in that country. The calendar of the courts in Azania is heavily loaded with cases related to the statutorily imposed segregation of the races. The prisons are full of people convicted under the maze of those statutes.

As in Zimbabwe, the Europeans in Azania settled there as conquerors. They fought many wars, first against Africans and secondly among themselves, as was the case in the Boer War at the turn of the century. It is true that Europeans have been living in that country for 300 years, but it is submitted that, as in Zimbabwe, their having lived there as conquerors for 300 years did not take away the right of the Africans to get back what is their own. Everything the Europeans got out of Azania was obtained by force, therefore it stands to reason that it is by force that they will have to give it back.

The Europeans of South Africa have been known to argue that they are a "white tribe" of Africa and, as such, have no other country to go to if they were forced to leave Azania. This kind of argument suffers from more than one defect. First, if they were indeed a white African tribe as they claim to be, they would not have imposed segregation by statute on their fellow black brothers. Furthermore, they would not have elected to take for themselves more than 80 percent of all arable land in the country. They would not have, by force of law, relegated the Africans to a position of permanent slavery and regarded them as sojourners outside the so-called African homelands. They would not have created unbelievable differentials in salaries and wages between themselves and the Africans. In short, they would not have dehumanized and debased fellow Africans by reducing them to robots with a pair of hands and a pair of legs to serve the needs of the Europeans in the mines, factories, farms, and private homes.

The so-called homelands or Bantustans can be described as Sanatoria to take care of those persons who, because of age, are no longer fit to work for the Europeans. They are sent back to these undeveloped homelands to die in conditions of absolute squalor and poverty. They have no rights which the Europeans respect. They are forever destined only to render duties with no hope of ever securing corresponding rights. The entire body politic in South Africa pulsates on only one topic of race. No wonder that the Europeans in Azania suffer from one of the highest rates of suicides in the world and drug addiction.

It is against such background that the rise of the movement of Black Consciousness has to be seen. The black youth are in revolt. They have rejected once and for all the patience of their parents, because they have realized that to the Europeans they are chattel without rights or needs, but to serve the Europeans as slaves. They know that the only way to achieve their goal is to launch an attack on the entire system and dismantle it. This explains the causes of the recent riots in Soweto township near Johannesburg and elsewhere in the republic.

THE FUTURE OF THE OAU

It is true that the existence of colonialism on the African continent is one of the strongest unifying factors cementing together peoples of different cultures to pursue the goal of eliminating colonialism from their continent. The question may be posed as to what would be the future of the OAU after colonialism is eradicated. It has already been pointed out in this paper that the member states of the OAU are in two groups: the radicals and the moderates. At every conference of either the heads of state or the council of ministers, these two groups have always manifested themselves. On several occasions the composition of the groups has changed, as, for instance, Nigeria which until a few years ago was regarded as a moderate state and is now a foremost leader of the radicals. The Peoples Republic of the Congo (Brazzaville) is now among the radicals. However, states like Senegal and the Ivory Coast have remained moderate to this day.

It is submitted that the OAU will have a future even after the colonial era has passed, because it will have to face the numerous problems of development in all areas of human endeavor: political, economic, and social. The existence of colonialism is like a running sore sapping all the strength of the OAU, thereby preventing it from addressing its mind to the urgent problems of development. One only hopes that the colonial era will come to a quick end.

THE ROLE OF THE UNITED STATES

There is no need to emphasize the fact that to the great majority of the American people, colonial rule is essentially oppressive and contrary to their tradition of freedom and equality which are the cornerstone of the founding of this great republic. The brutal query on the lips of the millions of oppressed people in southern Africa—Zimbabwe and Azania—is whether the United States can, as one of the world superpowers, influence events in that unhappy part of Africa and produce a situation that will grant independence and self-determination to the Africans before the Europeans in the area are faced with a long war which they will never win.

Time, technology, and numbers are all on the side of the Africans. In spite of the fact that immigration laws in both Zimbabwe and Azania favor European immigrants who want to live in privilege and believe in European supremacy, these laws will not deter Africans from fighting for what the entire international community regards as a just cause.

SUGGESTIONS

It is suggested that a new "Conference of Berlin" be called, this time not to partition Africa among the great powers but to liberate Africa. Such a conference must consist of the United States, the USSR, China, all those European powers that colonized Africa, the African Liberation Movement, and the emerging African superpower Nigeria. The usual accusation of the Soviet Union by the Western powers of interference in Africa will never be justified in the eyes of the African masses until the United States and her European allies demonstrate by deed that they wish to see colonialism brought to a quick end.

The recent events in Angola serve

as an example of the wrong approach by the United States to African affairs. The United States was very reluctant to permit Angola to take her seat in the U.N. and, in the end, allowed Angola into the U.N. by the negative tactic of abstaining from voting in the Security Council instead of positively supporting the application of Angola.

Secondly, and more importantly, the declaration by the United States that she would not establish diplomatic relations with Angola unless Cuban troops leave Angola smacks of unwarranted arrogance and intolerable patronage with serious overtones of racial discrimination. It is a well-known fact that after Angola had become independent, European troops of Azania invaded Angola on the flimsy pretext of protecting the giant hydroelectric dam on the Cunene River some 40 kilometers inside Angola. The dam was a joint venture between Azania and Portugal when the latter was still the colonial power in Angola. Angola requested and got Cuba to come to her rescue. As a result, the European troops from South Africa were repulsed after having nearly reached the Angolan capital of Luanda. Nigeria and other black African countries regarded the South African invasion as an affront, and all went to the assistance of Angola's MPLA government. They did not think about ideology; their priority was to deal a blow at South Africa. The two nationalist parties in Angola, UNITA and FLN had, by accepting assistance from South Africa, committed a "kiss of death" and found themselves without a single ally in Africa.

The United States has diplomatic relations with nearly all European Communist governments in Europe. Further, when the Soviet Union invaded Hungary in 1956 and Czecho-slovakia in 1968, the United States disapproved of both invasions but did not sever diplomatic relations with the Soviet Union or with Czechoslovakia or Hungary. Why then, the question may be asked, is the United States putting a condition to the establishment of diplomatic relations with the young republic of Angola, who has so far merely declared that its government shall follow Marxist-Leninist scientific socialism?

This kind of stance can be partly explained as yet another kind of racial discrimination. It is quite alright for the United States to have diplomatic relations with a Communist country as long as the country is European, but not when the country is African. The United States, without even waiting to see how Angola will interpret what she means by scientific socialism—which, by the way, is open to many interpretations—is refusing to extend to Angola a hand of friendship and goodwill. There is no need to overemphasize the desirability of having an effective U.S. diplomatic presence in Angola to let the Angolans have a choice and not shutting the door of the great Western superpower in their faces. It is ironic to see that it is U.S. corporations and not corporations from Cuba or the USSR who are exploiting the oil resources of Angola.

EDUCATION AND WELFARE

Many people agree that the pen is mightier than the sword. The United States could play a vital role in south Africa, Angola, and Mozambique by aid grants in the field of education to young Angolans and others to get higher education in American universities and colleges. The military hardware has its limits, but education has no limits. A whole generation of the people of Angola and Mozambique would welcome such a program. It goes without saying that the implementation of such programs would go a long way in convincing Africans that the United States wishes them well. Africa is in need of an unequivocal U.S. commitment which in the long run will, without a doubt, be a blessing to the economic interests of the United States and at the same time enable Africa and the OAU to appreciate everything that is good in the U.S. system.

CONCLUSIONS

The OAU has survived the first decade of its foundation, but it must learn to condemn its member states for violations of human rights.

The OAU resolution on decolonization, passed at the first summit conference in May 1963, is still the chief driving force that pervades all its deliberations and actions. The present trend is ever-increasing pressure on the two remaining colonial powers in Africa, that is, Rhodesia and South Africa, to surrender to the wishes of the African majorities in those countries. A Conference of Berlin in reverse should be called before a general conflagration occurs in south Africa. The United States is duty bound to play a big role in all these developments and not leave everything to the USSR.

The future of the OAU is bright even after colonialism is dismantled throughout Africa, because there will always be a need for a unifying forum to process development programs and enhance the realization of the objectives of the charter of the OAU.

*   *   *

QUESTIONS AND ANSWERS

Q: You mentioned the dictatorships in Rhodesia and South Africa and spoke eloquently about their misdeeds. We know that there are approximately 40 states in Africa, and less than half are bona fide democracies. Of the others, Idi Amin's in Uganda is the worst, but not the only one. Since the speaker did not criticize Idi Amin at all, I am asking isn't this racism?

A (Anyanwu): I try the best I can to present the views of Mr. Binaisa, who did admit that the African organization fails to intervene when there are issues concerning national entities. The denial of human rights in Uganda has now become a major question of OAU, but from the day the organization was started, about 1963, the number-one business on the agenda was the decolonization of Africa. They still see Rhodesia, South Africa, and South West Africa as territories occupied by whites. It is not discrimination but a matter of principle that all African territories must be free. After that, I think that the Africans would begin to challenge themselves.

President Sadat is a member of the OAU. There is no discrimination against him. He is light in complexion, but he is African. The major problem is that many Europeans in South Africa or Rhodesia, do not accept themselves as Africans. They call themselves Europeans and see themselves as superior to other Africans. Egypt does not see itself as superior to Africans.

ment openly and stop siding with the white minorities in South Africa, not to take over the activities of the African liberation movement.

Q: You made a strong plea against colonialism. Then you made a strong plea to the United States, for a superior power to come in and direct the affairs of developing nations. Isn't this in essence a contradiction?

A (Anyanwu): On one hand, if the Africans ask the United States to help, isn't it an invitation to colonialism? I would say no, it is a recognition that the United States has an interest in the world, the United States and the Soviet Union are superpowers, and they can influence issues in the world system. For example, the Organization for African Unity would appreciate the United States reminding Europeans that time has come for these countries to give up their colonies. The United States speaks the language that South Africa and Rhodesia understand. For example, President Carter's repeal of the Byrd Amendment, is a step in the right direction. This is what the Organization of African Unity is asking the United States to do—to support the African move-

Q: How do you reconcile the humbling ineffectiveness of the OAU to bring about some tangible results in the process of the liberation with the high-level rhetoric that has marked the language of the heads of African states or the organization itself since 1963?

A (Anyanwu): We tend to have some misconception of the role of or the power of OAU. OAU is not a superstate. It is a gentlemen's club of heads of state. If you follow protocol, there are certain things you don't talk about when heads of state meet. If OAU wanted to be effective in the way you want, it could have been an assembly of the people. It has not been so. Given the structure of OAU, I am not disappointed about what they have done.

My criticism is that the charter should be changed in a direction that would help OAU to be effective, but given the charter it doesn't have much power. It cannot do anything that any state does not want to discuss, and that is why it has not done very much.

The Challenge of Cultural Transition in Sub-Saharan Africa

By Victor C. Uchendu

ABSTRACT: It is the cultural content of the challenge posed by the new states of tropical Africa that is the subject of this paper. Post-colonial societies are transitional; they are making deliberate efforts to redefine their cultures. Cultural engineering, the deliberate political effort to channel behavior toward maximizing national objectives, particularly national integration, demands the notion of culture as an interventionist agent. Since independence, African politics has focused on the search for institutions and strategies to promote nation-building, economic development, and national and continental unity. African nations face the problem of how to select national, inspirational symbols that do not alienate their traditions. A related problem is the conflict between national cultural identity and growing cultural convergence. To be effective, cultural policy must be lived by the people who are the culture-builders. It cannot be achieved without cultural strain, and even among countries sharing a similar colonial experience, cultural policy may vary.

Victor C. Uchendu has been Professor of Anthropology and the Director of African Studies Center at the University of Illinois, Urbana-Champaign, since 1971 and was formerly the Director of the Makerere Institute of Social Research and Reader in Sociology/Anthropology at Makerere University, Kampala, Uganda. He has done field work among the Navajo Indians, in Uganda, Kenya, Tanzania, Zambia, and Ghana. Among his publications are The Igbo of Southeast Nigeria; *(co-author)* Agricultural Change in Kisii District, Kenya; Agricultural Change in Geita District, Tanzania; *and* Agricultural Change in Teso District, Uganda.

THE death of European empires gave birth to many sovereignties—new nation-states—in Africa, Asia, and the Americas. Ordinarily, new states constitute a problem in themselves. But the post-colonial states, which by accident of history must make conscious efforts to define and assert their cultural autonomy in a world characterized by increasing institutional convergence, pose a special challenge to the world and our age. Since institutions have their cultural basis, it is the cultural content of the challenge which the new states in tropical Africa pose that is the subject of this paper.

Students of African societies and cultures are increasingly becoming cautious in making generalizations about the African continent. This is particularly true of the sub-Saharan region, where a diversity of social arrangements and cultural patterns prevail. The imposition of European rule, which resulted in many contradictory colonial policies and cultural programs, further complicated the picture. We trust that we are not adding to the plethora of annoying stereotypes about Africa in the limited generalizations we think justified by the common experience of Africans in trying to forge post-colonial territories into modern nation-states.

Post-colonial states are forced to carry the cultural load of their departing imperial master, just as they must, at least initially, work with the institutional infrastructure created by colonial rule. Policies of new states—whether they aim at disengagement from or cooperation with the former colonial ruler or assert autonomy or seek diversification of dependency—have important cultural consequences. We will explore the cultural consequences of political action in three areas that practically every African state has identified as a challenge. These areas are: the task of nation-building; the challenge of economic development and modernization; and the problem of identity.

CULTURE AND TRANSITIONAL SOCIETIES AS ANALYTICAL CONCEPTS

All important events take place within the setting of history and some culture. In fact, events and events-systems derive their significance from the cultural setting in which they occur. The notion of "cultural transition" embodies both the ideas of culture and processes of history which must be understood in the African context if our exploration is to prove fruitful.

Our understanding of the nature and dynamics of human society has led to an expanding view of the concept of culture. The traditional conception of culture in dualistic terms—culture people versus nature people—has been abandoned. Although culture is defined in many different ways, and each definition has its major emphasis, there is now common agreement that the term culture refers to man-made aspects of our social environment, including the ideas and symbols we use. Culture is more than just a heritage, an historical product; it is more than the expression of man's mode of living, something that individuals in each society must undergo as a kind of fate or rites de passage. In an age when man has taken political control of his social and cultural destiny, and technology facilitates the control and subjugation of the environment and forces of nature, culture must be seen as an instrumental agent, as another mode of intervention in our social and economic life.

Cultural engineering,[1] a term Ali Mazrui uses to describe the deliberate political effort in Africa to channel behavior in the direction that maximizes national objectives, particularly that of national integration, demands the notion of culture as an interventionist rather than a passive agent. While technology has enabled modern man to tame and exploit the turbulent forces of nature, the notion of culture as an interventionist agent has led man to subsume the rules of nature within normative rules that are subject to cultural direction. Cultural rules are no longer sacred and do not have to be followed blindly. Elaborating on this theme, van Peursen reminds us that "every culture can be regarded as programmatic, a guided course of activities. . . . All culture may be regarded as man's way of imposing form upon the forces around him."[2] How African political leaders try to impose cultural form on many aspects of their transitional societies is not only interesting to explore but also challenging to understand. This raises the other conceptual problem—the notion of a transitional society.

Most typologies in social analysis, particularly in sociology and anthropology, tend to be dualistic or dichotomous. We have noted that the early notion of culture embodied a duality—culture versus nature peoples. It is in the concept of society that the notion of duality is most embedded. A few examples may be cited. Society is often conceived of as either civilized or uncivilized; folk or urban; cosmopolitan or local; sacred or secular; and Gemeinschaft or Gesellschaft. The processes of socio-legal development have been viewed as unidirectional, usually from status to contract; and the level of cultural achievement and institutional elaboration has been characterized as embodying either a Great Tradition or a Little Tradition. Post-colonial societies do not fit these models. The many contrasts they present among themselves, on the one hand, and between them and Western societies, on the other, have raised serious questions about the utility of these dichotomies. The concept of the Third World is more than a political concession to the emergence of new states on the world stage. It represents, in my view, a recognition of our inability to capture and contain the major social processes and societal complexities of the new states within the bounds of these dualistic categories.

We assume that Third World societies are in transition. But we are still far away from a theory of transitional social systems. We tend to project our view and characteristics of transitional society from either our model of traditional society or from the empirical characteristics of contemporary, industrial Western society. By selective use of diagnostic cultural traits, we define or refer to the traditional society as pre-literate and backward in cultural achievements, pre-Newtonian in its notions of causality and in general attitude to the natural environment, and often voiceless in political issues which shape its destiny. Because we have learned to associate traditional society with resistance to change, we are likely

1. Ali A. Mazrui, *Cultural Engineering and Nation Building in East Africa* (Evanston, Ill.: Northwestern University Press, 1972).

2. C. A. van Peursen, *The Strategy of Culture* (Amsterdam: North-Holland Publishing Co., 1974), pp. 11, 21.

to describe its attitude to innovation as one of stubborn tradition. Energy use, its source and amount, is often used to define traditional society. In this view, the traditional society is a low energy user, one that depends on human and animal sources of energy rather than on the inanimate sources of energy.

Working with the assumption that the transitional society lies between the traditional and the modern societies and that the direction of social change is unidirectional and practically irreversible—from traditional to modern patterns—it has become conventional to analyze the great political and cultural ferment of our times in terms of a confrontation between the two polar societies. According to Levine, this analytical model

. . . has helped us cope with the diversity of world cultures, substituting an image of commonality for one of bewildering variety, and prodding us to ask again and yet again in what ways the modern Western world is different from all other worlds. . . . As understanding of non-Western societies has deepened and ideas have refined, the ideal type of polarity between traditionality and Westernism has degenerated into a stereotype. . . .[3]

Given the limitations of dualistic categories and ideal types in social analysis, attention has increasingly turned to triadic categories. Daniel Lerner has used the triadic typology with good effect. Working from the hypothesis that "high empathic capacity is the predominant personal style only in modern society, which is distinctively industrial, urban, literate and participant," Lerner projects traditional society as "non

participant" and the transitional society as literally one in motion.[4] Sub-Saharan Africa is in motion in the sense that, with independence, it has taken the cultural destiny of its peoples in its hands. Its cultures are being defined and managed by its political leaders. This raises the question: What is the direction of cultural change in Africa?

THE CULTURALLY EMERGENT AFRICA

Since independence, the focus of African politics has been on the search for institutions and strategies which will promote nation-building, economic development, and the preservation of national and continental unity. Everywhere in sub-Saharan Africa, African governments have had to face a common problem: the political and cultural management of a plural society. African society is divided by ethnic, cultural, linguistic, and religious loyalties. It is a society in which unevenness in social and economic development is easily politicized because unevenness in the distribution of scarce resources and privileges of the new state are ethnically linked. It is a society in dire need of an overarching, shared symbol—a national ideology—but one which operates in a political environment that frowns upon or reluctantly accepts foreign symbols when regional symbols are politically difficult to nationalize.

The cultural agony of black Africa is deep-rooted. Africa is a continent whose cultural achievements were either ignored or attributed to foreign donors. It is the most thor-

3. Donald N. Levine, "The Flexibility of Traditional Culture," *The Journal of Social Issues*, vol. 24, no. 4 (1968), p. 129.

4. Daniel Lerner, *The Passing of Traditional Society* (New York: The Free Press, 1964), pp. 50, 94.

oughly colonized continent in recent history. Its leaders face what Barbara Ward calls "a double challenge" in their political effort to redirect and manage African cultural destiny: "They face an enormous challenge of change. But, in addition, they face an equally vast challenge of choice."[5]

THE CHALLENGE OF CHOICE

The very idea of culture implies change—adaptation and readaptation of forms, institutions, and ideas and their application to changing situations. Culture change, a dynamic process, implies among other things choice-making in society.[6] Choice-making involves individuals and groups as primary actors and the various alternatives provided by society. Choice-making is not an end in itself; it is simply instrumental. The type of choices which will help redirect African cultures are now politically directed. If you believe newspaper reports, it is not infrequent that the use of mini-skirts and foreign hairstyles, including wigs, by African women becomes the subject of presidential concern, if not court intervention. The content of African culture is largely an unchartered problem because choice-making, even in the area of culture, is no longer a simple affair for new nation-states.

Although politically managed cultural programs make choice-making problematical for individuals, the evidence suggests that every country in sub-Saharan Africa pursues what Lloyd Fallers calls a conscious policy of "cultural management."[7] The policies often vary and suffer from instability, but they are nevertheless designable. Some countries emphasize the continuity of African cultural systems, others recreate ancient abandoned institutions, and a few are highly selective, drawing from local and foreign cultural forms. McKim Marriott tells us why cultural policy is such an essential pillar of African post-colonial reconstruction: "No state, not even an infant one, is willing to appear before the world as a bare political frame. Each would be clothed in a cultural garb symbolic of its aims and ideal being."[8]

How do new African states want to be culturally clothed? And how are they, in reality, culturally clothed? The answer to the first question would require a documentation of ideological statements by African political leaders; and for the second question, the answer is an empirical one. It is reflected not by what leaders say, what Joseph Spengler calls "the contents of the mind of the elite who direct and of the men who man . . . underdeveloped society,"[9] but rather by the lifestyles and cultural responses of the individual members of African society.

5. Barbara Ward, *The Rich Nations and the Poor Nations* (New York: W. W. Norton & Company, Inc., 1962), p. 61.

6. V. C. Uchendu, "The Passing of Tribal Man: A West African Experience," *Journal of Asian and African Studies*, vol. 5, nos. 1–2 (1970), p. 59.

7. Lloyd A. Fallers, "Ideology and Culture in Uganda Nationalism," *American Anthropologist*, vol. 63 (1961), pp. 677–78.

8. McKim Marriott, "Cultural Policy in the New States," in Clifford Geertz, ed., *Old Societies and New States* (New York: The Free Press, 1963), p. 27.

9. Joseph J. Spengler, "Theory, Ideology, Non-Economic Values, and Politico-Economic Development," in Ralph Braibanti and J. J. Spengler, eds., *Tradition, Values, and Socio-economic Development* (Durham, N.C.: Duke University Press, 1961), p. 5.

CONTENT OF CULTURAL POLICY

The content of the cultural policy in modern African states is, in many ways, determined by the various colonial experiences and the indignity suffered by the black man in his recent history. McKim Marriott argues that

. . . most of the new states of sub-Saharan Africa [must] struggle to compensate culturally for their lack of full participation in any recognized civilization. . . . in Africa expanding literacy and education create a void, while considerations of political dignity and national purpose require that the void be appropriately filled. If the Africans do not suffer from civilizational *embarras de richesse* that now typically confronts the Asians, they suffer instead from the dilemma of having either to relate themselves to some foreign great tradition or somehow to convert elements of their many indigenous . . . cultures into a new entity worthy of civilized respect.[10]

It is in the use of "inspirational" symbols and symbolism that cultural policies in post-colonial African societies are most explicit. The names of the most important pre-colonial states and kingdoms in western Africa have been adopted by new nation-states. Ghana, Mali, and Benin may be mentioned in this context. In central and southern Africa, new place names, drawn from Africa's glorious past, are being revived, as Zimbabwe makes clear; and new place names like Zambia, Malawi, Tanzania, Azania, and Zaire have been coined to replace colonially imposed place names. Africa is witnessing, in the post-independence decades, a cultural renaissance in dress. This is most pronounced in western Africa where cultural continuity seems strongest. The absence of a dominant, non-African, immigrant settler population probably explains this. Many west African societies did not have to use the small European ruling class as a reference status symbol in matters like dress, as is the case in Kenya, Zambia, Rhodesia, and South Africa. Besides dress, Zaire, under President Mobutu Sese Seko, is probably unique in its apparently successful campaign to devalue foreign names, which are essentially Christian names.

Despite the inconsistency in the cultural policies of many African countries, religion remains one important area of African cultural life that is marked by a consistent policy. Sub-Saharan African states are basically secular in orientation, and there is good political reason to expect them to remain so. Religious symbols are as divisive in a plural society as ethnic symbols. Since both the Christian and Islamic faiths that command the loyalty of most Africans are foreign to black Africa and, more important, are regionally centered, the symbols they provide do not and often cannot command national acceptability.

EXPRESSION OF CULTURAL POLICY

Cultural policy is not just proclaimed; to be effective, it must be lived by the people. It is the people, the culture-bearers, who are the culture-builders.

Nation-building is one important national activity that every African leader must face. In a fundamental way, nation-building is more than a political activity; it is essentially culture-building. Ali Mazrui[11] has

---

10. Marriott, "Cultural Policy in the New States," p. 48.

11. Mazrui, *Cultural Engineering and Nation Building*, p. 277.

identified five major processes of nation-building. First is the necessity to achieve a degree of cultural and normative consensus; second is the promotion of economic inter-penetration among the different strata and actors of society; third is an effort at social integration through cross-cutting links, including marriage bonds; fourth, the building of effective conflict management institutions; and fifth, the accumulation of shared, national experience and the psychological empathy that this experience entails. In the African context, we must add a sixth factor: the diligent pursuit of even socio-cultural and economic development—in short, a policy of equity and justice, not as abstract principles but as social realities.

The cultural implications of each of the above processes of nation-building are obvious. The pursuit of cultural autonomy is essentially a segmentary process. A plural society that resents cultural domination from foreigners faces a dilemma of appropriate symbols when it makes decisions about national symbols, those instruments of the Great Tradition that may alienate the regionally centered Little Traditions that already exist in the society. How to evolve national symbols without alienating local or regional symbols is a central problem for transitional societies.

Language policies, or lack of them in many African states, provide a case study of the political dilemma of African states. The question is not whether African states need or deserve a national language. They do. Africans do not need just any language; they need to agree on a language that will give cultural expression to the dignity they must have and get others to respect.

For Africans at this stage of their political and cultural development, a national language must be seen as more than a vehicle of communication. As Berger reminds us, language is words, and words

. . . describe the realities of human life. But words also have the power to create and shape realities. The words of the strong carry more weight than the words of the weak. Indeed, very often the weak describe themselves in the words coined by the strong. Over the last two centuries or more the strong have been the technologically advanced nations of the West. As they improved their military, political and economic power over most of the world, they also improved the power of their words.[12]

The political dignity of the new states demands that the colonially inherited official language, which divides the elite from the masses, be decolonized. But the political realities, the problem of alienating one group or the other, forces language policy to take an evolutionary rather than a revolutionary approach. The pronouncement of African elite notwithstanding, it is only in Tanzania, among black African states, that a language policy backed by an active language program now exists.

In modern Africa, nation-building is tied up with economic development. Economic development, like nation-building, requires political guidance. It is the nature of a transitional society, or the post-colonial society, that the economy and the society must be developed as a simultaneous process. The reason lies partly in the strong linkage between resource endowment and population and partly in the role of

12. P. L. Berger, *Pyramids of Sacrifice, Political Ethics and Social Change* (New York: Anchor Books, 1976), p. 7.

the African state as a major entrepreneur in the economy, a responsibility that older industrialized states did not accept.

IDENTITY AND CULTURAL CONVERGENCE

Transitional societies are identity-builders. The most important instrument for building a national identity is an ideology. Ideology defines the boundaries of a cultural system as much as it gives it content. Fallers defines ideology as "the apologetic part of culture." In his view, ideology is "that part of culture which is actively and explicitly concerned with the establishment and defense of patterns of value and belief."[13]

Post-colonial societies which came into their own through protracted political struggles are more likely to cultivate and promote explicit ideologies than those that achieved independence through constitutional evolution. As societies mature, they tend to routinize their ideology through a general growth of political and value consensus. It should not be surprising, therefore, that ideological struggles are still going on in transitional societies. The ideology-moving political systems in black Africa are no less in transition than the political systems whose leaders have not been challenged sufficiently to formulate and promote explicit ideological goals.

The pursuit of national identity goals is in conflict with the notion of cultural convergence, another societal pattern which results from the fact that transitional societies are drawing from the same basic ideas of science, management theory, and technology in the solution of what appear to be common problems. The world may be divided by the harsh realities of social and economic inequality and the memory of past and, in places, continuing exploitation and injustice. Equally true, the world is more interdependent today than in any period in man's recent history. Cultural convergence is, therefore, in competition and sometimes in conflict with national cultural identity.

Given the pattern of choice-making in black Africa and the limited inventories for cultural engineering, the question has often been asked: Are African societies becoming like the West? This question is rooted in the relatively common effects of similar cultural choices which the history and the character of the transitional society impose upon its culture-bearers. It further reflects a convergence hypothesis which argues that, almost everywhere, common choices made under similar prevailing constraints, whether that of ideology or technology, tend to generate similar structural or cultural patterns. The evidence from sub-Saharan Africa suggests that while similar structural patterns are emerging in response to common constraints, their cultural content tends to be divergent.

Transitional societies in Africa have a common political value which they probably derived from the African past. They tend to view progress, cultural and economic, in purely political terms. Like all transitional societies, they have won their freedom through political action and, unlike the older, industrialized states, they have no ideological obstacle to intervening in various aspects of the people's welfare. Since politics in the transitional society is a major source of power, social mobility, and prestige, poli-

13. Fallers, "Ideology and Culture," pp. 677–78.

tics is practically coterminous with society rather than just a part of it. This development is probably unique. It cannot be said to be a cultural carry-over from the traditional society or from the recent colonial experience. Whatever its origin, the result is the same: the tendency to polity primacy. The dominance of every aspect of social and cultural life by politics, and particularly the extreme reliance on political solution for every problem in society, has tended to increase cultural strain. Cultural strain is multiplied by political competition, not just by politicians but by bureaucrats and other individuals who seek access to the privileges and scarce resources of society. Competitive politics in a society where government is the most important industry increases cultural strain.

SUMMARY

Post-colonial societies are transitional societies. They are societies that are making deliberate efforts to redefine their culture and guarantee its autonomy. They are also societies which must function in a contemporary world in which choice-making is complicated. One important challenge which cultural management faces in such societies is how to select and maintain national, inspirational symbols that do not alienate the Little Traditions that exist in the society. A related problem is the inherent conflict between national cultural identity on the one hand and growing cultural convergence on the other hand.

Culture-building is a guided process. In a society where politics is pervasive, it cannot be achieved without a large measure of cultural strain. The African experience shows that cultural policy, as a deliberate political exercise, may vary even among countries which shared a similar colonial experience. The difference between the cultural policy of Guinea and the Ivory Coast must be sought in the political styles and personal, political experiences of the presidents of these states rather than in the colonial experiences of the two countries.

*   *   *

QUESTIONS AND ANSWERS

Q: What measure of democracies do the tropical nations of Africa have? What kind of legislature do they have or could they originate?

A. (Uchendu): Americans have a folk view of democracy, but they have a very short memory of its history. If democracy really means going to the polls, not many African states have it. If it means participation in running one's own country, the Tanzanian government, for example, is democratic in the sense that people are given the opportunity for discussion before policy is formulated and representation before government takes action. Given the nature of the society, democracy is interpreted in different ways. American democracy is quite different from British democracy. This is true in other areas of the world, so there is no one pattern of democracy. There are different responses to democratic institutions.

Of course, in West Africa particularly, we have had a number of disappointments, where soldiers took over from or for elected officials and are in power. But these problems are not insoluble. Remember that black Africa has only been independent for the last 17 years. A child born 17 years ago cannot even vote in this country. What then about a country? You must look at the number of years that African countries have been independent and study the kind of institutions they inherited. We are dealing with two problems, not just the problem of democracy. We are also dealing with the problem of institutional development. Whether it would take a democratic character like the one you have in Washington, in Britain, or in Switzerland is something we are trying to find out. I think the essential ingredient in democracy is one that recognizes the right of everybody to live a dignified life. It doesn't matter whether soldiers, the boss, or parliament is running it. We are trying to find out what would be the appropriate institution. We haven't succeeded yet, but 17 years is not a long time for a nation.

The Developing States of Africa

By RUTH SCHACHTER MORGENTHAU

ABSTRACT: The colonial era, with its monopoly of wealth by whites, is over. None of the withdrawing colonial powers were very good at preparing the African nations for independence. It took a decade for the invisible structures of empire to start giving way. Most African countries inherited insufficient administrative and economic infrastructures, borders that made little economic sense, and small markets. As a result, they were vulnerable, at independence, to fluctuating world prices and feast or famine conditions, making economic planning almost impossible. The economies of African states are governed by forces largely out of their control, and growth does not bring development for many because of lopsided distribution. There is, however, industrial potential, and manufacturing, though limited by low purchasing power, is growing. With the oil crisis, a few African states may hope to catch up soon with industrialized states in living standards, but meanwhile producing resources doesn't ensure equal distribution. Multinationals also weaken some African states by making them dependent. If they are to gain a sense of shared stake, they must cease to feel like horses driven by jockeys from the industrialized states.

Ruth S. Morgenthau has been Professor of Politics at Brandeis University since 1969, Chairman of the Department of Politics since 1974, and Adlai Stevenson Professor of Politics since 1972. In the past she has served as Research Fellow at the Center for International Affairs of Harvard University, Research Associate of the African Studies Program at Boston University, and Lecturer at the Institute of African Studies of the University of Ghana. Her publications include Political Parties in French-Speaking West Africa *and* "Strangers, Nationals and Multinationals in Africa."

F EW people realize how great
are the variations in wealth
among, as well as within, the many
African states. Indeed, African extremes between rich and poor are
probably growing. However, they
are no longer, since the rise of the
Organization of Petroleum Exporting Countries (OPEC), quite the
same extremes which provoked the
Bandung meeting in the fifties and
the U.N. Conference on Trade and
Development (UNCTAD) meetings
in the sixties, to speak of the fatal
enlarging gap between rich and
poor, superimposed upon the gap
between developed and underdeveloped, white and black. Class
cleavages in Africa are no longer
superimposed upon white-black
cleavages as much as in the past.
Rich is no longer always white; poor
is no longer always black. Since
the rise of OPEC, the alignment
has changed in Africa. There are
policy implications well worth
pondering.

THE END OF THE COLONIAL ERA[1]

The colonial era, with its monopoly
of wealth in white hands, is over.
It matters more what the African
governments now do than what the
colonial governments did. It matters
less who the colonizer was than how
deep a modernizing impact the
colonizers made on African society.
By that I mean what ports are there,
what airports, roads, bridges, what
hospitals, factories and mines, power
plants and broadcasting stations?
What kind of schools, who went, what
did they learn, and how many
Africans learned how to run shops
and garages, hospitals, laboratories,

1. See my "Old Cleavages among New
West African States: The Heritage of French
Rule," *Africa Today*, April 1971, for a fuller
discussion.

plants and ports, commercial farms
and fisheries? There were greater
differences in the modernizing impact within the French empire, for
example, between Algeria and Chad,
than between the French and British
impact on the Ivory Coast and
Ghana, respectively. Depending on
the modernizing impact, some new
states did, others did not inherit
viable economies, institutions, and
governments staffed by trained
people.

We can now look back and say,
though the colonizers varied, they
had much in common. A common
feature of the colonial systems
was to monopolize the top positions,
administrative and economic, for the
Europeans. All the European powers
declined after World War II and
pulled back from African commitments, usually less decently where
there were European settlers and
more gracefully where there were
none. All went, not in a coordinated
fashion, but one after the other,
with Portugal last. The U.S. and
USSR, though they intervened little
in decolonization, in various ways
contributed to making it necessary.

The African military balance
changed also, as the European
nations saw little sense in maintaining expensive African bases in
an era of changing technology and
refined techniques of long-range
missiles, satellites, and supersonic
aircraft. They searched for occasional tiny island bases, for refueling
and retooling, but not for African
installations on which to house many
men trained to control large countries. And they sought to shrug off
military responsibility. The withdrawal of the Europeans lifted the
barriers against entry by the United
States and the Soviet Union; both
gradually, somewhat gingerly, proceeded to seek footholds. And on

occasion as in the Congo in the
sixties and in the Horn in the
seventies, they confronted each
other. Meanwhile, some African
countries, particularly Algeria, Nigeria, and Zaire, built up their
own forces. So did white South
Africa and Rhodesia.

None of the withdrawing colonial
powers were terribly good at preparing the African nations for independence. Representative systems,
if they existed at all, often were
more apparent than real. Within a
decade, many of the parliamentary
institutions hastily planted by the
withdrawing colonizers had disappeared, many elections became
loyalty parades, multiparty systems
became one party systems and then
no party systems. Belgium and
Portugal left so fast, once they decided to go, there was no time to
plant any parliamentary institutions.
There are, of course, some exceptions, and a few African party regimes do exist. For the most part,
however, the leaders of the new
African states, severely pressed by
the realities of the multiple tasks
they inherited, found many constraints and frequent crises. In more
than half, the military took power.

Though the colonial empires had
practically disappeared by the mid-
sixties and only the Portuguese hung
on, it took another decade for the
invisible structures of empire to
start giving way. Some English-
speaking African leaders suspect
those speaking French lacked
"African personalities" and still followed orders from Paris. Informal
and formal relations, financial, economic, educational, and social persist to some degree even to this
day. There are common policy processes and mutually recognized
obligations between former metro-
pole and former colony. Strategic

and intelligence information flows
along the networks of the Commonwealth and between Paris and
the French-speaking African states.
Sometimes small issues are regulated in this invisible system-matters
of health, scholarships, exchanges of
diplomatic visits. A large number
of expatriates from the former metro-
pole work in the ex-colonies.

Some of the economic barriers
left by the colonizers in Africa
are coming down. One reason is
that Britain joined the European
Common Market. This altered the
reaction of the English-speaking
African Commonwealth members to
associated status with the European Community. Whereas before
associated status to the European six
meant a need to cut with Britain,
once Britain joined the Common
Market there was no need to choose.
Thus, the British European decision had a unifying effect in Africa.
Another reason that the African,
Caribbean, and Pacific states were
able to join together with the European states in the Lomé Convention was that after the rise of
OPEC the associated developing
states had considerably more strength.
Some were rich and expected to
become richer. Nigeria, Gabon,
Cameroon, and others knew their
resources meant a great deal to the
Europeans. By cooperating among
themselves, they were in a position to obtain genuine advantages
in Africa and Europe.

The Lomé Convention guarantees
preferential treatment in Europe
to the manufactured exports of the
ACP states. Although these are, for
the time being, quite limited, it is
likely that they will grow. Some
observers believe Africans might
become offshore producers of consumer goods for the Europeans. The
convention also sets up aid plans

and cooperative processes on trade, on a program stabilizing earnings from exported commodities (STABEX), on treatment of foreign companies, payments, and movements of capital.

The Lomé Convention represents a fresh departure, a structural change that reinforced, to some degree, both African and European cohesion. Lomé substitutes "Eurafrican" links for the earlier more fragmented imperial ones. To some degree, of course, the Lomé Convention was designed to discourage non-European industrial nations from trading or entry in the former colonies. But the African nations themselves have insisted on their right to open their doors to the highest bidders— be they from east, west, or middle east. Many United States enterprises, moreover, with branches in the European nations, find it convenient to enter the ACP states through their European affiliates.

The difference with past practice is that the Lomé agreements end the exclusive limits set around individual European empires and set up a single system embracing somewhat more than all of them put together.[2]

COLONIAL RESTRAINTS ON AFRICAN ECONOMIES

From colonial rule, most countries in Africa inherited insufficient administrative and economic infrastructure, borders that made little economic sense, and markets that are small. For example, "the typical West African country, with about four million inhabitants, has a demand for industrial products equivalent to that of a middle sized European provincial town."[3] Local manufacturing conflicted with the rules laid down by the colonial powers which confined trade largely to African raw material exports. As a result, at independence, most African economies were vulnerable to fluctuating world prices and subject to feast or famine conditions, which made economic planning almost impossible. In a few instances—Togo, Dahomey, Ruanda, and Burundi—the population was perhaps better off during and possibly even before the colonial era than after.[4]

In varying degrees, though the colonial powers were modernizers in tropical Africa, structural transformation of the African economies was confined to European needs. That is why the new countries had tremendous difficulties adjusting after independence. As the slave trade ended, roads and ports and railroads were built designed to facilitate the export of cash crops to Europe, such as palm oil, rubber, peanuts, cocoa, coffee, and bananas. The colonizers saw African colonies as private preserves, suppliers, and markets for the metropolitan factories.

Of course, there were variations in policy. The British, confident of their capacity to compete, were somewhat more flexible than the French, the Belgians, or the Portuguese, who followed mercantilist policies well into the twentieth century. The colonizers used large merchant companies, descendants in some cases of the great charter companies, to regulate mutual trade.

2. See Guy F. Erb, "Africa and the International Economy," mimeographed, February 1977.

3. Robert Smith, "West African Economic Cooperation—Problems and Prospects," *Foreign Service Journal*, April 1974.

4. Samir Amin is an eloquent exponent of this view. See his *Afrique de l' Ouëst bloquée* (Paris: Minuit, 1971).

Though they encouraged regional mobility within their zones,[5] most colonial powers tried to prevent intra-African trade across their monetary zones.

Such export economies, in turn, imported manufactured goods. The factories were in Europe. Spare parts also came from Europe—the wheels, tires, nails, screwdrivers, gasoline, cars and trucks, even matches. Technological superiority helps explain the Europeans' success. Their technology did not spread evenly throughout African societies. Rather it remained in enclaves, in cities, where there were roads, in the fertile rain forests, where cash crops grew, and coexisted with iron-age agriculture, stone-age hunting and gathering, and nomad cattle raising.

There were many effects. Where the Europeans introduced palm oil, coffee, cocoa, rubber, peanuts, cotton, and sisal, they spread new wealth among Africans. Newly rich Africans, in turn, had access to the bicycles, refrigerators, cars, and other goods made in Europe that distinguished them from the rest of the African population. The result was an African middle class, including cash crop farmers, from among whom came many new leaders of African sovereign states. These escaped from the pattern of low skill, low wage-earning jobs which still blights the lives of most Africans in the towns. If it is true that the money economy was small in places like Ghana, for example, it was large enough to involve, in addition to a consuming middle class and political leadership, cash crop farmers and an African entrepreneurial class. What prevented

their combination to support a program of local manufacturing?

One answer is it did not happen because it did not need to. Foreign firms grew with their markets. Only when a threat to an existing market occurred were overseas producing affiliates created by parent companies.[6] As long as the colonial system kept out the market threat and Africans were not strong enough to insist on their own manufacturing there was no need for foreign firms to manufacture locally. There were simply branches of European trading companies. Some were equal in size and impact to the colonial government bureaucracy. Not only did the trading companies face little competition, they excluded Africans from the ranks of management.[7] For a long period of time, the European trading houses did their best to crowd Africans out of even the export trade in African produce like palm oil, peanuts, coffee and cocoa, fruit and rubber. Without colonial rule, the big European trading houses, which became, for example, the United Africa Company (UAC), a subsidiary of Unilever, and the Société Commerciale Ouëst Africaine (SCOA), could probably not have taken over an estimated two-thirds to three-quarters of the overseas trade. The European companies relegated African traders to subordinate positions and reduced them to subsidiary retail trade.

This is not to imply that they were unimportant. African traders had a strong tradition in some parts of Africa. Nevertheless, be-

---

5. Akin Mabogunje, *Regional Mobility and Resource Development in West Africa* (Montreal: McGill, 1972).

6. See Mira Wilkin, *The Emergence of Multinational Enterprise* (Cambridge, Mass.: Harvard University Press, 1970).

7. Anthony G. Hopkins, *An Economic History of West Africa* (New York: Columbia University Press, 1973), pp. 284–85.

tween the trading houses and the villages, there were also foreign intermediaries. In East Africa, Indian traders accompanied the Europeans and cut out Africans from much of the retail trade. In Zaire, Greeks, Pakistani, and Portuguese did it. In West Africa, although Lebanese, Syrians, and some Indians took over the wholesale circuit, African traders managed to stay in the retail trade. Indeed, they had almost a monopoly of the unofficial or clandestine trade.[8] A very high proportion of the active population was in trade in Ghana, a country considered to be predominately agricultural.[9]

African traders might have flowed naturally into the big time in trade and from there into investment. They were inhibited by the officially protected European trading companies. There were African trading families that trace their roots through centuries of economic and political upheaval. Examples are the associates of Baidy Guèye of Guinea, and of Kebe of Senegal. Many African trading families rejected the Europeans and European schools. Their sons were often not the best prepared to beat the Europeans at their own game. Those who carried on heretical traditions, religious as well as political, were forced to turn to commerce. For them, it was a livelihood; they had no alternative. It was not a matter of preference. Some of the most active builders of Islamic brotherhoods in West Africa belonged to such a heretic business tradition, illustrating that "heresy promotes the business spirit."[10]

The European trading companies stimulated long-distance trade but held Africans back. European colonialism created a limited infrastructure for its own rather than African national purposes. Until recently, most Africans invested their money in real estate, good living, and charity. Only slowly are some African traders becoming direct investors, as traders did in many industrializing countries. They, like the larger foreign-owned enterprises, are becoming a new force in parts of Africa and providing alternatives to exclusive dependence on government for income.

Many important African trading families were internationally minded, and few stopped their transactions at the borders of the new states; many were aliens, not born in the country where they lived. In the first independence decade of almost autarchic African nationalism, some new governments viewed multi-African connections as suspect. An anti-stranger reaction against Indians, Syrians, Lebanese, and Africans of foreign origins extended to Africans. Strangers, like the *Hausa* in Ghana, the *Dioula* in Ivory Coast, the Dahomeyans in many parts of West Africa, the Somali, the Burundi, and Southern Sudanese, were sometimes even expelled.[11]

8. Ibid.; Peter Bauer, *West African Trade* (Clifton, N.J.: Augustus M. Kelley, Pubs., 1954).

9. Peter Garlick, *African Traders and Economic Development* (Oxford: Oxford University Press, 1971).

10. Spanish proverb cited in F. L. Nuss-baum, *A History of the Economic Institutions of Modern Europe* (New York: F. S. Craft and Co., 1937), p. 138. A fascinating discussion of the interconnection between religious heresy and trade can be found in Lansine Kaba, *Evolution of Islam in West Africa: The Wahhabi Movement and Its Contribution to Political Development 1945–58* (Ph.D. diss. in history, Northwestern University, Evanston, Ill., January 1972).

11. See my "Strangers, Nationals and Multinationals in Africa," in *Strangers in Africa*, ed. William Shack and Elliot Skinner (Berkeley: University of California Press, forthcoming).

For about a decade, in most politically independent African countries, the economic legacy of colonial rule was little disturbed, although there were internal struggles for power. Many new African governments followed policies that postponed the emergence of a group of African entrepreneurs, even though some African traders have the contacts to link the economies of several states. Some such activity has occurred, illegally, in diamonds, foreign currency, cattle, fish, and cola nuts, linking, for example, Angola, Zaire, and West African states.

This was inhibited by the disparate tax, tariff, and currency barriers among French-, English-, and Portuguese-speaking African countries. There were no effective payment arrangements among the monetary zones. It could take a year to pay legally for cattle coming into Upper Volta from Ghana. Some countries like Ghana (1974) had an over-valued currency. It was worthwhile for its merchants to import at the official rate of exchange and export at the parallel market rate of the depreciated *cedi*. For political reasons, the Ghana government did not want to devalue. Clandestine trade thrived, including transit trade, in Dahomey and Togo or Gambia. Official statistics recorded that almost all West African states received no more than 5 percent of their imports from neighbors. Unofficially, however, Nigeria absorbed at least 75 percent of Niger's exports and provided at least 20 percent of her imports. Legal imports from Nigeria were subject to 30–50 percent tariff in the franc zone states. Officially, therefore, importing European goods was often cheaper. What would the inter-African trade figures be if all countries in Africa favored economic co-operation? If barriers were reduced and economic cooperation became the official goal in West Africa, a different economic pattern might well emerge than one oriented to export overseas.[12]

Who controls resources has been a hot political issue in Africa from way before the Europeans came. At independence, even the countries with the most active nationalist movements, such as Ghana, the Ivory Coast, Guinea, and Mali, did not easily acquire economic power. For a variety of reasons, African entrepreneurs were shouldered aside, often by African political leaders. Many new governments made their peace with chambers of commerce controlled by European businessmen. The exceptions were a few socialist states — Guinea, Mali under the Union Soudanaise, Tanzania, Moçambique, and Angola.

The first generation of new African leaders had little experience with economic matters. Since the Europeans kept economic controls in their own hands, at independence few African technocrats existed, and few of those had any special standing with the original national founding fathers. There were many conflicts among the political leaders, wage earners, and African managers of economic institutions, private or public, who often allied themselves with the military. In time, most founding fathers have stepped aside, while a new generation of African leaders reassessed their economic alternatives.

PRESENT CONDITIONS VARY

The economics of developing African states are governed by forces largely out of their control. For

12. Smith, "West African Economic Cooperation."

many, moreover, even growth does not bring development, since distribution remains sadly lopsided. The typical developing African nation has a sparse population, small internal markets, limited infrastructure, new and fragile borders, and economies vulnerable to fluctuating world prices. There remains a large near-subsistence sector in most African economies, which with a few exceptions are export economies that exchange in the international market African raw materials—animal, vegetable, or mineral—for manufactured goods. Some manufacturing has started, but outside of South Africa it is largely limited to import substitution, petroleum and nonferrous metals, and processing or semi-processing.

Nigeria, with perhaps 80 million, has by far the largest population. Egypt, Ethiopia, South Africa, and Zaire each have more than 20 million people. All the rest have fewer. Including the islands, some 33 countries have a population of under 5 million and approximately 18 have fewer than a million.[13] The majority of the population is under age, and the growth rate is very high. The continent, made up of more than 50 countries, is sparsely settled. Most Africans are vulnerable to famine and death, and it is not unusual for one child out of two to die under the age of five. While a few African nations are prosperous, most are not. The Organization for Economic Co-operation and De-

velopment (OECD) figures show that of the world's 28 least developed countries, at least 18 are located in Africa; 28 of the 45 countries most seriously affected by recent rises in cost of fuel and food are also in Africa.[14]

There are, in contrast, the fortunate few. Even the petroleum-producing countries are only recently rich, with Nigeria, Algeria, and Libya heading a list that includes Angola, Egypt, and Gabon. The United States needs other mineral exports: columbium from Nigeria, manganese from Gabon and South Africa, cobalt from Zaire, chromium from South Africa and Rhodesia, gold and platinum, antimony and vanadium from South Africa. There is copper in Zaire and Zambia; uranium in Gabon, Niger, and South Africa; iron in Liberia and Mauritania; fluorite in Kenya; and Moçambique Guinea is estimated to have the world's largest reserves in bauxite.[15] Nigeria exported $3 billion worth of petroleum products to the United States in 1975, which was almost a billion more than the total value of South Africa's exports to the United States.

There is industrial potential. Of the world's known hydroelectric potential, 13 percent is in Zaire where the Inga project alone is expected to produce as much electricity as is presently used in the United Kingdom. African rivers—the Senegal, the Niger, the Zaire, the Nile, the Zambezi—have cheap power potential. Dams at Akosombo (Ghana), Kainji (Nigeria), Aswan

13. For figures, I have frequently relied on *Africa South of the Sahara 1976* (London: Europa Publications, 1976). Nigeria's figures, announced for the November 1973 census, 79.7 million, are widely disputed. See *Africa Confidential*, 17 May 1974. See, also, the statistical annexes in John W. Sewell, and the ODC Staff, *The United States and World Development, Agenda 1977* (New York: Praeger, 1977).

14. See Maurice J. Williams, Chairman, Development Assistance Committee, *Development Cooperation, 1976 Review*, (Paris: OECD, November 1976).

15. Sources: *Mineral and Materials*, a monthly survey, U.S. Bureau of Mines, (Washington, D.C.: September 1976).

(Egypt), Gouina (Mali), Konkoure (Guinea), Kafue (Zambia), Rufuji (Tanzania), Inga (Zaire), Cabora Bassa (Moçambique), and Cunene (Angola) actually or potentially produce cheap power for industry. When oil prices quadrupled, these hydroelectric installations increased in value. Ambitious plans to expand ore processing are being laid in the rich mineral exporting states.

Manufacturing in the African developing states, though limited by low purchasing power, is growing. Algeria, Morocco, Ghana, and the Ivory Coast export considerable manufactured goods; so do Tunisia, Nigeria, Egypt, Cameroon, and Kenya. If European wages continue to go up, prospects improve for African light industry. The European market for textiles and other clothing, leather goods, canned goods, and other consumer goods is likely to expand. Already slacks made in the Ivory Coast, leather goods and furs in Kenya, shoes in Dakar, and dresses in Morocco are shipped to European consumers.[16]

Like the United States a century or two ago, a number of states—Kenya, the Ivory Coast, for example— maintained respectable growth rates after independency by exporting agricultural products, some in a processed or partly processed state. The more fortunate states depend on several exports, the more vulnerable ones are subject to one product's price fluctuations, like Ghana with cocoa, Mauritius with sugar, Chad with cotton. Temporary world shortages—in cocoa, coffee, rubber, sisal—have created periods in which the African pro-

ducers have been able to acquire substantial, if irregular, incomes. Higher costs of imported fertilizer, seed, energy, and containers have hit these agricultural countries hard.

Some of the poorest African countries subsist precariously on foreign remittances. This is true for many of the sahel states whose people migrate in search of income to the richer West Africa. Workers from Malawi, Moçambique, Lesotho, and other "frontline" states migrate to the farms and factories of South Africa.

While agricultural production has been rising in a number of countries, foodstuffs still constitute a disquieting proportion of African imports. Even larger food shortfalls are expected in the future.[17] Meanwhile, the poorest African states, for example, Niger, Mali, Chad, and Upper Volta, export dried fish and cattle to the coastal states in return for money that helps pay for the governments in the towns. But in the countryside, as during the drought of the early seventies, people may die or sicken from starvation.

Only a comprehensive international food plan for the poorest states can help bring about a variable balance. With such a plan, African agricultural production could rise dramatically and be sufficient both for home consumption and, in some states, for abundant exports.

Meanwhile, few official institutions of economic cooperation exist among African states, though there is considerable grass-roots interdependence. In a global sense, moreover, most African leaders struggle

16. See Andrew M. Kamarck, "Sub-Saharan Africa in the 1980's: An Economic Profile," in *Africa from Mystery to Maize,* ed. Helen Kitchen (Lexington: Lexington Books, 1976).

17. See International Food Policy Research Institute, "Meeting Food Needs in the Developing World: The Location and Magnitude of the Task in the Next Decade," *Research Report #1,* February 1976, p. 37.

with the fact that they are unable to significantly affect the marketing or prices of exports and imports. No wonder that the call for commodity price agreements finds fertile soil in Africa. No wonder, also, that most developing African states, whether governed by socialists or conservatives, popular parties or military regimes, are following policies of economic nationalism at home and abroad.

ECONOMIC NATIONALISM AND MULTINATIONAL ENTRY

Policies of Africanization in trade, commerce, and small enterprises are political in origin and motivation, a reaction against economic colonialism. There are few signs of Africanization in white-ruled Africa. Even in some black-ruled frontline states, like Malawi or Swaziland, it is hard to find an African business employing as many as 10 people. Moreover, the many African governments carrying out Africanization policies realized that these policies alone could not give them control over their economies nor assure them of an expanding economy in which the size of everyone's share might grow. Many African governments which sought growth accepted the entry of foreign multinational enterprises or even sought them out. Insofar as international capital assistance became available to African states, it was mostly as loans or suppliers' credits. The problem for African developing states was often not so much one of credit, though certainly many had their balance of payments problems when they had to buy vital supplies at prices they could not afford; it was rather credibility—proving that they had the cadres, the technology, the market know-how to justify big in-

vestments. Foreign credit was more easily available to countries whose projects involved multinational enterprises.

Multinational investments have shown a remarkable capacity to survive instability or hostility. The largest foreign enterprises often survived intact from one kind of government to another without regard for ideological questions. The socialist government of Tanzania, though it nationalized banks and most medium-sized businesses, licensed offshore oil exploration to multinational oil companies. Despite shifts of economic policy by the Libyan government, some international oil companies have been able to reorganize and keep on working. Even in revolution, multinational affiliates are rarely destroyed. Gulf shored up the former Portuguese dictatorship in Angola, yet it survived a transfer of power from Portugal to Angola. Similarly many oil companies working in Nigeria have survived the shift from British to Nigerian nationalist rule despite a major civil war. Civil war in Zaire, genocide in Burundi, and a drought and a coup in Niger have not stopped operations by multinationals which develop copper in Zaire, oil in Nigeria, nickel in Burundi, and uranium in Niger. In the troubled Zaire countryside of Shaba (Katanga), U.S. based multinationals moved into openings left by departing Belgian rulers. In socialist Guinea, multinationals quickly filled the void left by the French and their sudden withdrawal. In spite of the Franco-Algerian war, multinationals quickly found new opportunities. Indeed, rival multinationals, many not European in origins, moved into openings that accompanied European decolonization, in the midst of social and political upheaval.

The quadrupling of oil prices in 1973–74 opened yet another phase. Indeed, the OPEC strategy is being tried by producers of other commodities. They realize that if the multinational oil companies had not been organized as a partial oligopoly, OPEC might not have been able to exercise as much global leverage. OPEC was the first clearly successful producer challenge to the prices paid by industrial consumers for raw materials originating in developing countries. Almost unanimously the new African states, whether oil importing or not, backed the OPEC struggle against the major oil companies. They identified with the economic nationalism of the oil producing countries in the Middle East even though at first they paid a high price.

Coups in Niger and Upper Volta and the army revolt in Ethiopia were related to the inflation that accompanied the rising prices of food- and oil-related imports. There were shortages of some packaging materials. Fewer long-term funds were available for investment from the developed world, less tourism, and a growing trade gap in many oil importing African countries. In some countries, food shortages worsened, as higher costs of transport, fertilizer, machinery, and manufactured goods led them to the edge of bankruptcy and to internal dissention. To them the effect of OPEC's rise to power has been demotion from the Third World to the Fourth. Many have had to reconsider their economic policies and to scrap plans for development.

A lucky few benefited immediately. Nigeria, Libya, Algeria, Gabon, and Angola produce oil. Cameroon, Congo-Brazzaville, Niger, and Zaire have active hopes. The new oil wealth raised them from poor to rich. Nigeria's GNP is expected to exceed that of South Africa in the near future. The new wealth in developing Africa flatly contradicts the old idea that the United States has the most at stake, economically, in southern Africa.

WEALTH AND ITS DISTRIBUTION

The changes accompanying the oil crises have made possible what African political leaders had never considered likely—that a few African states might soon catch up with the industrialized states in standard of living. Most serious students of industrialization in Africa, before OPEC, believed that with careful planning some African states might catch up with the 1950 standard of living of middle-range industrialized states by the twenty-first century. Some African economic nationalists, disillusioned by the post-independence reality, even espoused the cause of isolation and advised turning inward, cutting the links of dependency with the industrialized countries, and transforming African economies only from within.

Since oil producing countries succeeded in rearranging the international market in their favor, these lines of reasoning have lost their audience. Global economic interdependence bore fruit to the rich African states. African oil became precious, and so did its hydroelectric power, coal and iron, uranium, copper, and even rubber and vegetable oils. For the first time in many centuries, a few African leaders can shop the world for the best of what they need.

Meanwhile, producing resources says nothing about distribution. While international interdependence speeds up economic transactions and gives African governments some economic strength, it adds new layers of inequality. Entry of multinational enterprises in mining, for example, can exaggerate the disparity between city and countryside; it affects the location of infrastructure. Long lead time, much capital, and machinery characterize most mining, while only a few Africans work for the mines even where there are ore-processing plants. Often, though enterprises prosper, people do not. New money stays in the enterprise or in the capital city. Even in the better organized new African mining states, the top broadens out only a little. The resulting syndrome can be growth without development, even in the rich states. A great deal depends on political leadership.

If African countries had better distribution of income, more diverse and larger sources of revenue, stronger and more effective institutions connecting leaders and the rest of the population, more avenues of social mobility—then the entry of multinational enterprises and international interdependence would not so exacerbate the extremes of power, health, and wealth. Multinationals weaken some African national governments by making them dependent and yet bolster these same governments up.

The international economy has quickened the transfer of world market highs and lows to Africa, together with the effects of shortages or gluts in food or fertilizer or of inflation. It can be said that the present system of interdependence sometimes vitiates policies of self-reliance, decreases the likelihood that serious attention be paid local African markets and local needs, and drains vital resources like food from the national to the international markets.

POLICY PERSPECTIVES

No one nation is singly responsible for the way the international economy affects the distribution of wealth in Africa. Yet it is fair to say that the industrialized nations as a whole, and the colonial powers in particular, share responsibility for the economic weaknesses in new African states, the comparatively weak level of African entrepreneurship, the relatively low wages of African wage earners, and the vulnerable state of most African economies.

Aid is a help, though not by any means the only or the most effective one. The Russians still do not give their share. Russian military aid, directly or through Cuba, is going up, but not economic aid. The Chinese have done one big job, the building of the Tan Zam railroad. The Western powers, individually and through multilateral agencies, committed $3.9 billion in 1975. OPEC, through various donor organizations, committed $4.1 billion the same year, of which roughly $400 million went to African countries that are not members of the Arab League.[18]

More significant than aid are policies having to do with world commodity prices and markets, world trade, investment decisions, and allocation of financial and technical resources. The United States carries weight on these questions. Where do U.S. interests lie? Before replying, it is worth asking how important Africa is to the United States.

This question cannot be answered

18. See Gordon Bertolin, "U.S. Economic Interests in Africa: Investment, Trade and Raw Materials," mimeographed, February 1977.

simply in economic terms. Africa is part of the American heritage. The ancestors of at least 10 percent of our people came from there. Its human and cultural riches add to our society; its troubles affect us. As a multiracial nation, we resonate whenever racial conflicts take place in Africa. We become involved when white oppresses black in southern Africa, for example. Therefore we need to take full responsibility for our economic engagements in that part of the world. To African leaders of the developing states, moreover, racial equality is a principal goal, one that unifies them in the Organization of African Unity. Racial equality and majority rule to southern Africa are human rights over which we cannot afford to compromise. U.S. good faith on this issue, in African eyes, is almost a prerequisite to the growth of fruitful and mutually beneficial foreign relations.

Africa is important to us for economic reasons. Though Africa is one of the world's poorest continents, there are a number of rich African nations—particularly the oil exporting ones. Nigeria is the richest. Its GNP is shortly expected to surpass the GNP of South Africa; the value of Nigeria's exports surpassed the value of South Africa's exports a year or so after OPEC successfully quadrupled world oil prices. Already Nigeria is the second largest supplier of foreign oil to the United States. In addition, there are perhaps 10 African states with whom the United States has substantial and growing economic relations, who sell more to us than they buy, who could therefore become yet better customers.

Africa is a continent where U.S. interests are sometimes in competition with the former European colo-

nizers' for access to markets, investment opportunities, and raw materials. Though most African nations continue to sell most of their exports and to buy most of their imports in Europe, the picture is changing somewhat. Indeed, in the Lomé Convention the European Community made a number of real concessions to African economic demands, because they want to keep a big share of Africa's international economic transactions.

Nevertheless, Japan's share is growing, as is America's. To date, the African states are minor economic partners of the United States —with only 3 percent of our foreign investment and perhaps 6½ percent of our foreign trade. When it is remembered that until African independence from colonial rule, the United States and Japan were pretty well barred from access to Africa, the figures represent a considerable growth and can hardly be ignored. Since OPEC, the preponderance of trade lies with developing Africa, not the South.

Though the economies of the developing African states still remain more important to Europe than to the United States, the international economy is now so woven together that the United States is itself deeply affected by the prosperity or the lack of it in Europe. In this sense, African development becomes part of our growth, directly or indirectly. The fall of copper prices signals not only the decline in the economies and stability of Zambia, Zaire, and Chile, but also the decline in the automobile, communications, and the construction industries in the developed countries.

Africa is important, furthermore, because there are crises brewing that can threaten world peace. We might, if careless, find ourselves in an East-West confrontation with the Russians in the Horn of Africa, or worse still, in southern Africa, in a racial confrontation in which we are on the wrong side. We cannot afford to leave the initiative to the Russians in southern Africa that they acquired almost unexpectedly through the Cuban intervention in Angola.

The African nations now constitute a full third of the membership of the United Nations. Though the U.N. was born without them in the forties, its agenda and priorities have been altered by the new members. There are almost 50 African members, and they are in a position to make themselves heard on the two prime issues: racial equality in southern Africa and economic equality among rich and poor nations in the world. If the U.S. government wants African allies in international institutions on issues dear to us—like peace in the Middle East, arms control, or an end to nuclear proliferation—we must of necessity find ways to become useful to them. We need to reach for a way to build partnerships with the developing African states.

What policies, then, should the United States advocate? To encourage African trade, in UNCTAD and the General Agreement on Tariffs and Trade (GATT), we should announce concrete measures indicating sympathetic understanding of the marketing problems by African manufacturers, few though they still are.

Increased food production is vital even to the richer African states, which nevertheless have trouble feeding the people. We might even build new institutions—such as a Food Corps and an International Agricultural Foundation—through which techniques and support services for the interested African states could be made available. Special food assistance to the poorest nations could become available through these and other international structures that look beyond the limited horizon of relief and are dedicated to African food self-reliance. Food prices also relate directly to security. Food riots in Egypt preceded a call for more U.S. arms. Food riots in Ethiopia, Niger, Chad, Mali, Upper Volta, and elsewhere preceded military coups. Even Nigeria, though rich, was shaken by riots against the high price of grain.

It now appears that with the STABEX provisions of the Lomé Convention and OPEC support for a common fund and price stabilization of commodities, the idea is taking concrete shape. The United States has only the choice of joining in or standing apart. It is time that the United States joins within UNCTAD in negotiations on commodity agreements and a common fund.

We are used to thinking along these lines about domestic food policy, but have yet to demonstrate our knowledge of the relevance to foreign policy matters. Successful international control over international commodity highs and lows could significantly reduce the number of crises in Africa, hence the calls for economic aid, for emergency relief, or even for military assistance.

Other ways the United States could meet African development needs include educational assistance to speed the process of Africanization, encouragement of measures that favor inter-African trade, allowing African states to renegotiate their debts, and receiving emergency credit to tide them over unforeseen budgetary crises.

Such measures could meet African desires for an international economic system that works for them, gives them a sense of self-reliance, and removes blocks to more equal domestic and international distribution. Some of these suggested measures might be debated; a number might cost the United States some short-term advantages. In the long run, however, there would be gains in growth, security, and the creation of a stable world economic order.

CONCLUSION

This paper has been mostly about the changing circumstances in the developing African states, particularly social and economic, that accompanied first the imposition of colonial rule and then its withdrawal. It has been argued that many of the immediate economic by-products of separate colonial rule are indeed changing and that the European states are making a collective bid to maintain their primacy as the trading and economic partners of the new African states.

The majority ruled African states have development as a prime objective. It would benefit them, and the United States, if we found ways to respond to their expressed desires for more ways to become self-reliant even as they connect up with the international economy in which we play so large a part.

The extremes between rich and poor in Africa may well be growing, as they have been growing since before European colonization.

Yet there are new departures. Since oil prices rose, rich is no longer white, as in the colonial era, and poor is no longer always black. The extraordinary decline of white rule in Africa since the end of World War II, of which the withdrawal of Portugal from Angola and Moçambique were the latest examples, suggest the probability that majority rule is not far away from Rhodesia and Namibia. Racial equality must come in South Africa as well.

The United States has every reason to keep matters moving in that direction. Our economic interests in the developing states are more important, presently, than in white ruled southern Africa. If we must choose to place at risk U.S. economic interests in southern Africa so as to bear witness to the steadfastness of U.S. devotion to human rights for black and white,[19] the risks are likely to be temporary. The capacity to survive political changes, by U.S. enterprises performing essential services in African states, has stood out in the recent economic history of the area. If the African states are to gain a sense of shared stake, then the leaders must cease to feel like horses driven by jockeys from the industrialized states. Evidence that the United States favors policies of both racial and economic equality should help Africans feel they also own horses in the international economy.

19. See my "Security and Conflict in Africa," produced for the 30 March 1977 meeting in Washington of the Council on Foreign Relations.

*   *   *

QUESTIONS AND ANSWERS

Q: Do you think there is ever any possibility that UNCTAD and GATT could get together at least on some areas?

A (Morgenthau): If you are asking me if there is a chance that UNCTAD will not get deadlocked in a conflict between an industrialized and a developing country, as appears to have happened again in the most recent meeting, I think there is a possibility. I was trying to raise issues for redefining American interests, and reconsideration of the kind of position we take in international institutions, so that a real dialogue can start with developing countries. I think we are reaching a stage of understanding of our dependence on others which is a necessary preparatory stage for a reformulation of foreign policy. So I think there is hope that the level of dialogue in GATT and UNCTAD will change. Whether the change will be immediate I would hesitate to predict until I see the change.

Q: I was very struck by two particular points: your prophecy that Africa might well become a supplier of manufactured consumer goods to Europe and, secondly, that at present, the effective market in an average west African nation of about 4 to 5 million people is about the same as in an average European provincial town. What I wonder is where it leads, both for Africa and in terms of our present concern. Do you think there is any reason to suppose that the new form of international division of labor is going to be any more useful in the essential transition to development than the previous form of extroverted economies we all know about?

A (Morgenthau): I cannot really predict accurately beyond saying that there are leaps of change in the history of economic and social change. There are moments in which there is very great structural redistribution. We are living through one such period now. Look at what is happening to the price of consumer goods, in relation to income even in the industrialized countries. Becoming the supplier of consumer goods in 1970, 1980, and 1990 is a respectable position. Indeed, it is one that could lead to considerable or greater returns now than in 1950, given the relative claim on income of consumer goods now as opposed to where it was. By this I mean all of us are finding that our standard of living is declining, even if our salaries are going up, because of the price of consumer goods.

Q: The Sherman Anti-Trust Law states that all combinations in restraint of trade are illegal. I want to know how reducing trade would help economics.

A (Morgenthau): You are asking me whether the U.S. Anti-Trust laws have a bearing on the international economy. I would say not much. Look at the oil companies. Now the Anti-Trust laws keep the oil companies from publicly coordinating their policies and prices at home, but there is a remarkable uniformity in the range of prices. If you are asking me do the U.S. Anti-Trust laws affect what U.S. enterprises do internationally, I say not that I can perceive. The oil companies try to get the State Department's blessing before they publicly confer to combine their policy in negotiating with OPEC, but on the whole I don't think there is much effect.

China's Role in Africa

By GEORGE T. YU

ABSTRACT: Over 2 decades have passed since China made its first formal presence in Africa in 1955, and since then China has become a major actor with vital interests in the continent. The greater part of Chinese-African interaction occurred from 1960–65—a high point of African decolonization and a time of Sino-Soviet conflict. From 1965–70 Chinese-African interaction coincided with the Great Proletarian Cultural Revolution. It was post-independence for most African nations and a time of Chinese retreat. Since 1970, China has reemerged as a major actor in Africa. There are 3 major components of China's role in Africa: the Chinese model, the superpowers, and China's Third World policy. The call to liberation struggles has long been a hallmark of Chinese policy. The Chinese model also relates to China's developmental experience. China has stressed struggle against the superpowers, the U.S. and Soviet Union, identifying with the Third World against them. There can be no doubt that Africa occupied a central place in Chinese foreign policy and the U.S. and Soviet Union were important factors in it. China can expect to retain its presence in Africa if it responds to Africa's changing situation.

George T. Yu has served as Professor of Political Science and Asian Studies at the University of Illinois, Urbana-Champaign, since 1970 and was Earhart Foundation Fellow in 1976. He has been Chairperson of the Midwest Regional Seminar on China since 1970, and he served as Visiting Research Political Scientist at the Institute of International Studies of the University of California in the summer of 1975. Among his publications are China's African Policy, China and Tanzania: A Study in Cooperative Interaction, "Chinese Aid to Africa," in Chinese and Soviet Aid to Africa, and others.

O VER two decades have passed since the People's Republic of China made its first formal presence in Africa. In this period, beginning from an almost "zero base" of attention to and interest in Africa, China has become a major actor with vital interests in the continent. Indeed, as with interaction with the Soviet Union and the United States, relations with Africa—both in terms of interaction with individual African nations and with the African nations collectively—have served a variety of important functions in China's total foreign policy and behavior. In examining China's role in Africa, we will focus upon these primary components: the Chinese model, the superpowers, and China's Third-World policy.

CHINESE-AFRICAN INTERACTION

Before examining China's role in Africa, we need to review the major stages of China's relations with Africa. The years between the Bandung Conference of 1955 and the end of the decade constituted the initial stage of Chinese-African interaction. Contacts between China and Africa were started, and China made a cautious attempt to win African recognition and support. The United Arab Republic (then Egypt), one of the six African states at the Bandung Conference, was the first African state to recognize China in 1956. By the end of the decade China had established a wide range of contacts, including recognition of the provisional government of the Republic of Algeria, participation in the Afro-Asian People's Solidarity Organization, and the recognition of China by four African states. It should be mentioned that the initial period of Chinese-African interaction took place during the Sino-

Soviet alliance. China's primary adversary was the United States. One Chinese goal of developing an African connection was to win new friends and seek new allies to break out of the American encirclement.

The greater part of Chinese-African interaction occurred from 1960 to 1965, the second stage of China's African policy. Two factors explained the high tide of Chinese activities. First, these years constituted a high point in the African decolonialization movement. Between January 1960 and December 1965, no less than 29 colonies won independence, with 16 African states gaining independence in 1960 alone. At the height of China's offensive—1964–1965—a major campaign which included visits to Africa by Chou En-lai and Chen Yi was undertaken to win African recognition and support. An indicator of the success of the drive was that, by the end of 1965, China had won recognition and support from an additional 15 African states. However, China's successes were balanced by disappointments. The second Afro-Asian conference which China had campaigned for was doomed by a coup d'état in Algeria, the site of the proposed meeting.

A second factor that explained the high level of Chinese activism in Africa was the Sino-Soviet conflict. Following the open break with the Soviet Union in the early 1960s, China sought to challenge Soviet diplomatic influence and to subvert Soviet revolutionary credibility. Africa, therefore, became a battlefield in the Sino-Soviet conflict, just as Africa had earlier become an arena in the Sino-American competition. An example of the Sino-Soviet battle was manifested in China's campaign to win African support to exclude Russian participation at the abortive Afro-Asian conference of 1965.

The years 1965 to 1970 constituted the third stage of Chinese-African interaction, which coincided with the Great Proletarian Cultural Revolution in China. In Africa, except for Angola, Mozambique, and a few other colonies, this was the post-independent era; the new African states turned their attention to the problems of nation building and survival. Without question, this was a stage of Chinese retreat. This could be seen in the number of African states that continued formal relations with China. Whereas 18 African states maintained formal diplomatic relations with China in 1964–1965, in 1969 only 13 did so. The reversal of China's campaign to win African recognition and support was due to a complex of factors, including China's own ineptitude and the instability of African politics. Certainly China's exclusive and rigid policies won it very few friends; but, on the other hand, the instability of African domestic politics bewildered the Chinese. Finally, China's militant posture, both actual and perceived, of the Great Proletarian Cultural Revolution constrained relations with certain African states.

The fourth and final stage to date of Chinese-African interaction, since 1970, has witnessed a reemergence of China as a major actor on the African continent, part of China's new drive in the Third World. China has restored relations with those African states with whom relations were suspended, such as Ghana, Tunisia; improved relations with states whom relations were at a low level of interaction, such as the United Arab Republic; and established new diplomatic relations with additional African states, such as

Liberia, Mozambique, Nigeria, Zaire. However, China's reentry into Africa was not free from competition, especially from the Soviet Union. The Angola case represented an excellent example. American interest in the liberation politics of southern Africa also constituted a challenge to China. Since the death of Mao in 1976, the uncertainties associated with China's leadership transition was also a factor regarding China's African policy, though none had been manifested. Indeed, China's African campaign has continued unimpeded.

THE CHINESE MODEL

With this review of the stages of China's relations with Africa in mind, let us now turn to the three primary components of China's role in Africa: the Chinese Model, the superpowers, and China's Third World policy. It should be emphasized that these categories are closely interrelated. From an analytic viewpoint, however, there is much merit in considering them separately.

Since the coming to power of the Chinese Communist party and the founding of the People's Republic of China in 1949, few issues have been subject to more discussion and controversy than the Chinese model. Two parts of the model deserve our special attention with respect to China's role in Africa. The most often discussed, and certainly one of the earliest, parts of the Chinese model has been the struggle to capture power. The people's-war formula is well-known. Its major elements include the commitment to a comprehensive ideology, that the struggle must be led by a Communist party, that the party must control the masses, that the struggle must be basically self-reliant and headed by an indigenous leadership, and that the struggle should adopt a united front policy. Above all, the people's-war formula calls for the salvation of the exploited and the oppressed through armed struggle.

The summons to the peoples of Africa who were not yet independent to engage in liberation struggles has long been a hallmark of Chinese policy. In essense, China's constant reiteration of this theme has been to demonstrate the viability of the Chinese model to achieve liberation, to claim its universality, and to insist that the liberation struggle approach constituted the only route to victory. China has consistently expanded this feature of the model, including extension of specific support, both verbal and material, to those who seek their liberation, ranging from Algeria in the early 1960s to those in southern Africa in the 1970s.

There can be no doubt that China's own successful national liberation struggle and its support of the people's-war formula have caused others who sought liberation to look to China for support-material, moral, and otherwise. But it is equally important to point out that this feature of the Chinese model has its roots in the specific context of a given world unit. That is to say, though the people's-war formula has an appeal to those seeking liberation, what really determines their interest is not so much China's self-proclaimed leadership or even China's militant posture and support but the indigenous conditions in a given world unit and the goal of liberation.

Consider, for example, the case of the application of the people's-war formula in southern Africa. Here we are assuming that some form of the

formula, however imperfect, has been fought in southern Africa since the 1960s. Prior to 1964, the vast majority of the African colonies were being given independence by the European colonial powers. Consequently, there was only limited interest—except in specific instances, such as Algeria—in the people's-war formula. Indeed, for the most part the concept was unrelated to the context. Beginning only in the 1960s, when it became evident that the white minority governments in southern Africa and the Portuguese were not going to follow the pattern of "Africa for the Africans," did we begin to hear the cry for a revolutionary armed liberation struggle. What subsequently took place has become history; southern Africa became one of the focal points for the revolutionary armed liberation struggle. It is to be noted that the changing situational context in large part determined the form of the final struggle. For many Africans, it was a case of either accepting the status quo or taking up arms; the liberation movements of southern Africa and those African states that actively support them felt increasingly forced to adopt methods more applicable to the situation. As one African leader has put it: "When every avenue of peaceful change is blocked, then the only way forward to positive change is by channeling and directing the people's fury—that is, by organized violence, by a people's war."[1]

The second part of the Chinese model relates to China's developmental experience. There were a number of components to China's developmental experience inherent in the Chinese model. First, there

1. *Nationalist* (Dar es Salaam), 3 October 1969.

was the record of China's development, given the level of development at the time of the founding of the People's Republic of China in 1949. Second, the time factor has been of great importance. That is, the relatively short period during which China has been able to achieve a meaningful level of social and economic development. Third, China's successful bold experiments in specific social and economic sectors, such as education and public health. Fourth, the development of Chinese solutions to certain technical and organizational problems in line with Chinese requirements. Finally, there was the environmental-situational context of Chinese developmental experiences— China as a rural society amid the process of modernization. Through various appeals, similar to the people's-war formula, China has been equally quick to offer its experience, in this instance developmental, for other societies to follow.

The development feature of the Chinese model can best be understood from the viewpoint of those poor and small African countries seeking to develop their societies. It has been among those societies that China's experience has found the greatest appeal. A number of reasons account for this. First, many African countries have become increasingly dissatisfied with their own national developmental patterns, based upon the liberal Western model, which either was imposed upon them by their former European colonial masters or was self-imposed at an earlier date in an effort to achieve modernization. This has led many of them to search for alternative forms of development, from both East and West, capitalist and socialist societies. Second, the search for alternative

approaches and solutions to nation building has led many African societies to a closer examination of successful social systems similar to their own in historical and environmental-situational background. Third, most African countries have been impatient with the pace of their own national development. Indeed, the sense of urgency has been very great; rapid national development has become the goal of most countries in Africa. Finally, a significance of the developmental feature of the Chinese model has been the psychological appeal: the concern of African countries with the achievement of equality with the advanced West.

We can best explain this appeal as follows: The West has long held sway over much of Africa with its technological and scientific advances. China, beginning as an underdeveloped society, technologically, scientifically, and otherwise in the Western sense, had within a relatively short period achieved a meaningful level of development in these and other select areas, bringing to an end her total dependence upon and domination by the West. China's overall industrial and nuclear developments were seen in this light. The developmental feature of the Chinese model, therefore, appealed to many African countries, not only in the narrow economic and social sense, but also in the broader context of equality with the West based on developmental achievements.

An example of the general appeal of China's developmental experience can be found in the case of Tanzania. First, Tanzania had been dissatisfied with its past developmental pattern, for the most part under British influence. Since its independence in 1961 and especially following the Arusha Declaration of 1967, Tanzania has been seeking to create a new social system appropriate to its own historical and environmental-situational context. In building such a system, the Tanzanian elite had made it clear that there was no complete model for the nation to copy; Tanzania had to learn from both the East and the West, providing it was good for Tanzania. In short, the appeal of the developmental feature of the Chinese model has to be seen in the context of Tanzania's search for those aspects of a given model best suited to its needs. Second, Tanzania considered that it shared a common political experience and a common environmental-situational background with China. Therefore, China's developmental experience was pertinent to Tanzania's development. As President Nyerere put it: "The vast majority in both China and Tanzania earn their living from the land or in the rural areas. And both of us have only recently won freedom from that combination of exploitation and neglect which characterizes feudal and colonial societies. We have therefore much to learn from each other."[2]

Third, China's success and rapidity in nation building also constituted an appeal to Tanzania. Having rejected the Western model of development and searching for a new social system, Tanzania saw China as a successful model that could answer some of Tanzania's needs. Equally appealing to Tanzania has been China's rapid modernization in many sectors — that within a relatively short time period the living conditions and character of the Chinese people had

been transformed. Tanzania was also in a hurry and wanted things to change quickly. Finally, there was the psychological appeal of China as a "truly big power," a consequence of its development from a "semi-feudal backward country" to a "powerful independent industrial based . . . self-sustaining socialist economy." China, a country that had been "for long oppressed and exploited," had through development become a big power.

How are the two features of development and liberation of the Chinese model related to China's role in Africa? There can be no question that through direct aid to African liberation movements and economic and technical assistance to select African countries, the Chinese model or select parts of it had been directly and indirectly promoted by China. This had included at least 2 billion dollars in Chinese economic aid to the African countries between 1954 and 1974.[3] However, the true meaning of the Chinese model lay not in Chinese substantive endeavors, though to be sure assistance to African liberation movements and African countries have assisted the respective causes. Indeed, measured against African needs, China did not possess the resources or capabilities to support fully the liberation movements and the developmental endeavors. Rather, China's role in Africa, seen in the context of the Chinese model, has to be understood largely in symbolic terms. The meaning of China's developmental experience lies in the hope it provided, because in general terms the goals were seen as within the reach of most African societies. In short, it held the promise that

2. Information Service Division, Ministry of Information and Tourism (The United Republic of Tanzania), press release, 18 February 1965.

3. The State Department, *Communist States and Developing Countries: Aid and Trade in 1974*, February 1976, table 4.

certain developmental goals could be attained, because it had been the case in China. The people's-war feature of the Chinese model served an equally important role. For those seeking liberation, the formula served as not just a means to an end but as a proven scheme. It mattered not whether the formula could be duplicated and executed; in the eyes of the beholder, the people's-war formula represented the symbol of liberation. China stood as an example of what was possible for all who sought liberation.

THE SUPERPOWERS

A second component of China's role in Africa has stressed the "struggle against the super-powers," the Soviet Union and the United States. Two interrelated features of this struggle deserve our attention: China's policy of opposing the Soviet Union and the United States and China's attempt to discredit the two superpowers in Africa. China's African policy must be understood within the context of China's interaction with the two superpowers.

Chinese foreign policy was formally born in 1949, in the midst of the Cold War between the United States and the Soviet Union. This had an important impact upon the initial course of Chinese foreign policy and behavior. The 1950 alliance with the Soviet Union placed China in the Communist bloc, while the Korean War put China in direct conflict with the United States, which after the war sought to contain China. During the 1950s, with its security guaranteed by the Soviet Union, China turned to confronting American power. One Chinese approach to meeting the problem was the attempt to win friends and seek allies to counter the United States. A major campaign was undertaken to win diplomatic recognition. China's participation in the 1955 Bandung conference was directed toward this end. Although the conference was chiefly an Asian affair, 6 of the 29 states represented were African.

China's interest in Africa continued in the 1960s. In addition to establishing new linkages, China sought hard to get the African states to accept China's worldview and major policy objectives. One such case was China's notions regarding imperialism. Anti-imperialism has long constituted a major theme in Chinese foreign policy. This has included the Marxist-Leninist ideas of the division of the world into imperialist and socialist camps, the struggle between the two camps, and the unfolding world revolutionary struggle against the imperialists. Africa constituted a stage in the world's unfolding revolutionary struggle against imperialism. However, anti-imperialism had also its more immediate aspects. In practice, it was a Chinese policy directed chiefly against the United States. China portrayed the United States as the foremost imperialist —the successor to the old European powers. In the context of China's African policy, anti-imperialism served the primary function of "exposing" the imperialist character of the U.S. policy.

American imperialist character, according to China, was fully brought forth in developments associated with Zaire's—then the Congo—independence in 1960 and with Rhodesia's independence in 1965. In the first case, Zaire in 1960 had been the object of United States imperialism. China considered the sending of a United Nations force to Zaire as nothing more than a cover-up for U.S. armed intervention. The founding of Rhodesia in 1965 was regarded as another bridgehead, similar to South Africa, for use by the imperialists and friends "to commit aggression against and encroach upon" Africa. This the Chinese considered verified by Great Britain's refusal to use military force against Rhodesia and the support given to Great Britain by the United States.[4] Both instances were excellent examples of how the United States had sought to suppress the revolutionary and liberation movements in Africa. The United States as an imperialistic power had been exposed.

The United States constituted one Chinese problem; another has been the Soviet Union. Since the early 1960s, the Sino-Soviet conflict has been a major factor in China's African policy. We need not repeat here the well-known facts regarding the reasons for the conflict; suffice to say that they included unfulfilled expectations and demands on both sides, including the course of China's domestic development, the Soviet Union's relations with the United States, and the question concerning the best strategy for revolution, especially in the Third World. Following the open break with the Soviet Union, China sought to challenge Soviet influence and to subvert Soviet revolutionary credibility. Africa became a battlefield in the Sino-Soviet conflict.

In the 1960s, China approached the Soviet problem on two primary levels. On the one hand, China sought to identify the Soviet Union with the United States; on the other, China campaigned to politically exclude the Soviet Union from Africa. China accused the Soviet Union of undertaking joint action with the United States, including voting with the United States in the U.N. to send troops to suppress the liberation movement in Zaire and supporting Great Britain and the United States against the use of military force in Rhodesia.[5] China also charged that the Soviet Union disapproved of national liberation wars. Meanwhile, China sought to exclude the Soviet Union from Africa. One of the most overt examples of attempts to achieve this objective was China's campaign to win African support to exclude Soviet participation at the abortive Afro-Asian conference of 1965. In sum, the Soviet Union was not a revolutionary force; it did not belong in Africa, and its policies were identical to those of the United States, an imperialist power.

China's policy of seeking to mobilize Africa as a battlefield on its behalf against the United States and the Soviet Union had slowly emerged; China's role of identifying Africa's enemies and assisting in their exclusion from Africa was also clear. The pattern of China's involvement in Africa became even more evident following China's reentry into the international arena in the late 1960s, upon the conclusion of the Great Proletarian Cultural Revolution. This was greatly aided by developments in southern Africa, including the Soviet role in Angola and U.S. interest in the area as a result of the Soviet presence.

Events in southern Africa in the 1970s offered China new examples of superpower domination; U.S. imperialism and Soviet hegemonism were clearly the root cause of Africa's

4. See "A Chapter on African People's Anti-Imperialism," *Jen-min Jih-Pao*, 18 December 1965.

5. Ibid.

plight. According to China, while the Soviet Union had dispatched mercenary troops to Angola and started "a barbarous armed intervention," the United States was trying hard to hold on to its vested interests in southern Africa.[6] The two superpowers were engaged in competition for the control of Africa. But this was not all bad, the struggle had further awakened the African people to the true nature of the United States and the Soviet Union.

If the 1960s was the era during which the United States was the primary focus of China's international attacks, the 1970s must clearly belong to the Soviet Union. This has been due, in part, to the continued Sino-Soviet conflict, on the one hand, and the reduction in tensions between the United States and China, on the other. Indeed, the Soviet Union has replaced the United States as the focus of China's attention as the foremost dominating world power. From Peking's viewpoint, while in the 1960s the world learned of the imperialistic nature of the United States, during the 1970s the world "began to know Soviet social-imperialism." This was especially true in Africa.

Let us look at Chinese charges against the Soviet Union in Africa.[7] First, Soviet interest in southern Africa has been part of Soviet plans for world domination and Soviet search for raw materials. According to China, Soviet social-imperialists sought to gain access to African natural wealth, including gold, diamonds, and uranium. The Soviet

Union's interest in southern Africa also stemmed from its design to control Europe. By controlling the South Atlantic sea route through which oil and other supplies to Europe were transported, the Soviet Union would then "encircle Europe in a roundabout way." Second, Soviet appeals to Africa on the basis of a common stand against racial discrimination "is pure humbug." Such appeals, according to China, constituted a method to infiltrate the African countries; they were also intended as "a smokescreen to cover up its own expansionist designs and to bring Africa into the Soviet orbit." Third, China also charged the Soviet Union with dividing the African states. This was achieved through Soviet division of the African states into two groups: reactionary and progressive. The Soviet intent, said China, was to foster a split among the African states, set Africans against Africans, thereby weakening Africa's struggle against external forces. Fourth, the Soviet Union had sought to dominate African states and organizations through a third party. Under the appearance of cooperation, the Soviet Union had forced others to act on its behalf, "to serve as its cannon-fodder and colonialist tool." China claimed that the Soviet Union utilized a third party or an organization of that country to occupy an African state. Such was the case of Angola. Fifth, Soviet aid, including military assistance, constituted yet another form of control; it also was a method whereby military bases were secured. Finally, Soviet behavior had necessitated an adjustment in U.S. policy toward Africa, thereby increasing the level of competition between the two superpowers in Africa. China put it thus: faced with the Soviet Union's African offensive,

6. For an example of China's views, see Hsin-hua News Agency, "Tempestuous Storm Sweeps African Continent," 27 December 1976.

7. See, Hsin-hua News Agency, "Intensified Soviet-U.S. Rivalry over Southern Africa," 23 September 1976.

the United States had been compelled to take measures to defend its interests and to check Soviet expansionism.

The Soviet Union was clearly on the march in Africa, at least in the view of Peking. This was part of the Soviet Union's attempt to dominate the world. Similar to interaction with the United States in Africa, China's relations with the Soviet Union have to be understood in the total context of China's struggle against the superpowers: that is, the linkage of the struggle in Africa—and elsewhere—to China's opposition to the United States and the Soviet Union. Indeed, this has been a key factor in China's African policy.

THE THIRD WORLD

As Teng Hsiao-ping made plain in a speech before the United Nations in 1974, China perceived the world separated into three major units: the superpowers, the Second World, and the Third World.[8] The new world struggle consisted of the latter two units against the first. While supporting the Second World's opposition to the domination of the United States and the Soviet Union, China identified with the Third World of Africa, Asia, and Latin America. China's role in Africa, therefore, can also be seen in the context of China's Third World policy.

The origins of China's interests in the Third World can be traced to the mid-1950s; then it was principally seen as one approach to meeting the American encirclement.

8. Mission to the United Nations, People's Republic of China, "Speech by Teng Hsiao-ping, Chairman of the Delegation of the People's Republic of China, at the Special Session of the United Nations General Assembly," press release, 10 April 1974.

The primary area of operation was Asia. The next important development of the Third World policy occurred in the late 1950s and early 1960s. A series of situational-environmental factors combined to change China's international status; it also led to a reassessment of its foreign policy and behavior. Two major events that influenced China's Third World policy were the Sino-Soviet conflict and the emergence of the newly independent African states. China considered the latter event as an opportunity to secure recognition and support for its cause. A consequence of these and other developments led to China's search for the formulation of a new international strategy.

The new strategy contained two primary objectives: China's breaking out of the encirclement imposed by the United States and the Soviet Union and challenging their international domination and China's mobilization and organization of a new international force. In the 1960s China perceived the Third World, symbolized by developments in Africa, offering the greatest political developments. The old order was fast disintegrating, there was great sensitiveness by the new states toward the powers, there was a longing for economic and social development, and there was the promise of a new international force. China's new international strategy was formally announced in 1965; it called upon the Third World of Africa, Asia, and Latin America—"the rural areas of the world"—to challenge the domination of the powers, the "cities of the world of North America and Western Europe. Earlier, Chou En-lai and Chen Yi in late 1964 and early 1965, during their visits to Africa and Asia, sought to operationalize China's policy. However, neither the formulation nor the operationalization of China's new Third World strategy succeeded. Many Third World states were indifferent to China's strategy, seeing it as serving China's interests alone, and China was subsequently to be preoccupied with internal events.

The full implementation of the Third World policy awaited China's reentry into the international arena following the end of the Great Proletarian Cultural Revolution in the late 1960s. China's redefinition of the world into three primary units and the increasing political and economic contradictions among the units also presented new opportunities. As then Foreign Minister Chiao Kuan-hua repeated in 1975, China saw the world separated into three major units and China belonged to the Third World.[9] In the 1970s, after the two false starts of the 1950s and the 1960s plus the temporary interruption due to the Cultural Revolution, China's Third World policy was finally launched. The goals of opposing the superpowers; identification with Africa, Asia, and Latin America; and of creating new international structures were not operational.

China's Third World policy was manifested on a variety of levels in Africa. On the one hand, China sought to interact with most African states and liberation movements; China's diplomatic activism after the Cultural Revolution of cultivating and establishing formal relations with African states represented an example of this behavior.

On the other hand, China also sought to build political ties in harmony with and in support of common interests generally with African states; this has been expressed in China's strong support of Africa's demand for the total liberation of Africa, a restructuring of the international economic order, African and Third World unity, and other issues.

The operationalization of China's Third World policy in Africa can be seen from China's relations with Tanzania.[10] Situated on the shores of the Indian Ocean in East Africa, Tanzania was one of the African states with which China developed a close connection, becoming a model of China's much repeated "international relations of a new type." Beginning with Tanganyika's independence in 1961 and Zanzibar's in 1963, China sought and received the friendship of these new African states. After the union of Tanganyika and Zanzibar to form the United Republic of Tanzania in 1964, an increase in China's interaction with the new republic followed. From Tanzania's viewpoint, this was due to China's support of Tanzania's internal goal of economic and social development and external objective of Africa's total liberation and a just international order. The relationship was formalized with the conclusion of the Sino-Tanzanian Treaty of Friendship of 1965, signed during President Nyerere's first state visit to China. In the same year, Chou En-lai visited Tanzania.

China initiated an extensive economic, technical assistance, and military program to Tanzania; in 1974 Chinese aid (excluding mili-

9. Mission to the U.N., People's Republic of China, "Speech by Chiao Kuan-hua, Chairman of the People's Republic of China, at the 30th Session of the U.N. General Assembly," press release, 26 September 1975.

10. For an account of Chinese-Tanzanian interaction, see George T. Yu, *China's African Policy: A Study of Tanzania* (New York: Praeger Publishers, Inc., 1975).

tary) totaled $331 million in grants and loans. The Great Proletarian Cultural Revolution had neither an overly adverse political influence upon, nor caused a reduction in, the level of Chinese-Tanzanian interaction. Indeed, relations continued at a high level, marked by China's commitment to finance and construct the Tanzania-Zambia railway in 1967 and by President Nyerere's second state visit to China in 1968. Sino-Tanzanian relations continued to flourish in the 1970s, symbolized by President Nyerere's third state visit to China in 1974 and by Vice-President Jumbe's official visit to China in December 1976. To be sure, tensions have existed between the two actors, such as over different Tanzanian and Chinese policies toward Angola; possible tensions also existed over the level of Tanzanian-Soviet relations. Notwithstanding, through the mid-1970s relations with Tanzania constituted a model of China's Third World policy.

Through relations with Tanzania, China has established an important presence in Africa. The significance of Tanzania in China's Third World policy can be seen on four primary levels. First, there was the dimension of China's interstate relations which stressed China's common cause with the world's small and medium states, especially those in the Third World. In the words of *Jen-min Jih-pao*, "Both China and Africa belonged to the Third World. In the great struggle against imperialism, colonialism and hegemonism, the Chinese people . . . will always stand on the side of the fraternal African people and firmly support their just struggle till final victory."[11] The Third World was

singled out as playing an increasingly important role in international affairs. This was demonstrated at the Fifth Non-Aligned Conference held in 1976. According to China, the conference had restated the Third World countries' opposition to the superpowers.[12] China and Tanzania both belonged to the Third World. Thus, relations with Tanzania symbolized China's support for and relations with a small Third World state.

Second, there was China's support for national liberation, in terms of support for Africa's total liberation from colonial rule and white minority governments and support in the broader definition of opposition to imperialism and superpowerism. China contended that the United States and the Soviet Union had not only opposed Africa's liberation but had also sought to control, economically and otherwise, the independent African states. African opposition to such forces could only be achieved via African and Third World unity. As a leading member of Africa's frontline states, Tanzania fully supported Africa's total liberation; Tanzania was also an active participant in the Third-World non-alignment movement. Tanzania's friendship with China, therefore, was not only support and recognition of China's stand for Africa's total liberation, but also a united front, Africa and Third World, against the forces of imperialism and superpowerism.

Third, Tanzania's relations with China were seen in terms of China's developmental model and its contribution to Tanzania's economic and social growth. China, as we have mentioned earlier, had long cited

11. Editorial, "Strengthen Unity and March Onward," *Jen-min Jih-pao*, 8 July 1976.

12. Editorial, "March Forward in the Struggle against Imperialism, Colonialism and Hegemonism . . . ," *Jen-min Jih-pao*, 25 August 1976.

its developmental experience as a model for the Third World; one had emphasized the importance of agriculture. China had also stressed self-reliance. China had been aware of its economic and social achievements and the international implications should its developmental model, or specific features of it, be adopted by others, especially by those in the Third World. Tanzania was attracted to certain features of the Chinese developmental model, thus giving credence to China and its approach to development. Finally, Tanzania had been a major recipient of Chinese economic and technical aid, which constituted a new type of economic cooperation. This had included the famous Tanzania-Zambia railway, completed in 1975. According to China, Third World countries could only make true economic and social progress by supporting and closely cooperating with each other. Only thus could they shake "off dependence on the imperialists and hegemonists." Such Third World cooperation would eventually replace "the evil old international economic order" with a new one. Chinese-Tanzanian economic cooperation was a model of the future new economic order in the Third World.

China's relations with Tanzania was an important instance of China's role in Africa; it also represented an example of China's growing relationship with the Third World. From Peking's viewpoint, no doubt Africa was a vital international arena and world force; if Africa could be united with the rest of the Third World, an even greater new international force could be formed. We should not see China's Third World policy only in terms of its opposition to the superpowers; equally important was the development of a new Third World structure. The promotion of

African, Asian, and Latin American unity, therefore, must be seen as a role of China in Africa.

CONCLUSION

What conclusions might one draw on the basis of this survey? Three points will be emphasized. First, one cannot single out a specific Chinese role in Africa. Similar to other major powers, Chinese foreign policy has neither been totally consistent nor sought a single objective. It should be also understood that China's African policy developed over a considerable time period and in response to a variety of factors. But whatever the reasons contributing to China's interest, there can be no doubt that Africa occupied a central place in Chinese foreign policy.

Second, there can be no question concerning the importance of the United States and the Soviet Union as a factor in China's African policy. Opposition to imperialism and social-imperialism have become hallmarks of China's policy in Africa and elsewhere. Indeed, as we have demonstrated, the origins and development of China's African policy have been closely linked to China's interactions with the United States and the Soviet Union. Furthermore, the level of China's activism in Africa has often been directly related to the importance China assigned at a given time to its struggle with the United States and/or the Soviet Union. Notwithstanding, we cannot attribute in total to the United States and the Soviet Union the important place Africa has occupied in Chinese foreign policy. Nor can we assume that China foresaw Africa's world role in the early 1960s. Rather, one explanation for Africa's growing importance can be attributed to China's search for a new international strategy. This, of course, must be seen in the context of China's Third World policy.

Finally, in the last analysis China's role in Africa has been determined as much by China as it has been by Africa and the Africans. By that I mean, while China's policies and behavior have been responsible for whatever successes that have been achieved, the African response to China's policies and behavior have been equally vital. China's successes have not been because China was China or China willed them; they have been due in large part either to the response to a specific need or to the capture of a common aspiration. Herein lies China's future role in Africa: China can be expected to retain its presence in Africa providing China responds to Africa's changing situation.

*   *   *

QUESTIONS AND ANSWERS

Q: I am a little confused about the First World, Second World, and Third World. I had assumed the First World was the world of the Western industrialized countries headed by the United States and the Second World the Soviet Union heading up the industrialized countries. I thought you were talking about the First World as being the superpowers. Is there any usefulness in separating the Third World of the developing but potentially prosperous countries and the Fourth World where there is a state of predevelopment which will require considerable help?

A (Yu): As to what is the Third World, I am merely using the Chinese definition. The First World, in the Chinese view, consists of the U.S. and the U.S.S.R., the two superpowers that are the main forces in the world at this moment. The Second World includes the Western European industrial nations, Japan, Australia and New Zealand, as well as our neighbor to the north. Then everybody else is included in the Third World, which is primarily Africa, Asia, and Latin America.

As for a further differentiation among Third World nations, the Chinese recognize that some are more developed, advanced, or even affluent than others. One has to give different treatment. Insofar as the Chinese are concerned, the key consideration is the place of the members of the Second or Third World. The Chinese, at least in verbal statements, are seemingly optimistic about the future of the Third World. Among other things, they believe in numbers. Furthermore, there is a new assertiveness and awareness on the part of the Third World. The Chinese are trying to structure the Third World and maybe the Second World into a meaningful international force.

———————

Q: Don't you think that the current Chinese interest in Africa is ideological—that the Africans really only get ideological resources for nation-building and not the material resources which they get from the former colonial powers.

A (Yu): I would certainly agree that the ideological or symbolic components are the major and most important parts. However, the Chinese have to supplement those symbolic, ideological components with some measure of substantive aid, though it is not very large.

U.S. Relations in Southern Africa

By WILLIAM E. SCHAUFELE, JR.

ABSTRACT: U.S. policies in southern Africa are essentially founded on political interests, a significant ingredient of which is our concern for human rights. We believe the minority governments of Rhodesia, South Africa, and Namibia violate fundamental human rights. We cannot remain a spectator in the decolonization of Rhodesia and Namibia and the system of apartheid in South Africa. This administration's policy has been to try to ensure peaceful changes in these countries. Violence would cause untold human suffering and also create a climate for intervention by forces from outside Africa. We firmly believe African problems should be solved by Africans themselves. The situation in South Africa is different from that in Rhodesia and Namibia, since the whites have been there for 300 years and Africa is their home. Though we have demonstrated our opposition to the apartheid system, South Africa's problems should be resolved in Africa. There are examples on the African continent which give hope that political leaders can build a future in which blacks and whites can co-exist and prosper rather than have the future imposed on them.

William E. Schaufele, Jr., has been Assistant Secretary of State for African Affairs since December 1975. He holds the rank of Career Minister in the Foreign Service and has served as Inspector General of the Foreign Service since April 1975. He has served as Deputy U.S. Representative to the U.N. Security Council and Senior Adviser to the U.S. Permanent Representative to the U.N. In 1969 he was designated U.S. Ambassador to Upper Volta. Prior to that he served in the Department of State as Desk Officer for the Congo, Deputy Director of the Office of Central African Affairs, and Director of the Office of Central West African Affairs.

A FEW years ago, I would not have chosen this subject to provoke discussion among a distinguished group of academic scholars. The African continent in general, and the southern part of it in particular, excited sustained attention and debate only among a small band of specialists in academia, business circles, and the government except in time of crisis. This has also changed radically. Probably never in the history of American diplomacy has the governmental and public interest, even absorption, in one relatively small and remote area of the world increased at such a rapid pace from quasi-academic to substantial.

Our concern about southern Africa is quite unlike our interest in other parts of the world which are important to the United States, such as Europe, the Far East, and the Middle East. Our interest is not strategic. We have consistently made clear that the United States does not wish to play a military role anywhere in Africa. It is also not based on economic interests, although we do want to see that Western Europe as well as the United States retain access to the mineral wealth of southern Africa. Under the proper political circumstances, I can visualize a very substantial growth in two-way trade with that part of the continent. Our recent actions with respect to the Byrd Amendment should make clear that we are fully capable of subordinating our economic interests to other, more vital concerns.

HUMAN RIGHTS

U.S. policies in southern Africa are essentially founded on political interests. A significant ingredient of that interest is our concern for human rights and human dignity. Our policy toward southern Africa is guided by our ideals of liberty and equality and by our commitment to oppose racial and social injustice. We believe that the minority governments of Rhodesia, South Africa, and Namibia violate fundamental human rights as spelled out in the U.N. Declaration of Human Rights. We have spoken out on this subject forcefully and repeatedly so that there can be no mistaking our position. In conformity with our own fundamental principles as a nation, we have based our policies on the belief that the peaceful transfer of power to the black majority is not only necessary and desirable, but also possible.

The foreign policy of the United States, if it is to be successful, must be firmly grounded in our own fundamental beliefs. Lacking this vital element, it would not obtain the requisite backing from our people. It is self-evident, therefore, that the United States must be engaged in southern Africa if we want to remain true to ourselves. Given the dangers involved, we cannot remain an idle spectator while the decolonization process takes place in Rhodesia and Namibia.

Similarly, I believe that our history dictates that we have a role to play with respect to the system of apartheid in South Africa. It has been a long and frequently painful process for the black and white elements of our population to work out their relationship based on the ideals of the founding fathers. Very substantial progress has been made in recent years in this respect, and more needs still to be done. But at least there is now hope where there once was only despair, and we are on the right road. Having come through this experience, we can, I believe, without resort to the zealotry of the converted, also contribute to the resolution of the apartheid issue. Our history as a people of many races able to live together more or less in harmony can be, within limits, a guide and inspiration to others.

Apartheid, of course, simply means apartness. It enshrines the concept of separateness, without even the leavening thought of equality. The system of apartheid currently being practiced in South Africa is, therefore, still a considerable distance from the slightly more progressive concept finally struck down by our Supreme Court a quarter century ago. It is a measure of the distance South Africa must travel to overcome the burden of its racial heritage.

DECOLONIZATION

The rapid changes in Portugal brought about the decolonization of the Portuguese empire in Africa. This development of the last few years has, in turn, hastened the demise of the remaining two vestiges of the era of the empire, Rhodesia and Namibia.

The policy of this administration, and that of its predecessor, has been to try to ensure that the changes which we consider inevitable for both Rhodesia and Namibia take place in a peaceful manner. There are those who believe that the transition to majority rule can come about only by force of arms. These advocates of violence believe that Ian Smith's record of procrastination in Rhodesia and South Africa's continuing important role in Namibia preclude a peaceful settlement. I strongly disagree with that view. Progress has already been made, perhaps more than we had reason to hope for only a year ago. Ian Smith has agreed to the principle of turning over power to the black majority

within two years. Although negotiations broke down in Geneva over the complex questions surrounding the modalities of the transition of majority rule, I hope that talks can again be started. I am convinced there is a reasonable chance for success.

Rhodesia

We believe that the United Kingdom should continue to take the lead on the Rhodesian question, since it is the sovereign power in Rhodesia. We have worked closely and well with them in the past; during February we had several intensive meetings with them in Washington to coordinate our policies. And Foreign Secretary David Owen is currently in southern Africa to assess further the situation on a trip planned in consultation with the United States. It is also a significant accomplishment that, in the course of working toward a peaceful settlement of southern African issues, we have strengthened our ties with the frontline states of Zambia, Tanzania, Botswana, and Mozambique. Ambassador Andrew Young, on his trip to Africa during the early days of the Carter administration, received valuable new insights into the thinking of the African leaders on those issues of mutual concern. I want to emphasize that the frontline states continue to support the view that a peaceful solution is desirable in Rhodesia and Namibia even as armed struggle goes on. We are working closely with them to that end.

The advantages of a peaceful transition to majority rule should be manifest to all of us. The transfer of power is going to be difficult under any circumstance, and some disruption of the economic processes may be inevitable. But both Rhodesia and Namibia are potentially prosperous countries with existing structures upon which further sustained economic growth can be built. How much more desirable it would be for the black majority to inherit a country with a running economy than one so severely damaged or destroyed by prolonged strife that the immediate fruits of independence may be meager indeed.

Given the strength, on the one hand, of the Zimbabwe liberation forces, many of which are now in training camps in Mozambique and Tanzania, and the strength of the Rhodesian security forces on the other, we believe that a "solution" by combat of arms would inevitably be protracted. There would not be a quick knock-out by either side. Therefore such a solution would be bloody and involve untold human suffering and misery which we want to avoid if at all possible.

Prolonged violence would create a climate, moreover, conducive to intervention by forces from outside the African continent. The frontline states have thus far successfully resisted the counsel of those contending that only armed struggle can produce success in Zimbabwe and Namibia. We cannot be sure, however, that they will always see the situation this way. We firmly believe that African problems should be solved by the Africans themselves. Our policy has been guided by the principle that the big powers or their surrogates should not play a military role on the continent. We have seen how long it takes an outside power, once engaged in an African conflict, to withdraw its forces and the many undesirable consequences such involvement brings in its train in terms of African stability and unity.

Following rejection of the latest British proposals in January, Ian Smith has apparently decided to attempt what he euphemistically calls an "internal solution." This involves negotiations with certain black groups and individuals, some of whom were already members of the Smith regime, to bring about majority rule. We do not believe this will lead to a solution. It ignores not only the desires of the Zimbabwe guerrilla forces and important nationalist elements but also of the frontline states. In our view, this internal solution cannot last; to attempt it would inevitably lead to increased bloodshed and violence.

Finally, we believe that a peaceful solution in Rhodesia and Namibia would provide a useful stimulus to orderly change in South Africa itself. Conversely, the escalation of violence in the adjoining territories could well polarize opinion in South Africa and make more difficult the achievement of any progress in the direction of racial justice in that country.

We recognize, of course, that our dedication to a peaceful, rapid, and orderly transition to majority rule needs to be backed up with concrete measures. We worked hard for the repeal of the Byrd Amendment by the Congress, passed by a decisive margin in both houses and placing the United States in observance with pertinent U.N. resolutions. Repeal should convince Prime Minister Smith, if he still had doubts, that he cannot count on the United States to bail him out when his policies fail. We hope now that he will give real negotiations another chance.

We intend to ensure that the sanctions against Rhodesia are strictly enforced. We will be consulting with other nations to see what can be done about tightening compliance with sanctions. We are looking into additional measures that our government might undertake to place additional pressure on Rhodesia and to convince it of the gravity of the situation.

We have provided economic assistance to the governments of Zambia and Mozambique, in recognition of the economic losses suffered by these two countries owing to the closure of their borders with Rhodesia and the interruption of the hitherto profitable transit traffic in Rhodesian goods.

I would like to make it clear that we have no solution that we wish to impose on the various elements of the Zimbabwean political scene. We have no favorites whom we support. We will not take sides, since we believe that the Africans want to work out African solutions to African problems. We will continue to counsel maximum flexibility and readiness to compromise, maximum unity among all of the nationalist liberation forces, and a maximum effort to create the kind of atmosphere that will allow the negotiations to succeed. Both sides should come to the conclusion that their objectives can be achieved more surely and effectively by negotiation than by resort to arms.

Namibia

While the contentious issue of Rhodesia tends to dominate the headlines, we have not been unmindful about the need for rapid progress on the Namibian issue as well. Our policy with respect to that territory has been consistent and clear. In 1966 we voted to terminate South Africa's mandate. We have supported the finding of the International Court of Justice that South Africa's occupation was illegal. We remain committed to the U.N. Security Council Resolution No. 385 calling for free elections under U.N.

auspices, South African withdrawal of its illegal administration, and the release of all Namibian political prisoners.

As in the case of Zimbabwe, we have cause for at least some optimism that the Namibian problem can be peacefully resolved. Some progress has been achieved. A target date of December 1978 has been set for independence, and the South Africans have fully endorsed the concept that Namibia should become independent on that date.

A major difficulty, as we see it, has been that the present efforts to establish an interim government for Namibia have excluded the Southwest African Peoples Organization (SWAPO), which is recognized by the Organization of African Unity (OAU) and the U.N. as the sole Namibian nationalist movement. These efforts have centered on a meeting of Namibian groups in Windhoek seeking to establish an interim government to lead the country to independence. For its part, SWAPO has not wished to participate and insisted that independence could come about only as a result of direct negotiations between itself and the South African government. On this issue, also, we urge a spirit of compromise on both sides in the belief that what may be achievable in a peaceful manner would almost certainly be preferable to anything that can be won through the force of arms alone.

In the case of Namibia, too, it seems to us that, while the positions of some of the principal contenders are far apart, goodwill on both sides can produce agreement. We believe that all political groups in Namibia, specifically including SWAPO, have a role to play in the process leading to independence. We consider that the United Nations should have a role to play in giving birth to an independent nation from a territory which the community of nations accepts as being under U.N. authority, at least in theory. We have proposed that an international conference on a Namibian settlement take place under U.N. aegis at a neutral site, with all the concerned parties.

In support of our policy, the United States has, since 1970, officially discouraged American investment in Namibia. The facilities of the Export-Import Bank are no longer available for trade with the territory. No future U.S. investments there, made on the basis of rights acquired from the South African government following termination of the mandate, would receive U.S. government protection against the claims of a future legitimate government in Namibia. We have urged American firms doing business in Namibia to assure that their employment practices are in conformity with the principles of the Universal Declaration of Human Rights.

South Africa

Our policy toward South Africa is necessarily different from our policy toward Rhodesia and Namibia. We have had diplomatic relations with South Africa since that country became independent. In addition to our embassy in Pretoria, we have three consulates general which keep us informed about what is going on in that country. South Africa is not a colonial remnant. Even the leaders of black Africa do not challenge the right of the white minority to live in South Africa. The white settlers began to cultivate the lands of South Africa 300 years ago. They are also Africans, and they have no other place to go. The problems of South Africa should therefore be solved in South Africa—not by outside powers.

Our maintenance of diplomatic relations with South Africa is by no means an indication that we accept that country's institution of apartheid. We have not minced our words in stating our unalterable opposition to apartheid and shall not do so in the future. This system is a clear violation of the fundamental human rights. Last summer the United States joined a consensus in the U.N. Security Council resolution strongly condemning the South African government for its role in the Soweto violence. On that occasion, the Acting U.S. Representative called on South Africa to "take these events as a warning" and "to abandon a system which is clearly not acceptable under any standard of human rights."

As elsewhere in southern Africa, we are dedicated to the proposition that peaceful change must succeed, if only because the alternative is so unacceptable. We have watched with dismay the escalation of violence in South Africa, beginning with the Soweto riots last year. We are deeply concerned that, unless the spiral of violence can be arrested and reversed, there will be such a polarization of forces within South Africa that peaceful change will become immeasurably more difficult than it is already. We shall employ all reasonable channels to get this message across to the South Africans and to facilitate this change to the maximum possible extent.

It is appropriate, however, to insert here a cautionary word. Of all people, we Americans should probably be chary about providing excessive and unsolicited advice to others about how they should solve their racial problems. True, we have made impressive progress within our own country in removing the stain of injustice and discrimination based solely on race. But we must also admit that we have a considerable way to go before our achievements approach the ideals set forth in our Declaration of Independence and our Constitution. But perhaps more important, our recent history provides testimony to the fact that change in the racial sphere came about gradually, unevenly, perhaps even grudgingly, not because outsiders or foreigners told us what was right, but because the realization finally dawned on our people that the status quo was wrong and had to be changed for our own good. This self-realization must be given an opportunity to do its creative work in South Africa also, although I will readily agree that the time for results is limited. It is in no one's interest if the South Africans move into an isolationist shell, closed against outside influences, there to defend themselves from all enemies, foreign and domestic. Such a development would have an effect opposite from the one we wish to achieve.

Our diplomacy toward South Africa must, therefore, be carried out with a good deal of finesse and skill. We shall have to weigh carefully the relative merits of speaking out and of restraint.

In the circumstances I have described, the United States is necessarily pursuing a nuanced policy vis-à-vis South Africa without compromising our principle. As I have already indicated, we have repeatedly made clear our opposition to a system under which an 18 percent minority limits the black majority economically, discriminates socially, and deprives the blacks of political rights.

As a corollary to this policy, the

United States has opposed the South African government's policy of creating a series of "bantustans" or homelands. The Transkei was the first of these homelands to become independent, but others are expected to be given that status by South Africa. The United States has not recognized the Transkei, and, aside from South Africa, neither have other members of the United Nations. We have no intention of recognizing any of the other homelands that will be declared independent.

In fact, the creation of these so-called states is an extension of the apartheid policy. Stripped of all euphemisms and rationalizations, the concept of the homelands is unfair to the black majority. The effect of their creation is to deprive substantial elements of the black urban workforce of their civil rights in South Africa and to force many urban blacks to take on citizenship of a homeland they have never known. The homelands were established without counsulting the blacks. They are generally conglomerations of the remnants of tribal lands without contiguous borders, without the basis for economic viability, and without any basis for true political independence from South Africa.

It is worth noting that there have been some encouraging signs on the South African scene. Events of the past year have not been without their effect on the white community of South Africa. Many signs point to considerable soul-searching, even on the part of the Afrikaner community which forms the primary political base of the ruling party. A number of leading Afrikaner intellectuals have urged that the government reconsider important elements of its policy, such as present plans for the homelands, the denial of all political rights to Africans outside the homelands, and various forms of economic discrimination.

South African businessmen, too, have begun to urge steps to improve the daily life of Africans in such areas as housing and training. In certain areas of activity which are not directly under government sponsorship, such as athletic and religious organizations, we detect some breakdown in previously rigid racial barriers. We have been encouraged by the actions of the Catholic church to permit some integration of its schools and by the tolerance of this decision displayed by the South African government. In terms of the daily life of an African in South Africa, these are small steps. But we believe they reflect that the faith of many South African whites in the possibility of maintaining indefinitely racial separation and white supremacy is being fundamentally reexamined.

The United States has adopted certain policies to demonstrate our opposition to the apartheid policy of South Africa. Since 1962 we have maintained a voluntary embargo on the sale of military equipment to South Africa. U.S. naval vessels do not call at South African ports except for emergencies, although they regularly make courtesy calls in some black African ports.

We have redoubled our efforts to intensify our contacts with blacks in the South African population. President Carter recently invited Gathsha Buthelezi, a prominent black moderate, to the White House, underlining the administration's interest in establishing better ties with black leadership in South Africa.

Along these same lines, we have intensified the informational activities of the U.S. Information Service in South Africa, especially among the black population. We have also expanded our exchange program under which a cross section of the South African population, mostly blacks, visits the United States for month-long stays. Our diplomatic and consular officers, including black foreign service officers, cultivate a wide range of contacts in South Africa.

The United States has also encouraged American firms doing business in South Africa to improve working conditions for their black employees. We believe this could be a significant American contribution to the principle of social justice and provide a vehicle for promoting economic and social progress. We have been encouraged by the progress that many American firms have demonstrated in working toward the principle of equal pay for equal work, adequate pensions, improved medical and insurance benefits, and expanded opportunities for advancement based entirely on merit rather than race. Although there is clearly room for improvement in the performance of their labor practices, South African-based American companies have shown considerable sensitivity in dealing with their black employees. By their example, they have already set in motion some of the kinds of change that are so desperately needed.

A recent step in the right direction was the March 1, 1977, announcement by 12 major U.S. corporations with business interests in South Africa expressing support for a set of principles designed to promote equal employment rights for blacks and nonwhite minority groups. These principles call for the nonsegregation of races in all dining facilities and places of work and the concept of equal pay for all employees doing equal and comparable work. We hope that these constructive steps will be emulated and expanded by other U.S. firms engaged in business in South Africa and perhaps even be adopted by the South African business community itself.

We fully recognize that American corporations genuinely wishing to institute social changes in their labor practices may fear contravening South African laws and traditional practices which discourage evolutionary changes. Moreover, many of the white unions are resistant to change. They will not countenance having a black supervisor over a white worker, and they restrict the movement of black workers into the ranks of the skilled workers despite the fact that South African industry desperately needs more skilled workers. There is no reason why American firms cannot enter into collective bargaining agreements with black unions. Unlike the white unions, these are not officially registered. However, they are not illegal, and companies can deal with them. Several weeks ago, the second largest supermarket chain in South Africa announced that it would recognize and negotiate with a black trade union. We hope this will encourage American corporations to follow suit where the existence of a black union makes this feasible.

There are those, of course, who argue that American corporations in effect have no business being in South Africa in the first place, that they are either an impediment to social change or have no real effect on change, and that their net result is to buttress the status quo elements that want apartheid to go on. Others have come forth with opposing arguments. They claim that U.S. invest-

ment assists the economic development of South Africa, which sets in motion certain powerful currents of change that will be too much to withstand. Increased investment, the argument goes, helps create more jobs for blacks, inevitably some upgrading of their job skills, and this process has already resulted in new and different perceptions and attitudes that have made themselves felt on the South African political scene.

The South African blacks seem to be divided in their views on this issue. Some favor foreign, including U.S., investment while others have opposed it. There is certainly no clear consensus on the question.

As a government, we have stayed neutral on this issue so far. We have neither encouraged nor discouraged American investment in South Africa. This is one of many facets of our policy toward southern Africa that is currently under review.

Potential American investors have been free to decide the issue on their own, although, if asked, we provide them with all the information we have available. We make certain they are aware of the controversy about such investment, explain our official neutrality, note the moral and social as well as economic and political problems of working in an apartheid society, and urge that if they do invest they give priority attention to the matter of fair employment practices.

We have, however, placed some restrictions on our bilateral economic relationship. For example, we restrict the Export-Import Bank facilities in South Africa. Export-Import Bank direct loans to South African importers of U.S. products are prohibited. However, the bank does guarantee privately financed loans as a service to U.S. exporters.

CONCLUSION

As I indicated at the outset of my remarks, there are a number of positive elements on the southern African scene. Perhaps the most promising aspect is the fact that unlike a number of African countries, Zimbabwe, Namibia, and South Africa itself have strong economic assets. Southern Africa is richly endowed with a generally favorable climate and with natural resources that the world needs. We have already announced that we stand ready to assist Zimbabwe and Namibia with training programs to promote further economic development when majority rule comes.

The rest of the African continent has, in a relatively short time, made tremendous progress from the colonial period to independence to collectively playing a major role on the world scene. The record has inevitably been an uneven one, but there are a number of African countries where Africans and Europeans cooperate in harmony for the betterment of all. I would not suggest that the situation in southern Africa is analogous. But I do suggest that there are examples on the African continent which give hope that political leaders can creatively build a future in which blacks and whites can co-exist and prosper in peace rather than have the future imposed on them.

For the sake of Africa, and for our sake, I hope that the leadership in southern Africa will choose wisely. For our part we wish them well, and we will remain committed to doing everything in our power to ensure that the outcome will be a happy one.

MEMBERS' FORUM

With this volume we are introducing a new section of the ANNALS. Its purpose is to encourage our members to exchange opinions on matters of major public concern. To introduce this feature, we have provided the following list of issues and questions which arose in the course of the Academy's Bicentennial Conference on the Constitution. The papers for that conference comprised the July 1976 issue of the ANNALS. The full text of the three-day discussion will be published in a few months as a separate monograph.

Elmer Staats, a member of our Board of Directors and Comptroller General of the United States, chaired the key sessions on the Constitution and the structure of our government. He has abstracted from that discussion the major issues which were raised concerning the suitability of our present governmental style for the next 200 years.

We invite our members to comment in writing on any of these fundamental issues. Over the course of the next year, we will publish brief excerpts from the most outstanding letters from our members in the hope of encouraging an informed dialogue on these vital topics. If you wish to participate, please send your letter to:

Richard D. Lambert
Editor of the *Annals*
American Academy of Political and Social Science
3937 Chestnut Street
Philadelphia, PA 19104

So that we can acknowledge the source of the comment, please include your full name and any organizational designation you wish us to use in identifying you.

For members who are interested, reprints of the following are available in units of 10 for $6.00.

ANNALS, AAPSS, **432**, July 1977

The Bicentennial Conference on the United States Constitution
The Shaping of Public Policy—Issues and Questions for Discussion

Abstracted by ELMER B. STAATS

I. What is the best way to select candidates for the American presidency?

A. Is the nominating process of primary importance in identifying and selecting the strongest candidates? In other words, are we likely to get stronger candidates simply by improving the selection process as such? Are we too greatly concerned about methodology or should our concern be to create an environment and an attitude toward government which will bring forth the best leadership in our society?

B. Has the direct presidential primary, which emerged in the early 1900s as an alternate to the party convention and which has sharply increased in the past 10 years, met the expectations of its founders that it would produce stronger can-

didates and provide increased grass-roots support for such candidates?

C. Is the selection of candidates by party conventions inconsistent with the basic principle of democracy as set forth in the Constitution and the Declaration of Independence?

D. Does the presidential primary provide too much of an advantage to the winners in the early primaries by giving that candidate undue momentum and visibility, particularly where these involve special regional or state problems and possibly unrepresentative of the majority of other states? Does it give too great advantages to an individual like Governor Carter who was able to give full time to his candidacy as against other candidates who served in such capacities as a

Elmer Staats became Comptroller General of the United States March 8, 1966, after 26 years' service in the federal government. Before his appointment as Comptroller General, he had served as Deputy Director of the Bureau of the Budget under Presidents Johnson, Kennedy, Eisenhower, and Truman. He is a graduate of McPherson College, McPherson, Kansas, and has an M.A. from the University of Kansas and Ph.D. from the University of Minnesota. He received the Rockefeller Public Service Award in 1961.

senator, congressman, governor, or mayor?

E. Now that approximately 30 states have presidential primaries, has it become too expensive and too wearing on the candidates? Is there a danger that the public will be saturated and "turned off"? Are we placing a burden on both candidate and voter beyond that expected or judged necessary by the majority of our citizens?

F. Would the regional primary alternative which has been suggested provide a better arrangement by reducing the amount of candidate and voter exposure and providing a regional test as against a state-by-state test? (The regional primary concept most frequently supported is an arrangement whereby all states in a given region desiring to hold primaries would be required to hold these primaries on the same day.)

G. Has the extensive use of the mass media, particularly television, been good or bad from the standpoint of political party leadership in the selection of candidates? Does the influence of the media make the political organization or the party machine more or less obsolete? Would the voting public any longer be willing to turn back the clock and place greater reliance on local, state, or regional conventions to select presidential candidates?

H. Is there a danger in the presidential primary system of selecting a candidate largely because of his charisma, a good TV personality, and a national figure because of his prominence in some field not necessarily related to political party support or his qualifications to make a good president?

I. Should we get away from the pledging of delegates and would "unpledging" still further weaken the role of the political party in the selection of presidential candidates?

J. Should we limit the amount of time and money devoted to primaries as is done in Great Britain?

II. What should be the role of the political party in the formulation of national policies and goals?

A. Would a parliamentary system which combines party responsibility and governmental responsibility be a better arrangement than the present system which divorces to a greater or lesser degree party activity from governmental activity and responsibility, and in which the voters do not necessarily make a direct linkage by frequently voting for the individual rather than the party? (The parliamentary system automatically vests control of the legislative branch and the executive in the same party.)

B. Does the fact that so few people vote in both primaries and in the final election arise from the belief that political parties and political party leaders exercise too great a control over policy formulation?

C. Is the concern about a monolithic party and a monolithic policy a real one in view of the fact that there are great divergencies in political philosophy in both the Republican and Democratic parties? For example, the Republican party includes liberals such as Senator Javits and Senator Mathias and conservatives such as Senator Helms, Senator Tower, and former Governor Reagan. Under these circumstances, should not the primary concern be that the party provide a forum for the reconciliation of views within a very broad spectrum? Or should we deliberately encourage a multiple party system?

D. With campaign funding dependent on prior experience and vote-getting, are we now foreclosing the possibility of redesigning parties? Since a new coalition desiring to form a new party could not be funded under the federal funding system, have we curtailed greatly the possibility of such new formations?

E. Is so-called voter apathy due to the voters not liking any of the candidates? For voters that are not enamored of any of the candidates, perhaps there should be a box labeled "None of the above" so that they could express their views also. Why is the voter turnout so low? Is this a reflection of the failure of the political party and political party leadership, or are there more fundamental reasons for voter apathy?

F. Why does the political party play a stronger role in elections to Congress and for state and local offices than for the presidency? How do we reconcile this fact with the oft-repeated statement that voters do not trust political parties because of their reputation for bossism and the feeling that their primary concern is self-gain and self-perpetuation of political party leaders? What is the impact of party identification? Do people vote for a party when they do not know the candidates or are not sure how to vote on an individual? How important is this concept?

G. Have geographic boundaries for state and local government made parties unresponsive in many cases to special regional or local problems? For example, the New York City-Upstate New York schism or the differences in the concerns between Philadelphia and Pittsburgh.

H. Is there any solution to the problems which arise when different political parties are in control of the legislative and executive branches of the government? (Former Senator William Fulbright once suggested that the president-elect resign under this circumstance and the majority party in the Congress select his successor.)

III. Is the constitutional provision for separation of powers and checks and balances between the president and the Congress suited for today's problems?

A. Has not the growth and the powers of the president, arising from the economic depression of the 1930s and the World War II period, weakened the role of Congress in a way which threatens the original concept of separation of powers? Should we take the risk that a future president might develop procedures which would render Congress a subservient body, lacking effective means to check the president?

B. Would some of the disadvantages of separation of powers be overcome with a creation of an "executive-legislative council" made up of the president's cabinet and congressional leaders which would share in the formulation of legislative proposals and in the consideration of major presidential decision making?

C. Would the role of Congress be strengthened vis-à-vis the president through reform of the legislative process itself by making Congress a more efficient and effective body?

D. Would the role of the House of Representatives be stronger with a 4-year term of office to coincide with that of the presidential term of office?

E. Does the separation of powers and the growth in the size and complexity of the federal government make it infeasible for Congress to participate effectively in the development of solutions to major national problems such as an energy policy, tax legislation, or foreign affairs? Would a rearrangement of committee structure to consolidate present committee with broader perspective help?

F. Is Congress too constituent-oriented, as in the case of its intervention and thwarting of the president's handling of the Cyprus crisis, to be able to effectively participate in foreign policy negotiations?

G. Should Congress establish specific procedures for long-range planning for the economy, natural resources development, environmental programs and so on, in order to be able to exercise greater initiative in these areas rather than awaiting a presidential initiative and then reacting, modifying or rejecting presidential proposals? Does not the present system result in delays, stalemates, and confusion as to why better planning is not achieved? Is there an alternative which would provide that Congress insist upon presidential initiatives in proposing longer range plans and establishing by statute better machinery in the executive branch to engage in long-range planning, providing the results to Congress for review, debate, and consideration of subsequent legislation?

H. Is the proposal to provide for "sunset legislation" viable and would it provide an improved means of oversight and evaluation of executive-agency performance? (Sunset legislation generally is defined as periodic mandatory detailed evaluation of major programs by Congress to determine whether they would be continued, modified, or discontinued.)

I. How detailed and in what way is it desirable and feasible for Congress to exercise its oversight responsibilities? Are there dangers in the growing practice of requiring approval of executive regulations or other actions by one house of the Congress or by oversight committees? Is there not a constitutional question with respect to such provisions when the full Congress does not participate and the president has no opportunity to exercise his constitutional powers of approval or disapproval of congressional actions? When does oversight become so detailed that it takes over the decision-making function of the executive agencies?

J. Would it be useful to delay the effective date of major new legislation in order to give Congress an opportunity to discuss and advise on implementing regulations as a way of assuring compliance with legislative intent?

K. To what extent does the growing independence of the bureaucracy, particularly regulatory agencies, undermine presidential responsibility? Are there dangers that career service employees will develop close ties with committees of Congress, thus bypassing executive branch channels in dealing with Congress? Does the civil service have an obligation to pass information and recommendations directly to committees of Congress where they feel the executive branch may be partisanly motivated or withholding important information?

IV. Are present constitutional and statutory provisions adequate to deal with the president who is suspected of crimes, who is disabled, or who has lost the confidence of the Congress and the general public?

A. Should we move toward a system which makes it easier to remove a president? Was Watergate a real proof that "the system works" or was it more nearly the result of an accident? If the tapes had not been made or had been kept secret, would not the likely result have been that President Nixon would have filled out his term of office?

B. Should the Constitution be amended to provide an arrangement, prevalent in parliamentary governments, of votes of confidence in the president? If so, should the arrangement also give the president the right to dissolve the Congress and make them stand for reelection? Under a vote of confidence arrangement, should not Congress also have to stand for reelection, that is, put themselves on the line and incur the risk and the expense of reelection? What would be the consequence of a situation where the president of one party was pitted against a majority party which was instrumental in bringing about a vote of no confidence?

C. Did the framers of the Constitution deliberately make the removal of the president extremely difficult as a means of stabilizing or insulating the president from a "passion of the moment"?

D. If Congress had the power to vote no confidence in the president, would the likely result be that the president would take Congress in his confidence to a greater extent? Would he be more likely to consult with Congress to a greater extent before the fact rather than afterward, and would he be less

likely to use executive privilege to deny Congress information to the same extent as he has in the past?

V. Have the courts increasingly been pushed in the direction of legislative decision-making?

A. Has the failure of Congress to legislate definitively resulted in having these issues passed to the courts? Have the courts been too willing to take jurisdiction on issues which are essentially non-judicial in nature, such as deciding on adequacy of environmental, health, or safety standards?

B. To what extent has the development of public interest groups been a factor in pushing the courts into decision making better suited for the executive branch or Congress?

C. Is there a feasible alternative to the regular court system to deal with issues involving the environment, safety, and health? Should we not consider the establishment of an administrative court or a science court with technical competence to make highly complex scientific and technical judgments and trade-off analyses, or should we equip the courts with scientific, technical, and other advisory panels to provide expert testimony in cases of this type?

D. In the area of civil rights, have the courts assumed the function of Congress in the shaping of policy and has this resulted in the courts now being willing to undertake decisions involving health, the environment, safety and in other areas traditionally reserved to Congress?

VI. How can we reconcile the need for developing national policies with the need for local self-government?

A. Has the sovereignty of state and local governments been eroded over the past 200 years with the growing role of the federal government in delivering public services? Given the large array of public functions currently performed by the federal government and the greater interest shown by voters in national elections as compared with state and local elections, are state and local governments still the layers of government closest to the people?

B. To what extent have the following factors contributed to the shift in control in government to Washington: (1) the unequal distribution of wealth and opportunity, (2) the perceived inability of local government to function efficiently and effectively to meet citizen needs, and (3) the outmoded and inadequate structure of state governments and boundaries?

C. Has the inadequate structure of state governments and state geographic boundaries been a major factor in the acceleration of the trend toward centralization?

D. Is it feasible to develop adequate theory and criteria to explain why functions should be categorized as federal, state, or local? For example, how did education and welfare become essentially state and local concerns and pollution control a national concern? Can fixed criteria account for and allow changes in the relative roles of the different levels of government over time: for example, how could water and sewage treatment be transferred from a state or local responsibility to a federal function?

E. To what extent have the federal government's own programs created problems at the state and local levels which then require the federal government to intervene? For example, urban dispersal because of the interstate highway system, subsidized power which encouraged the New England textile industry to move to the South, and so forth. Do we have an adequate system of national assessment or planning with respect to the intended or unintended impact of federal actions on state and local governments?

F. How far should the federal government go in intervening directly or indirectly in the establishment of state and local government machinery as a condition for receiving federal assistance or in providing financial or other incentives to restructure government at these levels? An example of intervention is the requirement that grants to state and local governments for certain programs be required to conform with the regional plan. Should we reconsider the early proposals associated with federal revenue sharing legislation that such revenues be available only after the development of regional plans for restructuring and consolidation of units of local government as advanced by Senator Humphrey of Minnesota and Congressman Henry Reuss of Wisconsin?

G. Is there a conflict between the need for more effective and efficient state and local management and service delivery and the need for expanded citizen participation in government decisions? What should be the federal government's role in encouraging citizen participation?

H. How far should the federal government go in using its taxing powers to redistribute wealth among states and regions? Should it intervene when metropolitan areas suffer higher and higher taxes and rising public service needs as the result of migration from these areas to adjoining jurisdictions where the tax burden is lower? Should it intervene when metropolitan areas face increased service demands due to disproportionate influx of poor families and individuals?

I. Should we be concerned about the accountability of nonprofit and voluntary organizations which assume functions which are governmental or quasi-governmental in character? What should be the proper role of neighborhood advisory groups and organizations combined through community fund drives which may also receive financial assistance from federal, state, or local government sources?

J. Should the federal government have an obligation to intervene in financial crises such as New York City, Boston, Cleveland, or Detroit? And, if so, should this be done only through the state or states involved? Should there be a generic solution for all cities in fiscal distress or should each case be dealt with separately?

VII. How can we best organize at the state and local levels of government to most effectively meet governmental needs?

A. Are today's conditions so drastically different from the time that state boundaries were established as to require radical surgery and redrawing of state lines to meet the practical realities of governmental concerns, or is there enough flexibility under our Constitution to deal with problems which must be solved on an interstate basis?

B. Should high priority be given to strengthening the role of the

state governments vis-à-vis local governments, or has the time passed when we can usefully or practically avoid having federal programs bypass state capitals? Is the old constitutional argument of states rights as implied in Article I, Section 8, of the Constitution outmoded? Have not the courts always found enough flexibility to justify federal intervention in almost all areas previously considered to be reserved for state or local government? Should local or regional units of governments assume the legal sovereignty, rights, and responsibilities previously reserved for the states? On the other hand, should states insist on approval of all fiscal relationships between substate units and the federal government?

C. Have we fully utilized the interstate compact device to deal with regional problems, or is the interstate compact inherently limited by virtue of the fact that it requires approval of all states concerned? Are there any conditions under which the use of the interstate concept could be made more effective, such as giving the compact organization the right to levy taxes or to take regulatory actions without the approval of the state governments concerned? If this is not possible, are there incentives which the federal government could establish to encourage the use of interstate compacts?

D. To what extent can the federal government deal with regional problems by establishing a federal entity, such as the TVA, or creating regional groupings, such as the regional river basin planning commissions authorized by the Water Resources Planning Act? Could the federal government, for example, create a special federal entity—a Regional Development Commission—to deal with the economic problems of the New York City area with powers to make loans, provide subsidies, and carry on economic development activities in cooperation with the states and localities involved?

E. Has adequate recognition been given to the role which the state governments have played or could play in serving as pilots or laboratories for programs which later can be used, in whole or in part, on a national basis? Examples can be cited in such areas as health, land use, education, and so forth. Should the federal government encourage this and through what means?

F. Should formulation of metropolitan-wide governments be encouraged by the federal government so that local areas can tap a larger resource base and deal more effectively with common problems? Does the development of metropolitan-wide governments imply less opportunity for citizen participation in decision making, as is sometimes claimed by proponents of "neighborhood government"?

G. Should land-use planning and zoning decisions in complex metropolitan areas remain matters of local concern, or should they be transferred to state or regional regulatory authorities? Should the federal government encourage certain patterns of regional land-use development to promote national objectives such as energy production or air pollution control?

H. How can the trend toward centralization of powers and functions be slowed down or reversed? Would it be possible for the national government to set out a long-term and systematic program to strengthen state and local governments through improving legislative procedures, salaries for state and local government officials, and im-

proving the structure of state and local governments?

VIII. How can we improve the process of planning, goal making, and priority setting in a democratic society?

A. Is it possible to plan effectively in a democratic society without giving up the freedoms which were envisioned by the founders of the Republic? If the framers of the Constitution could have envisioned the complexity of present-day society, would they possibly have opted for something other than the concept of separation of powers and the division of responsibilities between the federal government and the state governments?

B. How do we reconcile freedom of individual action with the intervention of government which is involved in so many aspects of present-day life—the red tape and controls, for example, involved in protection of health, safety, and environment? How can we make these regulations and statutes flexible enough to meet varying conditions as among individuals and different localities and, at the same time, accomplish national objectives in a fair and impartial manner? Do the processes by which these regulations are developed take into account sufficiently the end impact on those being regulated? Should we contemplate a "paperwork impact statement" or a "regulatory impact statement" for each major bill or proposed regulation prior to its becoming effective?

C. Are planning and regulation necessarily synonymous? Is it not possible in a democratic society to accomplish national goals through means short of direct intervention? Can we use to a greater extent targets, social indicators, and better fact-gathering in a manner which will make it possible to obtain a consensus as to goals, such as inflation rates, unemployment rates, and improvement of the environment?

D. Do we need a better mechanism to establish the data base and an accounting or data retrieval system which will make it possible to better judge progress against national goals and objectives? Have we too lightly dismissed the concept of planning, programming, and budgeting in a system which links these concepts in the public sector?

E. In the economic arena, should we not experiment to a greater degree with deregulation? Are those who are now being regulated developing a vested interest in the regulatory system to avoid competition and fixed prices? In a free enterprise system, shouldn't we perceive the "right to fail"—which we may be losing—in such regulated areas as the air and surface transportation system? To what extent does the assistance of the regulatory type of organization contribute to the difficulties of administering regulation and deregulation? Would it not be better to have such regulations issued by a single-headed agency which is responsible politically to the president and Congress?

F. While the president is accountable to the electorate for setting national goals and objectives, are his hands too frequently tied by an unresponsive bureaucracy? Should the president have greater freedom to appoint to positions now protected by the civil service system? Does the high turnover (average 18 months) of top officials in the executive branch mean that we suffer from relatively inexperienced

people in these positions? Does this turnover undesirably strengthen the position of the bureaucracy and the civil service?

IX. How can we increase confidence in and responsiveness of governmental institutions?

A. How do we account for the fact that most public opinion polls reflect low confidence in governmental institutions, particularly at the federal government level? Is this due to the failure of political parties to effectively represent voter interests? Is it due primarily to growth in the size and complexity of government? Is it due to the growing centralization of governmental responsibilities at the federal level? Is it due to rising expectations of the role of government vis-à-vis nongovernmental organizations in society? Or is it a combination of several or all of these factors?

B. Voluntary organizations have always played an important role in American society, but how do we account for the rapid growth in recent years of public interest groups and citizen legal actions directed at requiring the government to act in the public interest? Is the public interest movement a temporary phenomenon or does it reflect something more basic in terms of the ability of citizens to obtain a redress of their grievances? Have these actions been too negative in character, designed to thwart initiatives by both Congress and the responsible executive agencies?

C. How far can we go in permitting public participation, granting of freedom-of-information requests, and opening up the courts for citizen action, compelling government action or restraining government action without immobilizing, delaying unduly, and generally weakening the ability of government agencies to exercise leadership in carrying out legislation enacted through the legislative process?

D. Does the creation of more mechanisms for citizen action add much if people are apathetic about voting? Does this mean that they are disillusioned with the electoral process? Or does it mean that the professional intervener or those with time and resources available are taking advantage of the widespread desire to have an open government? In other words, is it a case of the squeaky wheel getting the grease?

E. Have the public interest groups themselves—like Common Cause—become undemocratic when they do not permit members to participate in decisions as to what positions will be taken by these organizations or have any part to play in what matters the organizations will address themselves to? In other words, how do members of these organizations hold their officers accountable? Who is to decide, for example, issues of public morality and other value systems in society? Is it sufficient simply to have members free to join or not join such an organization if there is an undue level of financial support coming from large contributors? What about the accountability of the public interest law firm which has large resources at its disposal?

F. How do public interest groups differ from the more traditional trade and industry associations, labor unions, and such organizations as the League of Women Voters, councils on foreign relations, chambers of commerce, and so forth? Are the public interest groups en-

dowed with the ability to represent "all of the people" or "the public interest" in contrast to groups having special interests? Should public interest groups be required to register as lobbyists? Why are these public interest groups apparently a peculiarly American phenomena?

G. Are not many of the issues facing government today too complex to expect wide public understanding without the aid of special groups who can undertake research and public education activities in such areas as pollution control, tax policy, capital formation, nuclear proliferation, and so forth? Can these issues be resolved best through working directly with elected representatives and advisory groups established by executive agencies, by those directly affected, or is it necessary to have special groups in society represent the common good and the public interest? How does one define common good and public interest separate and apart from the self-interest of labor organizations, business organizations, professional societies, and other groups that are directly affected by governmental regulatory and other actions?

H. Why has not the formal ombudsman arrangement been more popular in the United States? Can the elected representative, in fact, serve this purpose or do we need a special mechanism, such as that which has been developed in some cities in the United States and in several foreign governments, to act on citizen complaints with respect to governmental action?

I. It has been argued that the federal government and the state governments are less responsive to citizens' needs and less accountable than local government, but is this true? Do the cities, such as New York, Chicago, and Los Angeles, provide for any more direct citizen involvement than the federal government? Are not special interest groups, criminal organizations, and so forth, equally effective—or perhaps more so—at the local level than at the federal government level? Is not the media—TV, radio, and so forth—more effective in maintaining openness and integrity at the national government level than at the local level? How effective is citizen participation in matters of local taxation, allocation of budget resources, decisions on capital improvement, and so forth?

J. It has been argued that responsiveness of government to citizen needs cannot be improved except through greater participation by voters in the electoral process, but how can this be done? Would a postcard voter registration system serve to increase voter participation, or is the "get out the vote" function one which should be primarily that of interest groups, such as labor organizations, public interest groups, and so forth? Would a system of compulsory voting or penalties for not voting increase citizen interest? Would it be useful to follow the example of most other democratic nations in arranging for a universal registration of all citizens for voting purposes? Should we shift elections from the traditional Tuesday to Sunday? If a compulsory voting system is adopted, should not there be a place for protest or "none of the above" votes which would be counted and published along with votes for or against candidates or issues?

K. Would confidence in government be increased if the president were elected for a single 6-year term and the House of Representatives elected for 4-year terms with a limit on the number of terms which representatives serve? Would confidence be increased if maximum age restrictions were placed on individuals running for public office or, at least, restrict the ability to serve as a committee chairman to individuals below a certain age? Would a system of automatic rotation of committee chairmen serve a useful purpose in this regard?

L. To what extent is confidence in government lowered by the publicity given to unethical practices of public officials, the failure to disclose financial interests, and the close association of some elected representatives with special interest groups? Is public disclosure of financial and other relationships adequate, or should divestiture be required, as well? What is the line between the objectives of privacy on the one hand and the disclosure of assets and financial relationships on the other?

M. To what extent is confidence in the federal government lowered by the manner in which the vice-president is selected and the role which he plays? Should the vice-president be selected following the presidential election by having the president-elect submit one or more names to the Senate and the House for approval (as in the case of President Ford and Vice-President Rockefeller)? Would it be desirable for the vice-president to serve in an administrative capacity such as a cabinet post? Would it not be wise for the Senate to select its own presiding officer rather than have the presiding officer represent the president and vote his position in case of a tie?

Delegates	Representing
Abbas, Dr. Jabir, Huntington, W. VA	Marshall University
Adams, Mr. P. W. T., New York, NY	Permanent Mission of New Zealand to the United Nations
Akuchu, Dr. Gemuh, Dover, DE	Delaware State College
Akuetteh, Mrs. Cynthia, Washington, DC	Action/Peace Corps/African Region
Alton, Col. Carlly, Carlisle Barracks, PA	U. S. Army War College
Alveranga, Mr. Glen, Haverford, PA	Haverford College
Andrews, Miss Roberta G., Philadelphia, PA	Children's Aid Society of Pennsylvania
Anyanwu, Dr. Rowland, Clayton, NJ	Glassboro State College
Appel, Prof. John, East Stroudsburg, PA	East Stroudsburg State College
Arnold, Mr. Kenneth L., Philadelphia, PA	The Association of American University Presses, Inc.
Arnott, Dr. Margaret L., Philadelphia, PA	Philadelphia College of Pharmacy and Science
Artz, Dr. Jefferson, Mississippi State, MS	Mississippi State University
Aviado, Dr. Domingo, Philadelphia, PA	Embassy of the Philippines to the United States
Badi, Mr. Solieman, New York, NY	Permanent Mission of the Libyan Arab Republic to the United Nations
Baker, Dr. Bettie J., Cleveland, OH	Cuyahoga Community College
Bartlett, Mr. David, Philadelphia, PA	The Association of American University Presses, Inc.
Batt, Ms. Joan, Philadelphia, PA	Association for World Education
Benjamin, Prof. Ernst, Detroit, MI	Wayne State University
Bentinck, van Schoonheten, Baron W., O., Briarcliff Manor, NY	Permanent Mission of the Kingdom of the Netherlands to the United Nations
Bletz, Mr. Donald F., Newville, PA	Wilson College
Botchway, Dr. Francis, A., Cincinnati, OH	University of Cincinnati
Bull, Mr. William V. S., Washington, DC	Embassy of the Republic of Liberia to the United States
Burk, Mr. James M., Pittsburgh, PA	American Association of School Administrators
Butler, Prof. Melissa, Crawfordsville, IN	Wabash College
Buzinkai, Dr. Donald, Wilkes-Barre, PA	King's College
Cagampan, Mr. Honorio T., Washington, DC	Embassy of the Philippines to the United States
Cahen, Mr. Alfred, Washington, DC	Universite Libre de Bruxelles, Belgium and Embassy of Belgium to the United States
Callaway, Dean Barbara, Newark, NJ	Rutgers University
Campbell, Mr. Joseph H., Jr., Philadelphia, PA	Americans for the Competitive Enterprise System, Inc.
Capaci, Miss Diane, Glassboro, NJ	Glassboro State College

DELEGATES	REPRESENTING
Caplan, Dr. Albert J., Philadelphia, PA	Charles Morris Price School of Advertising & Journalism
Carlson, Prof. Kenneth, New Brunswick, NJ	National Council for the Social Studies
Carone, Dr. Patrick A., Indiana, PA	Indiana University of Pennsylvania
Carr, Mr. David W., New York, NY	National Foreign Trade Council, Inc.
Carter, Mr. Vernon C., New York, NY	Permanent Mission of Barbados to the United Nations
Cassian Santos, Mr. Salvador, Philadelphia, PA	Embassy of Mexico to the United States
Chang, Mr. John, Washington, DC	Embassy of the Republic of China to the United States
Chang, Prof. Y. C., Newark, DE	The United Nations Association of the Republic of China
Chapman, Dr. Stanley H., Fairfield, CT	Norwalk Community College
Chew, Miss Beng Yong, New York, NY	Permanent Mission of the Republic of Singapore to the United Nations
Clark, Col. Donald O., Carlisle Barracks, PA	U. S. Army War College
Clark, Mr. Walter H., Philadelphia, PA	American Society of Civil Engineers
Comerford, Mr. Philip M., Haddonfield, NJ	The University of Michigan
Coombs, Dr. Norman R., Rochester, NY	Rochester Institute of Technology
Crabb, Dr. Cecil V., Jr., Baton Rouge, LA	Louisiana State University
Culver, Mr. William, Plattsburg, NY	State University of New York at Plattsburg
Daldy, Ms. Celia, Drexel Hill, PA	Jane Addams Peace Association, Inc.
Darboe, Mr. Momodou N., Philadelphia, PA	National Council on Family Relations
Davies, Mr. Lawrence, Carlisle, PA	Dickinson College
Davis, Mr. John W., New York, NY	NAACP Legal Defense and Educational Fund, Inc.
Davis, Mr. Williams B., Washington, DC	The National War College
De Grys, Ms. Mary, Carlisle, PA	Dickinson College
De Louise, Mrs. Barbara, Bethesda, MD	League of Women Voters of Maryland
de Pendleton, Mr. Eric B., Fairfield, CT	Norwalk Community College
Diallo, Prof. Geraldyne, Bronx, NY	Bronx Community College
Diallo, Prof. Mamadou, East Stroudsburg, PA	East Stroudsburg State College
Dindelgan, Mr. Gheorghe, Washington, DC	Embassy of the Socialist Republic of Romania to the United States
Disborough, Mr. M. R., Wilmington, DE	Delaware Council for International Visitors
Donohue, Miss Mary, Drexel Hill, PA	National Council of Catholic Women
Dumangane, Mr. Constantino, Sr., Rochester, NY	Rochester Institute of Technology
Dumas, Mr. Roburt Andre, Sr., Washington, DC	U. S. Department of State, African Bureau
El-Kattan, Mr. Ismail, Washington, DC	Embassy of the Arab Republic of Egypt to the United States
Eshleman, Dr. Kenneth L., Emmitsburg, MD	Mount Saint Mary's College

DELEGATES	REPRESENTING
Esteev, Mr. E. K., New York, NY	Permanent Mission of the Union of Soviet Socialist Republics to the United Nations
Fazekas, Mr. Istvan, Chevy Chase, MD	Embassy of the Hungarian People's Republic to the United States
Fokine, Mr. Yury E., New York, NY	Permanent Mission of the Union of Soviet Socialist Republics to the United Nations
Forrester, Mr. C. J., New York, NY	Permanent Mission of Australia to the United Nations
Foster-Carter, Mr. A., Leeds, England	The University of Leeds, England
French, Dr. George, Philadelphia, PA	The Philadelphia Board of Public Education
Frisby, Dr. David Allen, III, Philadelphia, PA	Antioch College
Gardner, Mrs. Priscilla A., Wilmington, DE	United Nations Association of the United States of America, Delaware Division
Goldfried, Mr. Edwin J., Philadelphia PA	City of Philadelphia, PA
Gordon, Ms. Vivian, Charlottesville, VA	University of Virginia
Green, Mr. William, Philadelphia, PA	The Philadelphia Board of Public Education
Greenstein, Mr. Lewis J., Bethlehem, PA	Moravian College
Griffith, Mr. Cyril E., University Park, PA	The Pennsylvania State University
Grimm, Prof. Kenneth, Sweet Briar, VA	Sweet Briar College
Grube, Ms. JoAnn, Baltimore, MD	National Security Agency
Hadas, Mr. Laszlo, New York, NY	Permanent Mission of the Hungarian People's Republic to the United Nations
Halfond, Dr. Irwin, Salisbury, NC	Livingstone College
Harries-Jones, Prof. P., Downsview, Ontario, Canada	York University, Canada
Harris, Mr. Donald, Newark, NJ	City of Newark, NJ
Harris, Prof. John R., Brookline, MA	Boston University
Harris, Ms. Ruth, Collegeville, PA	National Association for Women Deans, Administrators and Counselors
Harry, H. E. Mr. Ralph L., New York, NY	Permanent Mission of Australia to the United Nations
Hartsoe, Dr. Charles E., Philadelphia, PA	National Recreation and Park Association
Haugse, Dr. Eugene S., Waukesha, WI	Carroll College
Hawes, Ms. Janis, Philadelphia, PA	National Association for Women Deans, Administrators and Counselors
Haywood, Col. Willie M., Jr., Washington, DC	The National War College
Heard, Dr. Kenneth A., Halifax, Nova Scotia, Canada	Dalhousie University, Canada
Hecht, Lester, Esq., Philadelphia, PA	The University of Michigan
Heinsechs, Mr. Waldo, Jr., Philadelphia, PA	The Society for Historians of American Foreign Relations

DELEGATES	REPRESENTING
Hill, Ms. Catherine J., Washington, DC	The International League for Human Rights
Hin, Mr. William, Bayonne, NJ	American Association of School Administrators
Huitt, Mr. Ralph K., Washington, DC	National Association of State Universities and Land Grant Colleges
Hurst, Ms. Marjorie, Springfield, MA	Springfield College
Jackson, Dr. Andrew, Nashville, TN	Tennessee State University
Jackson, Mr. Henry, Salisbury, NC	Livingstone College
Jarvis, Dr. Chester E., Gettysburg, PA	Gettysburg College
Johnson, Dr. David, Greensboro, NC	North Carolina Agricultural and Technical State University
Johnson, Prof. G. Wesley, Santa Barbara, CA	University of California, Santa Barbara
Jones, Mr. Franklin D., Orangeburg, SC	South Carolina State College
Joseph, Prof. John, Lancaster, PA	Franklin and Marshall College
July, Prof. Robert, New York, NY	Hunter College of the City University of New York
Kalonji, Mr. Tshimbalanga, Washington, DC	Embassy of the Republic of Zaire to the United States
Kassai, Mr. Ervin, New York, NY	Permanent Mission of the Hungarian People's Republic to the United Nations
Kerrigan, Ms. Helen, Wilmington, DE	United Nations Association of the United States of America, Delaware Division
Kikhia, H. E., Mr. Mansur R., New York, NY	Permanent Mission of the Libyan Arab Republic to the United Nations
Kilson, Dr. Marion, Cambridge, MA	Radcliffe College
Kingsland, Mr. James, University Park, PA	The Pennsylvania State University
Kirikiri, Mr. Rauru, Washington, DC	Embassy of New Zealand to the United States
Kirsch, Mr. William, New York, NY	The Foundation Center
Klinghoffer, Mr. Arthur, Camden, NJ	Rutgers University
Knighton, Ms. Karen L., Providence, RI	Brown University
Koh, H. E. Mr. T. T. B., New York, NY	Permanent Mission of the Republic of Singapore to the United Nations
Kornegay, Mr. Francis A., Jr. Washington, DC	African Bibliographic Center
Kotecha, Dr. Kanti C., Dayton, OH	Wright State University
Kurtz, Dr. Donn M, II, Lafayette, LA	University of Southwestern Louisiana
Ladson, Ms. Gloria, Philadelphia, PA	National Science Teachers Association
Lalugba, Prof. Losay, East Orange, NJ	Upsala College
Lambert, Prof. Richard D., Philadelphia, PA	University of Pennsylvania
Langley, Dr. Winston E., Boston, MA	Commonwealth of Massachusetts
Lariviere, Ms. Elaine, Philadelphia, PA	The Indian Rights Association
Lasley, Mr. Michael, Takoma Park, MD	American Bar Association
Lawder, Dr. Elizabeth A., Philadelphia, PA	Children's Aid Society of Pennsylvania

DELEGATES	REPRESENTING
Ledbetter, Dr. Cal, Little Rock, AR	University of Arkansas at Little Rock
Lee, Dr. Allen B., Washington, PA	Washington and Jefferson College
Le Melle, Prof. Tilden, New York, NY	Hunter College of the City University of New York
Les Callette, Dr. M. G., Salisbury, MD	Salisbury State College
Levenbach, Ms. Roberta, Philadelphia, PA	The Association of Asian Studies, Inc.
Levitt, Dr. I. M., Philadelphia, PA	City of Philadelphia, PA
Lewis, Dr. William H., Washington, DC	U. S. Department of State, African Bureau
Lofchie, Prof. Mike, Los Angeles, CA	University of California, Los Angeles
Logan, Ms. Nancy, Wallingford, PA	Community College of Philadelphia
Long, Mr. Leslie, New York, NY	American Field Service International Scholarships
Lumsden, Prof. D. P., Downsview, Ontario, Canada	York University, Canada
Lye, Dr. William F., Logan, UT	Utah State University
Madigan, Ms. Marjorie, New York, NY	Marymount Manhattan College
Markovitz, Prof. Irving L., Flushing, NY	The City University of New York, Graduate Division
Mason, Mr. David J., Washington, DC	Embassy of Australia to the United States
McEvoy, Dr. Frederick, Huntington, W. VA	Marshall University
McKee, Prof. Donald K., East Orange, NJ	Upsala College
Mele, Mrs. Bette Crouse, Philadelphia, PA	The Indian Rights Association
Meriwether, Dr. Delano, Washington, DC	U. S. Department of Health, Education and Welfare
Merriam, Prof. Kathleen Howard, Bowling Green, OH	Bowling Green State University
Milburn, Prof. Josephine, Kingston, RI	University of Rhode Island
Miller, Dr. Eugene H., Collegeville, PA	Ursinus College
Miller, Mr. Joseph C., Charlottesville, VA	University of Virginia
Molotsi, Mr. Peter, Philadelphia, PA	American Friends Service Committee, Inc.
Morales Carrion, Dr. Arturo, Rio Piedras, PR	University of Puerto Rico
Morgenthau, Prof. Ruth, Waltham, MA	Brandeis University
Mueller, Ms. Martha, Philadelphia, PA	Brandeis University
Mukerji, Mr. Prafulla, Brooklyn, NY	Taraknath Das Foundation
Munoz Rios, Mrs. Diana, Philadelphia, PA	Embassy of Mexico to the United States
Mytelka, Prof. Lynn K., Ottawa, Ontario, Canada	Carleton University, Canada
Nellis, Prof. John R., Ottawa, Ontario, Canada	Carleton University, Canada
Nelson, Prof. Jack, New Brunswick, NJ	National Council for the Social Studies
Nelson, Dr. Ralph E., Morgantown, W. VA	West Virginia University

Delegates	Representing
Nickerson, Dr. John M., Augusta, ME	University of Maine at Augusta
Noonan, Dr. John D., Berwyn, PA	American Philological Association
Nzuwah, Prof. Mariiyo, College Park, MD	University of Maryland
Oakes, Ms. Rosalie, New York, NY	Young Women's Christian Association of the U.S.A.
Onejeme, Prof. Andrew, Carbondale, IL	Southern Illinois University
Otudeko, Prof. Adebisi, Lancaster, PA	Franklin and Marshall College
Parolla, Ms. Helen, New York, NY	Young Women's Christian Association of the U.S.A.
Peterec, Mr. Richard J., Lewisburg, PA	Bucknell University
Petulla, Mr. Louis W., Swarthmore, PA	American Society of Civil Engineers
Phillips, Mrs. Lloyd, New York, NY	National Council of Women of the United States, Inc.
Pierce, Mr. Richard A., New York, NY	Permanent Mission of Jamaica to the United Nations
Pinto-Coelho, Mr. Pedro, Washington, DC	Embassy of Brazil to the United States
Platt, Dr. Edward R., Indiana, PA	Indiana University of Pennsylvania
Pollak, Dean Louis H., Philadelphia, PA	Association of American Law Schools and The American Law Institute
Potter, Dr. George T., Mahwah, NJ	American Association of State Colleges and Universities
Presler, Mr. Franklin A., Kalamazoo, MI	Kalamazoo University
Quaynor, Dr. Thomas, Baltimore, MD	Morgan State University
Quigley, Dr. Robert, Philadelphia, PA	The American Catholic Historical Association
Ramsey, Ms. Jean C., Philadelphia, PA	Delaware State College
Rao, Mr. P. J., New York, NY	Permanent Mission of India to the United Nations
Rasmussen, Mr. J. Munk, Washington, DC	Embassy of Denmark to the United States
Raudebaugh, Dr. Robert J., Washington, DC	United States National Committee of the World Energy Conference
Redding, Dr. Jay Saunders, Ithaca, NY	State of New York
Reichard, Mr. John F., Philadelphia, PA	World Affairs Council of Philadelphia
Riley, Dr. Mark, Collingdale, PA	American Philological Association
Rodrigues, Ms. Rose, Bridgeport, CT	Fairfield University
Rolofson, Prof. William M., Media, PA	Widener College
Rosenberger, Mr. Lyle L., Souderton, PA	Bucks County Community College
Ruane, Prof. Joseph W., Philadelphia, PA	Philadelphia College of Pharamacy and Science
Sampson, Mrs. William C., Philadelphia, PA	Philadelphia Council of International Vistors
Sanderlin, Dr. Walter S., Washington, PA	Washington and Jefferson College
Sandgren, Dr. David, Moorhead, MN	Concordia College

DELEGATES	REPRESENTING
Sandstrom, Prof. Harald, Bloomfield, CT	University of Hartford
Saunders, Mr. Charles E., W. Hyattsville, MD	National Security Agency
Scranton, Dr. Philip B., Philadelphia, PA	Philadelphia College of Textiles and Science
Seton, Dr. Bernard E., Washington, DC	General Conference of Seventh-Day Adventists
Sevareid, Prof. Peter, Philadelphia, PA	Association of American Law Schools
Shannon, Dr. David T., Pittsburgh, PA	Pittsburgh Theological Seminary
Simon, Dr. K. Mathew, Teaneck, NJ	Fairleigh Dickinson University
Simpson, Mr. Stephen J., Hollins College, VA	Hollins College
Sister Margaret Gannon, Scranton, PA	Marywood College
Sister Mary Beth Anne, Cleveland, OH	Notre Dame College
Smith, Mr. James E., Washington, DC	U. S. Information Agency
Spencer, Dr. Eber, Northfield, VT	Norwich University
Sperry, Mr. Tim, Madison, NJ	Drew University
Stedman, Dr. Murray S., Philadelphia, PA	Temple University
Stephens, Dr. Alonzo T., Nashville, TN	Tennessee State University
Stoner, Mrs. A. J., Woodbury, NJ	Longwood College
Strack, Dr. Harry, West Chester, PA	Villanova University
Strong, Dr. Edwin B., Tulsa, OK	University of Tulsa and City of Tulsa, OK
Stuart, Dr. Charles, West Chester, PA	West Chester State College
Stub, Mr. Sverre, Washington, DC	Embassy of Norway to the United States
Sullivan, Dr. Michael, Philadelphia, PA	Drexel University
Suppe, S. J., Rev. Bernard A., Philadelphia, PA	University of Scranton "Jesuit University"
Tall, Mr. Booker T., Cleveland, OH	Cuyahoga Community College
Teachout, Dr. Roger S., Augusta, ME	University of Maine at Augusta
Tessler, Prof. Mark, Milwaukee, WI	The University of Wisconsin–Milwaukee
Thompson, Mr. Joseph, Rosemont, PA	Villanova University
Tilley, Mr. David, Henniker, NH	New England College
Tobin, Mr. James A., Wyncote, PA	Peirce Junior College
Tonkinson, Mr. John J., Philadelphia, PA	American Education Association
Tonkinson, Mrs. John J., Philadelphia, PA	American Education Association
Tropia, Mr. Thomas, Philadelphia, PA	National Science Teachers Association
Tsomondo, Prof. Micah, College Park, MD	University of Maryland
Ul Haque, Mr. Inam, New York, NY	Permanent Mission of Pakistan to the United Nations
Weeks, Dr. Albert W., Wynnewood, PA	The Geological Society of America
Weeks, Dr. Alice M., Wynnewood, PA	The Geological Society of America
Wheeler, Prof. David, Boston, MA	Boston University
Whitehorn, Mrs. Sarah, Silver Spring, MD	League of Women Voters of Maryland
Williams, Prof. Bernard D., Scranton, PA	University of Scranton

DELEGATES	REPRESENTING
Williams, Dr. C. Fred, Little Rock, AR	University of Arkansas at Little Rock
Williams, Mr. David C., Sumner, MD	Americans for Democratic Action
Williams, Mr. Frank E., Washington, DC	Action/Peace Corps/Africa Region
Williams, Mrs. Gwen, New York, NY	The International Association for Federal Union
Williams, Mr. Oliver, New York, NY	The International Association for Federal Union
Williams-Myers, Mr. Albert J., Northfield, MN	Carleton College
Wolfgang, Prof. Marvin E., Philadelphia, PA	University of Pennsylvania
Yang, Prof. Richard H., St. Louis, MO	The United Nations Association of the Republic of China
Young, Ms. Gretchen K., Washington, DC	Pomona College
Zemo, Mr. George, Uniontown, PA	California State College of Pennsylvania
Zimmerman, Mr. Zachary, Oberlin, OH	Oberlin College

MEMBERS	CITY AND STATE
Abbas, Dr. Jabir A.	Huntington, West Virginia
Abrams, Mr. Jeri Hamilton	Delran, New Jersey
Albright, Mr. David E.	Falls Church, Virginia
Appel, Prof. John C.	East Stroudsburg, Pennsylvania
Arnott, Dr. Margaret L.	Philadelphia, Pennsylvania
Artz, Dr. Jefferson G.	Columbus, Mississippi
Assenheimer, Mr. G. J.	Drexel Hill, Pennsylvania
Baer, Mr. John H.	Harrisburg, Pennsylvania
Baker, Dr. Bettie J.	Cleveland, Ohio
Barmore, Miss Sarah J.	Chicago, Illinois
Baumbach, Mr. August W., Jr.	Baltimore, Maryland
Bebek, Mrs. Tibor J.	New York, New York
Blake, Ms. Elaine	Philadelphia, Pennsylvania
Blatt, Judge Genevieve	Harrisburg, Pennsylvania
Bletz, Mr. Donald F.	Newville, Pennsylvania
Bluwey, Dr. Gilbert K.	Washington, D.C.
Bocher, Ms. Rita B.	Overbrook Hills, Pennsylvania
Bourodimos, Dr. E. L.	Somerset, New Jersey
Braxton, Mr. Reuben A.	Queen's Village, New York
Brown, Mr. Lawrence N.	Philadelphia, Pennsylvania
Brown, Mr. Mark L.	Reading, Pennsylvania
Byrnes, Mr. Malcolm	Ethel, Louisiana
Caplan, Dr. Albert J.	Philadelphia, Pennsylvania
Carageorge, Dr. Ted	Pensacola, Florida
Carter, Ms. Henrietta	Brooklyn, New York
Casciato, Ms. C. A.	Philadelphia, Pennsylvania
Chandler, Mr. James B.	Washington, D.C.
Chang, Mr. John	Washington, D.C.

MEMBERS	CITY AND STATE
Chase, Mr. Peter R.	Pleasantville, New York
Chiu, Mr. Peter C. T.	Parsippany, New Jersey
Clemons, Mr. Samuel H.	Milwaukee, Wisconsin
Clinton, Mr. Arthur	Forest Hills, New York
Crittendon, Mr. Edward	Detroit, Michigan
Dalton, Mr. Robert E.	Dearborn, Michigan
De Brady, Mrs. Mary L. Graham	Philadelphia, Pennsylvania
Delpino, Dr. Robert A.	Warminster, Pennsylvania
Doege, Mr. Richard L.	Minneapolis, Minnesota
Edgecombe, Mrs. Kay L.	Buffalo, New York
Eisenberg, Mr. Gerson E.	Baltimore, Maryland
Fitzgerald, Mr. Robert E.	Silver Spring, Maryland
French, Dr. George	Philadelphia, Pennsylvania
Friedman, Mr. Samuel H.	New York, New York
Furman, Ms. Marian Schwalm	Harrisburg, Pennsylvania
Georges, Mr. Stanley	Woodbridge, Virginia
Germ, Miss Mary	Swarthmore, Pennsylvania
Ghobadi, Mr. Djhangir	Washington, D.C.
Gill, Dr. Robert L.	Baltimore, Maryland
Gillison, Mr. Everette A., Jr.	Philadelphia, Pennsylvania
Gomez, Mr. Theodore P.	Haddonfield, New Jersey
Gordon, Dr. Vivian V.	Charlottesville, Virginia
Grady, Mr. Francis R.	Camp Hill, Pennsylvania
Green, Dr. Rose B.	Philadelphia, Pennsylvania
Greenwald, Mr. David E.	Bloomsburg, Pennsylvania
Greenwald, Dr. Frederick	Norristown, Pennsylvania
Greifer, Dr. Julian L.	Philadelphia, Pennsylvania
Hargrett, Mr. Andrew J.	Chicago, Ilinois
Hargrett, Mrs. Drucilla	Chicago, Illinois
Harris, Mr. Raymond J.	Philadelphia, Pennsylvania
Hecht, Mr. Stephen A.	Willow Grove, Pennsylvania
Harzenstein, Mr. Norris S.	Jenkintown, Pennsylvania
Heller, Mrs. Caroline L.	Bowie, Maryland
Hill, Ms. Billie Dennis	Frederick, Maryland
Horton, Mr. Egbert, Jr.	Media, Pennsylvania
Howard, Ms. Lorraine M.	Philadelphia, Pennsylvania
Hurst, Mr. Thomas E.	Norristown, Pennsylvania
James, Mr. W. E.	Newark, New Jersey
Jeyaraj, Rev. Michael, S. J.	Philadelphia, Pennsylvania
Jones, Mrs. Jimmie Lee	New York, New York
Jones, Dr. Lillian Hogan	Washington, D.C.
Kaplan, Mr. Charles D.	Camden, New Jersey
Kimball, Mr. Lewis	Meridan, Connecticut
Kinsey, Mr. William C.	Arlington, Virginia
Kramer, Ms. Harri J.	Washington, D.C.

MEMBERS	CITY AND STATE
Lauter, Mrs. Aaron M.	Claymont, Delaware
Lawton, Mrs. Ena G.	Philadelphia, Pennsylvania
Ledbetter, Dr. Cal	Little Rock, Arkansas
Lee, Dr. Allen B.	Washington, Pennsylvania
Leger, Dr. Love O.	Bryn Mawr, Pennsylvania
Les Callette, Dr. Millard G.	Salisbury, Maryland
Lewis, Mr. James H.	Philadelphia, Pennsylvania
Lineweaver, Mr. Paul K.	Chambersburg, Pennsylvania
Logan, Ms. Nancy	Wallingford, Pennsylvania
Magill, Mr. Samuel B.	Philadelphia, Pennsylvania
Manning, Ms. Nancy F.	Arlington, Virginia
Marshall, Dr. Donald S.	Alexandria, Virginia
Martin, Mr. Ray	Riverdale, Maryland
Medley, Mr. Bertram A., Jr.	Cleveland, Ohio
Merriam, Prof. Kathleen Howard	Bowling Green, Ohio
Monroe, Mr. Allen L.	Cedarville, Ohio
Moore, Dr. Richter H., Jr.	Boone, North Carolina
Morales, Mr. Carlos R.	Santurce, Puerto Rico
Morgan, Dr. Olive J.	Philadelphia, Pennsylvania
Nelson, Prof. Jack L.	New Brunswick, New Jersey
Newhill, Dr. E. E.	Indiana, Pennsylvania
Nichols, Mr. Nelson H., Jr.	Buffalo, New York
Nickerson, Mr. John M.	Augusta, Maine
Oakes, Ms. Katherine	Columbus, Indiana
O'Hara, Mr. John	St. Louis, Missouri
Osterndorf, Mr. Logan C.	Silver Spring, Maryland
Ostrander, Mrs. V. W., Jr.	Washington, D.C.
Ostroy, Dr. Joseph	Long Beach, New York
Packan, Ms. Mae	Clinton, Ohio
Papadakos, Mr. Nicholas J.	New York, New York
Perry, Rev. Harold C., C. S. B.	Houston, Texas
Pobbi-Asamani, Mr. K.	Washington, D.C.
Pollak, Dean Louis H.	Philadelphia, Pennsylvania
Price, Mr. C. Hoyt	Allison Park, Pennsylvania
Quaytman, Dr. Wilfred	Flushing, New York
Quinn, Dr. Joseph R.	Bethesda, Maryland
Raynolds, Mr. David R.	Lander, Wyoming
Reiff, Mrs. Dovie K.	Philadelphia, Pennsylvania
Rhoads, Mr. Edward O. F.	Philadelphia, Pennsylvania
Robbins, Ms. Stella M.	Reston, Virginia
Robinson, Ms. Rose M.	Hillcrest Heights, Maryland
Ruane, Prof. Joseph W.	Philadelphia, Pennsylvania
Russell, Mr. Harvey C.	Purchase, New York
Rutledge, Mr. Philip	Washington, D.C.

Members	City and State
Schmitt, Ms. Mary Margaret	Chicago, Illinois
Scuka, Mr. Dario	Oxon Hill, Maryland
Segal, Mrs. Joseph	Miquon, Pennsylvania
Serrano, Mr. Joseph D., Jr.	New Brunswick, New Jersey
Shepard, Mr. Charles W.	Atlanta, Georgia
Sherk, Dr. Warren	Tempe, Arizona
Shope, Dr. John	Salisbury, Maryland
Sims, Mr. Harold R.	New Brunswick, New Jersey
Smith, Mr. Elton R.	Harrisburg, Pennsylvania
Smith, Mr. James Iden	New Hope, Pennsylvania
Smith, Ms. Katherine de Dory	Annandale, Virginia
Smith, Mr. Philip W.	New Hope, Pennsylvania
Smyser, Dr. Willis M.	McLean, Virginia
Snyder, Mr. Robert M.	Lahmansville, West Virginia
Solari-Bozzi, Dr. Onofrio	Philadelphia, Pennsylvania
Solzbacher, Dr. William	Washington, D.C.
Sotirovich, Mr. William V.	New York, New York
Spiegelman, Sgt. Charles	Seymour Johnson AFB, North Carolina
Stedman, Dr. Murray S., Jr.	Philadelphia, Pennsylvania
Stiklorius, Dr. Jonas A.	Wallingford, Pennsylvania
Stoner, Mrs. A. J.	Woodbury, New Jersey
Streeter, Mr. James	Washington, D.C.
Taylor, Mr. Charles W.	Carlisle Barracks, Pennsylvania
Taylor, Mr. Leslie L., Jr.	Springfield, Pennsylvania
Teachout, Dr. Roger S.	Hallowell, Maine
Trent, Mr. Earl W., Jr.	Valley Forge, Pennsylvania
Van Eaton, Col. John H.	Xenia, Ohio
Walker, Mr. Alexander J.	Baltimore, Maryland
Wheat, Ms. Wendy	Philadelphia, Pennsylvania
Williams, Mr. Oliver	New York, New York
Wintering, Mr. Joseph G.	Wauconda, Illinois
Zeo, Mrs. Anthony J.	Longmeadow, Massachusetts
Ziegler, Mr. Ralph	Philadelphia, Pennsylvania

Report of the Board of Directors to the Members of the American Academy of Political and Social Science for the Year 1976

MEMBERSHIP

MEMBERSHIP AS OF DECEMBER 31

Year	Number
1966	21,043
1967	23,440
1968	25,158
1969	24,597
1970	24,544
1971	23,413
1972	21,963
1973	21,070
1974	19,473
1975	16,923
1976	15,516

FINANCES

Our bank balance at the end of 1976 was $46,582.58.

SIZE OF SECURITIES PORTFOLIO

MARKET VALUE AS OF DECEMBER 31

1966	$462,675
1967	481,123
1968	566,681
1969	539,083
1970	616,429
1971	612,046
1972	642,808
1973	533,024
1974	371,004
1975	440,450
1976	504,046

STATEMENT OF REVENUE, EXPENSE AND SURPLUS FOR THE YEAR ENDED DECEMBER 31, 1976

	1976	1975
REVENUES:		
Dues and subscriptions, net of agents' commissions and refunds	$218,511.59	$235,655.21
Sales of publications, net of discounts and refunds	47,426.27	35,435.67
Advertising, net of discounts	12,099.69	7,035.12
Royalty and reprint permissions	6,892.53	9,803.64
Annual meeting, net of refunds	7,193.09	7,224.76
List rental	2,253.90	2,000.00
Sale of review books	2,292.00	2,610.00
Miscellaneous	283.68	272.35
Total revenues	$296,952.75	$300,036.75
OPERATING EXPENSES:		
Annals printing, binding and mailing	$100,592.87	$ 96,866.45
Shipping and cost of publications sold	10,045.42	8,539.19
Salaries and related benefits	179,477.28	176,177.65
Annual meeting	8,328.43	9,505.08
Depreciation	591.85	564.00
Insurance	1,995.37	1,885.50
List rental and exchange	3,047.21	3,642.29
Postage	7,095.76	8,236.34
Printing, duplicating and stationery	21,155.46	15,951.61
Supplies	2,859.65	1,646.31
Telephone	1,438.21	1,495.24
Repairs, maintenance and utilities	7,274.43	8,511.63
Miscellaneous	8,010.94	7,707.24
Total operating expenses	$351,912.88	$340,728.53
LOSS BEFORE MONOGRAPH REVENUE	$ 54,960.13	$ 40,691.78
MONOGRAPH REVENUE, NET OF COSTS	429.94	1,728.31
OPERATING LOSS	$ 54,530.19	$ 38,963.47
OTHER REVENUE (EXPENSE):		
Dividends and interest	$ 25,188.60	$ 24,066.57
Investment fees	(2,254.64)	(964.52)
Gain on sale of investments	17,726.29	—
Bicentennial	17,361.96	11,122.00
Credit card income, net	1,075.73	—
Contributions	326.16	—
Total other revenue (expense)	$ 59,424.10	$ 34,224.05
EXCESS OF REVENUE OVER EXPENSE	$ 4,893.91	($ 4,739.42)
SURPLUS, BEGINNING OF YEAR	$342,156.50	$346,895.92
SURPLUS, END OF YEAR	$347,050.41	$342,156.50

PUBLICATIONS

MONOGRAPHS PUBLISHED

Date	Subject	Number Printed	Number Sold	Complimentary Distribution
1962	#1–Behavioralism	15,225	5,418	9,764
1963	2–Mathematics	30,725	2,565	28,162
1963	3–Public Service	17,230	1,142	16,105
1964	4–Leisure	37,488	3,646	33,844
1965	5–Functionalism	44,459	2,632	41,828
1966	6–Political Science	21,067	5,649	15,421
1967	7–Urban Society	22,578	1,507	21,073
1968	8–Public Administration	25,311	2,190	23,154
1969	9–Design for Sociology	16,191	3,754	12,540
1970	10–International Relations Research	10,055	1,347	5,823
1971	11–Technology	12,167	418	3,217
1971	12–International Studies	7,609	401	3,802
1972	13–Diplomacy	7,090	309	3,021
1972	14–Integration	8,096	391	7,000
1973	15–Public Interest	8,001	308	6,865
1973	16–Urban Administration	20,066	571	17,699
1973	17–Language Studies	5,109	573	837

During 1976, the six volumes of THE ANNALS dealt with the following subjects:

January — *Crime and Justice in America: 1776–1976*, edited by Graeme R. Newman, Professor at School of Criminal Justice, State University of New York at Albany.

March — *International Exchange of Persons: A Reassessment*, edited by Kenneth Holland, President Emeritus, Institute of International Education, U.N. Plaza, New York.

May — *Political Finance: Reform and Reality*, edited by Herbert E. Alexander, Director of Citizens' Research Foundation, Princeton, New Jersey.

July — *Bicentennial Conference on the Constitution: A Report to the Academy*, edited by Marvin E. Wolfgang, President of this Academy.

September *Role of the Mass Media in American Politics*, edited by L. John Martin, Professor of Journalism, University of Maryland, College Park, Maryland.

November *The American Revolution Abroad*, edited by Richard L. Park, Professor of Political Science, University of Michigan, Ann Arbor, Michigan.

The publication program for 1977 includes the following volumes:

January *The New Rural America*, edited by Frank Clemente, Senior Research Associate, Center for the Study of Environmental Policy, Pennsylvania State University, University Park, Pennsylvania.

March *Nuclear Proliferation: Prospects, Problems, and Proposals*, edited by Joseph I. Coffey, Professor of Public & International Affairs, University Center for International Studies, University of Pittsburgh, Pittsburgh, Pennsylvania.

May *Industrial Democracy in International Perspective*, edited by John P. Windmuller, Professor at New York State School of Industrial and Labor Relations, Cornell University, Ithaca, New York.

July *Africa in Transition*, edited by Marvin E. Wolfgang, President of this Academy.

September *Ethnic Conflict in the World Today*, edited by Martin O. Heisler, Associate Professor, Department of Government and Politics, University of Maryland, College Park, Maryland.

November *Social Analysis and Social Policy*, edited by J. Rogers Hollingsworth, Professor of History, University of Wisconsin, Madison, Wisconsin.

The rotating summaries of social sciences disciplines, established in 1961, are being continued.

During 1976, the Book Department of THE ANNALS published 300 reviews. More than three-fourths of these reviews were written by professors, and the others by college or university presidents, members of private and university-sponsored organizations, government and public officials, military personnel, and business professionals. Most reviewers were residents of the United States, but some were residents of Great Britain, Canada, Scotland, Ireland, Ghana, Japan, Thailand and the West Indies. Over one thousand books were listed in the Other Books section.

One hundred and seventy-six requests were granted to reprint material from THE ANNALS. Most of these went to professors and other authors for use in books under preparation.

MEETINGS

The eightieth annual meeting, which was held in April 1976, had as its subject *Bicentennial Conference on the Constitution*, and continued the tradition of our gatherings with respect to the diversity of organizations represented by delegates, the size of the audiences and the interest displayed. Fourteen embassies sent official delegations, as did 7 United Nations missions and 7 states, cities and agencies of the federal government. Delegates were also sent by 127 American and foreign universities and colleges and 82 international, civic, scientific and commercial organizations. Nearly 600 persons attended one or more of the sessions. The average attendance for a session was 500.

The theme of the 81st annual meeting, held April 15 and 16, 1977, at the Benjamin Franklin Hotel, Philadelphia, was *Africa in Transition*. This volume of THE ANNALS contains the papers presented at the meeting.

OFFICERS AND STAFF

Members Elmer B. Staats, Richard D. Lambert and Rebecca J. Brownlee were reelected for another three-year term.

The Board also renewed the terms of its counsel, Henry W. Sawyer, III, and accepted the resignation of Walter M. Phillips. Three new Board Members were elected: Matina S. Horner, Thomas L. Hughes and Lloyd N. Cutler.

All of the Board officers were reelected and both the Editor and Assistant Editor were reappointed.

Respectfully submitted,

THE BOARD OF DIRECTORS

Norman D. Palmer
Howard C. Petersen
Elmer B. Staats
Marvin E. Wolfgang
Lee Benson
A. Leon Higginbotham, Jr.
Richard D. Lambert
Rebecca Jean Brownlee
Covey T. Oliver
Thomas Lowe Hughes
Lloyd N. Cutler
Matina S. Horner

Philadelphia, Pennsylvania
1 June 1977.

148

The Huk Rebellion

A Study of Peasant Revolt in
the Philippines

Benedict J. Kerkvliet

This is a study of why peasants revolt.
Because Kerkvliet's account of the
Huk Rebellion considers its evolution
in both a local and a regional framework, it should interest not only
readers concerned with Philippines
society but also those involved in comparative peasant studies.
322 pages, 15 tables, 4 maps, $16.00

China after the Cultural Revolution

Jürgen Domes

Translated by David Goodman

Emphasizing political rather than social or economic aspects of the developments between 1969 and 1973,
Domes's acute insights help to make
the tortured course of the Cultural
Revolution more readily understandable.
293 pages, $15.00

Bureaucrats, Politicians, and Peasants in Mexico

A Case Study in Public Policy

Merilee Serrill Grindle

Grindle analyzes the activities of one
important federal agency as its officials planned and pursued a new policy
for rural development under the
Echeverria administration.
239 pages, 34 tables, 13 figures,
$12.50

The Origins of International Economic Disorder

A Study of United States
International Monetary Policy
from World War II to the
Present

Fred L. Block

Block analyzes the rise and decline of international economic stability since World War II,
and examines the prospects
for a return to order.
"Block is a thoughtful radical
who understands that the cy-
cles of the political economy
do not in and of themselves
create prerevolutionary situations. The issue is to employ
our intelligence to expand our
consciousness of the basic reality, and hence our awareness
of the need for structural alternatives. He has done precisely that and I salute him."—
*William Appleman Williams, The
Nation*
*A selection of the Library of
Political and International Affairs
Book Club*
294 pages, $14.00

Guernica! Guernica!

Diplomacy, Propaganda,
and the Press

Herbert R. Southworth

A panorama of one of the
greatest propaganda cam-
paigns of all time! Southworth
has created a lively study of
wartime journalism, an inquiry into government manipulation of news, and an investigation of the hypocritical
maneuvers of European diplomacy.
552 pages, $25.00

Book Department

INTERNATIONAL RELATIONS AND POLITICS

WELDON A. BROWN. *Prelude to Disaster: The American Role in Vietnam, 1940–1963.* Pp. viii, 278. Port Washington, N.Y.: Kennikat Press, 1975. $15.00.

I fail to see, completely, the author's reason for writing this book and the publisher's for publishing it. Mr. Brown does not bring any new material to bear in this topic: the U.S. role in Vietnamese politics, 1940–1963. Neither does he offer a novel or worthwhile interpretation of an already well covered area. The only new set of documents from which Mr. Brown could have extracted new insights on this period of history is the *Pentagon Papers.* Although these are listed in the bibliography, I did not see them once listed in any of the footnotes. On the contrary, the majority of the footnotes refer to secondary and generally outdated publications by Fall (1963), Trager (1967), H. V. Chi (1965), Shaplen (1966), Lancaster (1961). Some of these works are, furthermore, of doubtful historical value, as they were financially sponsored by U.S. governmental agencies and may be assumed to justify certain policies. Moreover, Mr. Brown relies excessively on his sources: long passages of this book are but summaries, paraphrases or analyses of portions of his sources. For example, in Chapter 1, out of 39 footnotes, 16 refer to H. V. Chi's

work. In Chapter 6, of 73 footnotes, 37 refer to Fall's *The Two Vietnams.* Why then, readers may well ask, should they rather read Mr. Brown than the sources he so closely follows?

The author's interpretation of the years 1940–1963 is in no way original and as little persuasive as earlier versions of the same outlook. His anti-communism leads him into constant contradictory statements. For example, Ho Chi Minh is labelled a traitor, a crook and, of course a communist. Whatever H. C. Minh does, whatever issues from him is evil. And yet, Mr. Brown recognizes, as would be hard for anyone not to, that "after 1946, the best disciplined, most dedicated and efficiently organized group in all Vietnam was communist" (p. 135), and that in 1945 "the only force capable of political leadership" in Vietnam was H. C. Minh's. Not surprisingly, Ho's communist group went on to lead the fight for independence from the French and to win it. In spite of Ho Chi Minh's military victory over the French at Dien Bien Phu, he was pressured at the Geneva Conference in 1954 by Big Powers both communist and non-communist, to claim less than his fair share of victory. He was made to yield the southern half of Vietnam to non-communist Vietnamese (those who had fought alongside the French up to Dien Bien Phu) on the understanding that the two Vietnams would, 2 years later, vote to select a single government of a united Vietnam. The Southern half, in the meanwhile, fell into the hands of Ngo Dinh Diem, "our ally" according to Mr. Brown. The author sees no wrong in his ally's refusal to proceed with the elections in 1956. Elsewhere, he sees many faults in Ngo Dinh Diem. His government was an autocracy when it was meant to be a democracy; he abolished freedom rather than defend it. Finally he was very ineffective, because "our ally seemed more interested in graft, corruption and war profits than in fighting for his own national freedom" (p. 127). These admitted travesties of Saigon in no way invalidated the U.S. support of Diem's regime which the author deems essential to stop North Vietnam's "despotism." The U.S. could not stop despotism itself so it remained wedded to the Diem despot in order that he might stall the American-perceived despotism of the North. Money, arms and hopes notwithstanding, Diem did not achieve what the Americans wanted. Mr. Brown's reasoning runs as follows: "How could we effectively pressure an Oriental people, endlessly patient, impoverished, illiterate, concerned with personal survival, plagued by excessive heat and humidity, and unable to do almost anything energetically" (p. 171). Are Orientals all of the above? If so, Mr. Brown should remember that "their side" is also composed of Orientals, the same Orientals!

After a decade of unreserved support, Diem's government had finally to be dropped; fortunately, that is where Mr. Brown's book also meets its end. Concerning this last chapter, I would suggest to Mr. Brown that the *Pentagon Papers*, among other documents, contain a great deal of new information that would have made his chapter look a little bit better than mere pages of an old newspaper.

The author promises a sequence to this book. I would sincerely hope that Mr. Brown has found, in the meantime, some other more rewarding activity. If his next book is anything like this one, then I am afraid that he is wasting his time as well as that of would-be readers.

TRUONG BUU LAM
University of Hawaii
Honolulu

STEPHEN HESS. *Organizing the Presidency*. Pp. ix, 228. Washington, D.C.: The Brookings Institution, 1976. $10.95. Paperbound, $3.95.

Stephen Hess seeks to improve presidential decision-making and managerial effectiveness. His thesis is that recent presidents, using a bloated and unwieldy White House Office, have attempted to personally formulate major policies and oversee their implementation in all areas of government. But, according to Hess, the actual result has been to draw increasing numbers of no-win problems to the president; cut the time the president can devote to any one problem; require the president to spend more time managing his staff; and increase the number of people who can "misspeak in his name." After considering and rejecting the possibility of increased use of outside consultants as a solution, Hess concludes that presidents must turn back to department and agency heads for advice and administrative help. Many have argued that cabinet members are of only limited usefulness for these purposes because most of them are selected according to their group affiliations and are more loyal to those interests than to the president's. This view may have been valid in the past, but, says Hess, it no longer applies because changes in the political system (for example, new campaign techniques and election laws) permit an individual to reach the presidency without committing cabinet positions to particular interest groups. Hess then outlines a strategy by which presidents can mold their cabinets into aids instead of impediments.

This is the first book on the presidency that leaves one with the feeling that he has read a comprehensive treatment of the subject. The others seem to concentrate on fragments such as legalities of the office, the presidency's severe limitations, or its potential to befuddle its occupant's good sense. Hess encompasses all of these plus presidential management and decision-making styles, cabinet and White House staff recruitment, and presidential—White House staff—cabinet interaction. He accomplishes this using a massive array of sources including his own personal experience in the White House, which make this a much "bigger" book than its modest physical length would suggest.

Considering the broad scope of this study, each reader will probably disagree with some of Hess' observations. For example, it may be that ever greater numbers of problems are being drawn into the White House not because of White House staff growth but because of the increasingly complex nature of problems which more and more tend to cross departmental boundaries. And many will doubt that the political scene has changed sufficiently to permit the president to significantly expand the cabinet's role. But, despite such disagreements, few will fail to be challenged and enlightened by *Organizing the Presidency*. It will be, deservedly, the most widely discussed work in this field since Neustadt's innovative study.

CARL GRAFTON
Auburn University at Montgomery
Alabama

ROBERT JERVIS. *Perception and Misperception in International Politics.* Pp. xii, 445. Princeton, N.J.: Princeton University Press, 1976. $22.50.

This study of perception (and misperception) in international relations is an important book: a masterpiece of disaggregation and of synthesis. Professor Jervis has broken his subject down into the processes of perception—showing for example how decision-makers learn from history, and how their attitudes change; and into a section on common misperceptions ("overestimating one's importance as influence or target," "the influence of desires and fears on perceptions" "cognitive dissonance"). Then drawing on his mastery of the literature of diplomatic and military history, political science, psychology, and even anthropology, he has brought together the insights of the disparate fields as they bear on international politics. It is the first serious attempt to do this.

Often the insights seem obvious or even trivial: "experiments have . . .

shown that people are less impressed and less likely to reciprocate favors if they believe that the other had no choice in helping them . . ." (p. 42). But the result is to systematize, in a loose way, the lessons of both experimental psychology and (in this case) diplomatic history, while bringing the former to bear on the latter.

Despite the ambition in an undertaking of this scope, the author is largely successful. This is in the final analysis due to the fact that he resists the fashionable impulse to build more sophisticated theory than the material of the study can bear or will allow. The loose, interrelated, "pre-theoretical" observations that underlie and inform the structure of the book are remarkably sophisticated conceptually, given the novelty of this terrain. The book is meticulously footnoted and, given the superb production by the publishers as well, worth its price.

Several quibbles are confined to the uses the author makes of his own models in looking at today's realities.

Jervis's advice is for the Prince, whom he sees, in the absence of evidence to the contrary, as no less "rational, sophisticated, and motivated to understand [his] environment than are scientists" (p. 5). But how cognitively complex? Jervis reports another insight from the world of psychology, in noting that people with "high cognitive complexity tend to be less confident of their judgment than do people of low complexity" when dealing with consistent information. One struggles to name more than a handful of senior officials in the American government in recent memory of whom that would be true: the reviewer thinks of the Pentagon official who gave him as evidence that the public was "pro-Defense" the fact that the businessmen seeing him everyday were "high on the pentagon." These were the contractors visiting the senior American official dealing with Defense industries; no oddity was seen. Jervis's book will influence the milieu from which the best of our statesmen will emerge, and one can at least dream of a world in which our leaders actually read and ponder books like this.

The other quibble goes to the heart of the material to which Jervis hopes his masterly study will be applied, Soviet-American perceptions. He concludes a very tentative and impartial treatment of spiral and deterrence models of perception with the suggestion that one (read, United States) should "procure the kinds and numbers of weapons that are useful for deterrence without simultaneously being as effective for aggression."

What if the adversary won't play that game, and chooses weapons whose agreed purpose is to provide a war-fighting capability that its doctrine explicitly justifies? What, then, for us, if deterrence fails? One can overdo his impartiality, as so many scholars did in the 1930s as they sought to avert a general war. True, as Jervis concludes, the "cost of overestimating the other's hostility is itself often underestimated" (p. 424), but the situation is highly assymetrical as there are no scholars like himself on the other side interpreting perceptions with such sophisticated impartiality for the scholarly and policy audience.

There are, after all, a few facts in this dispute, and they exist quite apart from the opinions of the separate schools with their different theories. It might have been better had the author either gone a little further in their pursuit (what, for example, of the Intelligence community's underestimation of the proportion of the defense budget to the Soviet GNP by a factor of at least two—and the American intelligentsia's dogged refusal to face the implications of this?) or gone a little less far and allowed the reader to apply the book's lessons to the present context without his own implicit or explicit assistance. For if there is a history of misperceptions, cognitive dissonance, or overestimating one's own importance, it surely is here and now, as we struggle to learn the meaning of a massive Soviet arms buildup countered by an approximately equally large cutback (in constant dollars) in our own defense spending. If Professor Jervis's book has lessons to teach, which it does, it would surely be to look carefully at what the two sides are currently doing:

and not to overreact to the "lessons of Vietnam" and whatever else is past.

W. SCOTT THOMPSON
Tufts University
Medford
Massachusetts

JEANE KIRKPATRICK. *The New Presidential Elite: Men and Women in National Politics.* Pp. 630. New York: Russell Sage Foundation, 1976. $20.00.

Jeane Kirkpatrick has written an important book. The delegates to the 1972 Democratic and Republican Conventions, a large sample of whom was extensively surveyed through mail questionnaires and personal interviews, are the presidential elite of her title. Her research was "inspired by the belief that American politics is being transformed in some important, fairly fundamental ways by the ascendancy to power in the majority party of large numbers of new men and women whose motives, goals, ideals, ideas, and patterns of organizational behavior are different from those of the people who have dominated American politics in the past." The hypothesized "new breed" of delegate was indeed found to exist, and Kirkpatrick analyzes their characteristics and reflects on their impact on the political system thoroughly and insightfully.

The McGovern delegates were the core of the new breed while the Humphrey and Muskie delegates were more likely to look at politics in traditional ways. Of particular note was the disproportionate number of "symbol specialists" (teachers, journalists, clergy, social scientists) in the McGovern ranks. The symbol specialists appear to be the vanguard of the future among political activists, and Kirkpatrick is not sanguine about their systemic impact. "A symbol specialist may be said to have a vested interest in the intellectual and moral aspects of politics because he is expert in articulating, analyzing, criticizing, and moralizing." Thus, politics under the new breed is marked by ideological conflict and criticism of traditional values. But Kirkpatrick does not see the rise of ideology leading to a renaissance for the parties; the new breed's commitments are to causes, not organizations. The continuation of party decomposition is likely as personalist factions surge and decline with the currents of events. And the health of the Democratic party will not be improved by the split between the "cultural transformers" in the new breed and the "cultural preservationists" who are predominant in the party's rank-and-file.

The richness of Kirkpatrick's analysis has only been touched upon. Her discussion of the limited impact of the quota requirements on the Democratic Convention, for example, is highly instructive. So are her comments on the prospects for women in the upper reaches of the party hierarchies. With all its merits it is regrettable that the price and length of *The New Presidential Elite* will make it inaccessible to most students. An editor and publisher who put out an abridged, paperback edition of this fine study would profit themselves and the many people who would surely buy their product.

PAUL LENCHNER
East Texas State University
Commerce

DAVID KNOKE. *Change and Continuity in American Politics*. Pp. 187. Baltimore, Md.: The Johns Hopkins University Press, 1976. $11.50.

Change and Continuity in American Politics is an examination of the social bases of American political parties using the method of quantitative data analysis. Dissecting "the parties in the electorate along the religious, racial, regional, and socioeconomic fault lines of the post-World War II period," the author produces a study that confirms much of the popular wisdom about political parties and that is also a reasoned, though sometimes ponderous and difficult, data analysis approach to problems in the social sciences.

The book's central theme is that there has been in the last three decades a considerable continuity in the pattern of social bases for party affiliation. Change, however, is not totally absent as is exemplified in the growing number of independent voters.

The author notes the affinity of Catholics and Jews for the Democratic party and the fact that as Catholics become more affluent, they tend to become more Republican. He says that Protestants are distinctly more Republican, "but important stable political cleavages within the large Protestant group were found. The high status Protestant denominations exhibit strikingly higher degrees of Republicanism than do the lower class denominations." A chapter on socioeconomic differences gives too limited a role to these concerns in structuring party differences. Another on the party system approaches but stops short of offering any significant conclusions.

Mr. Knoke does not attempt to probe the reasons why various groups act as they do in the political spectrum. Rather, he is content to take empirical data, analyze it, and present only those conclusions that can be objectively verified.

Few of the major themes of this study will prove particularly new to the seasoned political observer. Nevertheless, the book does have value in that it provides a model for data analysis study and by offering a number of perceptions, most of which are somewhat limited, about the social bases for political affiliations that will prove of use to future scholars.

GENO BARONI
FRED ROTONDARO
National Center for Urban Ethnic Affairs
Washington, D.C.

MICHAEL LEIGH. *Mobilizing Consent: Public Opinion and American Foreign Policy, 1937–1947*. Pp. xvi, 188. Westport, Conn.: Greenwood Press, 1976. $14.50.

Democratic theory has long attributed a special importance to public opinion. A "traditionalist" group has argued that policy-makers are constrained by public opinion while a "radical" group has seen policy-makers manipulating public opinion in favor of their predetermined policy choices. This book by Michael Leigh (a Tutor in International Relations at the University of Sussex) attempts to resolve this debate. This topic is of special importance if President Carter, following his campaign promises, does open up the making of foreign policy to both the public and the Congress.

Leigh's study spans the decade that began with Roosevelt's "quarantine the aggressors" speech and ended with Truman's proposal of economic and military aid to Greece and Turkey. Using the techniques of both the political scientist and the historian, he has drawn upon little-used archival materials, especially unpublished reports of various U.S. government agencies concerned with public opinion. His working hypothesis is that the more highly developed the government's information function, the weaker the public opinion constraint. His history of the various bodies created during World Wars I and II is especially interesting and useful.

Leigh finds that the change in Presidential prerogatives since the 1930s rests on "the transformation of the opinion-policy relationship. The President's sense of the possible has grown with his capacity to invoke his separate constituency, the mass public" (p. 168), which liberated the White House from dependence on congressional and other surrogates for popular opinion. The author believes that the "fine tuning of mass opinion is a patent impossibility. . . . the instruments for mobilizing consent, though comparatively sophisticated in the postwar period, remain crude and imperfect. . . . Yesterday's manipulation is today's constraint" (pp. 169–170).

He concludes that neither the radical nor the traditional model of the opinion-policy relationship is valid, since neither side has specified the linkages between what the public believes and how policy-makers behave. Both have failed to explain systematically how public opinion is crystallized, transmitted to, and interpreted by people at the top of the bureaucracy. "The participation of the outer circles of opinion in policy-making does not fall neatly into the category of manipulation or constraint. The form of participation, as well as its probability, is determined by a complex set of factors, some of which have been identified in this analysis" (p. 171). Thus, the author ends by admitting that his is not the final analysis of this important part of the governing process.

A minor comment on the work of either the author or the proofreader is that the incorrect spelling, in one place or another, of "Isaiah Bowman," "Emanuel Celler," "Cincinnati," "Hadley Cantril," "Kenneth McKellar," "Robert McNamara," "Vyacheslav Molotov," and "Llewellyn Thompson" (and a number of other words) mars what is otherwise a careful study.

DONALD G. BISHOP

Sun City Center
Florida

MICHAEL K. O'LEARY and WILLIAM D. COPLIN. *Quantitative Techniques in Foreign Policy Analysis and Forecasting.* Pp. v, 291. New York: Praeger Publishers, 1975. $20.00.

Prepared under the auspices of the State Department's external research department, this volume is an ambitious effort to apply advanced social science methodology to the study of foreign policy. The applications of quantitative data and techniques to foreign affairs analysis, with the full cooperation of the State Department, has led to a series of essays that aim at middle range theory: neither issue specific nor macro-level.

Part I of the book, one chapter, presents a report of the project and summarizes the work of the Bureau of Intelligence and Research for one year; that experience provided the data base for the project. Six case studies comprise Part II, selected to demonstrate the utility of a variety of social science techniques. The cases deal with instability in African politics; voting in Western Europe; the politics of bargaining between North and South Korea; military expenditures in Latin America; monitoring and predicting violence in the Middle East; and the politics of global oil flows.

Part III consists of the authors' analysis of the general usefulness of social science methodology to foreign policy analysts. An appendix contains the specific recommendations of the authors to the State Department about the limitations and advantages to be derived from the systematic employment of the advanced statistical and methodological techniques applied in the case studies.

As the authors discuss in their conclusion, the success of applying new methodologies to the work of the foreign policy analyst will depend on the hypotheses and assumptions of the analyst, first and foremost, and not with the quantitative techniques available. If it is possible to standardize the assumptions and hypotheses employed by the analysts; improve the quality and the quantity of available data; eliminate cultural and historical pre- and misconceptions, then the techniques demonstrated in the case studies should prove useful in three areas: information gathering, descriptive analysis, and forecasting. The first two categories, if time, effort and financing are available, will prove to be most useful in coming to grips with the complexities of the real world of foreign policy analysis. The capacity of such techniques to contribute significantly to forecasting will respond principally to the demands of the moment. Forecasting in crisis situations will leave little room for quantitative techniques. Long range prediction, if viewed as offering sets of alternatives and elucidating the complexities of sets of variables that impinge on specific foreign policy areas, will be more successful if integrated into the ongoing policy process and not left in the hands of the research and analysis specialists alone. The possibility of that happening in the foreseeable future is highly problematical.

RIORDAN ROETT
The Johns Hopkins University
  School of Advanced International
    Studies
Washington, D.C.

AFRICA, ASIA AND LATIN AMERICA

FREDERICK P. BOWSER. *The African Slave in Colonial Peru, 1524–1650.* Pp. xiv, 439. Stanford, Calif.: Stanford University Press, 1975. $16.50.

Here is the most intensively researched work ever to appear on African slavery in Latin America. The book is based on archival material found in Perú, Spain, and Portugal. Both coastal and urban Perú were so dependent on black labor and slavery that virtually every agency of civil and ecclesiastical government generated documents dealing with Afro-Peruvians. The book contains an index, appendices, excellent footnotes, a superior bibliography, and literary skill throughout.

The book traces the complex interaction between Spaniard, African, and Indian within the socioeconomic structure of colonial Perú. Primarily, it studies the function and evolution of African slavery as an urban institution centered in Lima, a city with the largest concentration of blacks in the Western Hemisphere. By the 1570s, slavery in Perú was an economic necessity, but it soon became entrenched in Spanish society. By 1650, social attitudes that made for the assimilation of the Afro-Peruvian had been firmly established. All in all, concludes Professor Bowser, the lives of most Afro-Peruvians in the 16th and 17th centuries were bleak and monotonous. The dominant note was not grinding hardship nor misery but drabness and indifference.

Several chapters are particularly outstanding: "African Versus Indian Labor" (Chapter 5) shows how the economic and demographic realities of Perú transformed forced Indian labor (*mita*) and African slavery into complementary and enduring institutions. "The Control of the African Cimarrones" (Chapter 8) relates the harsh penalties for runaway slaves. Captors legally could kill escapees who resisted apprehension; the head alone sufficed as proof for reward. In "Spiritual Concerns" (Chapter 9), slaveowners opposed the Christianization and marriage of blacks. Such attitudes and the sexual imbalance in rural and urban areas, moreover, encouraged promiscuity and illegitimate offspring. Finally, in "The Free Person of Color" (Chapter 11), the author notes how many free Afro-Peruvians gained modest fortune and acceptance, yet racial cohesion and identity were lost in the process. Race mixture—the widespread sexual mingling of Indian, African, and Spaniard—played an important role in creating and sustaining a class of free Afro-Peruvians. The key to socioeconomic advancement was "whitening" and "passing"—culturally if not racially. Spanish culture was therefore the model for most free Afro-Peruvians.

Professor Bowser, however, does not capture and communicate black emotions. What did it feel like to be a slave in colonial Perú? The author says it is difficult to make the black man come alive. His further admission that the vast and rich fund of documentation has but one flaw—that the African slave (even the free person of color) was rarely viewed as a person but as part of the masses—does not fill the void (p. ix). The author again states (p. 80) that the preferred *bozal* was the "Guinea" slave but does not give reasons for this preference in origin. He also does not wish to leave an impression that the urban residents of Perú owned slaves simply to establish their own social status (p. 103), but indeed he does (p. 101). At times, assumptions are made, for example (p. 158): ". . . a similar policy was probably followed elsewhere in Perú." Yet, despite very few and minor criticisms, this is an essential volume for historians and libraries everywhere.

FRANCIS J. MUNCH
University of Nebraska
Lincoln

A. J. DAWISHA. *Egypt in the Arab World: The Elements of Foreign Policy*. Pp. ix, 234. New York: Halsted Press, 1976. $24.50.

Shortly after the 1952 revolution, Nasser became the undisputed national leader of Egypt. After the nationalization of the Suez Canal and the failure of the Anglo-French-Israeli attack against

Egypt in 1956, he emerged as an influential leader in the Arab world. Moreover, his friendship with President Tito of Yugoslavia and his relations and adventures with Russia and the United States further enhanced his stature among the Third World leaders.

Did Nasser plan Egypt's foreign policy step by step in order to achieve his goals, or did he act spontaneously as he faced foreign policy decisions? This book attempts to answer this question methodically with emphasis on Nasser's decisions in regard to Egypt's foreign policy toward other Arab states in the Middle East.

Part I of this book contains five chapters and supplies the historical setting for Egypt's foreign policy during 1952–1970, using the union with Syria in 1958 as a focal point. It summarizes the pre-union involvement, the union experience, and the post union events which led ultimately to the June war of 1967. Part II is a methodical evaluation of the underlying elements of the events based upon what is described as action-response-reaction nexus.

In the final analysis, the author seems to imply that Nasser's major foreign policy decisions may be justified and even rationalized if certain circumstances and constraints involving these decisions are taken into consideration. On the basis of this assumption, the author supplies a number of reasons for Nasser's major foreign policy decisions. In one instance, however, he goes a little bit too far when he attempts to rationalize Nasser's decision to dismiss the United Nations Emergency Forces from Sinai in 1967 (p. 110).

There is no doubt that Nasser made many sound decisions in the conduct of Egypt's foreign policy, but he also made a number of other decisions in which he merely reacted to certain events without weighing the consequences. It is not difficult at all to cite several good reasons for any particular foreign policy decision, yet a sound decision in any situation is made only after all aspects are taken into consideration, including the all-important aspect of economics. In this respect, President Sadat is considered a master of foreign policy decisions, simply because he weighs carefully all the possibilities and constraints of any situation before he makes his final decision.

This book is well-written and well-organized. It is informative as well as challenging and thought-provoking. The author is to be complimented for his methodology and insight.

WILSON B. BISHAI
Harvard University
Cambridge
Massachusetts

ERNEST S. DODGE. *Islands and Empires: Western Impact on the Pacific and East Asia*. Pp. xvi, 364. Minneapolis: University of Minnesota Press, 1976. $16.00.

Islands and Empires is part of a new series from Minnesota called "Europe and the World in the Age of Expansion." Most of the projected ten volumes have now been published, and the publishers are to be congratulated on producing such a series at a time when "imperial" history is pretty much at a discount. Perhaps the whole series will *in toto* provide a new direction and rationale for this currently unfashionable area of inquiry.

The present book is a very readable survey of European activities in the Pacific and East Asia, beginning with the very earliest contacts and ending around 1900. Dodge covers various European "impacts" on the two areas—the work of explorers, missionaries, traders, diplomats, adventurers, settlers—and also sketches reverse influences, such as the fashionable adulation of Polynesian visitors in Regency England, and the chinoiserie fad in Europe and America. Many topics are deftly handled in a light colloquial style. There is little new here, but this book should appeal to a wide public, for much ground is covered in a very attractive manner.

I don't know who decided that this book should cover both East Asia and the Pacific, but this is what must give qualms to Dodge's fellow scholars. He himself says both that "This is the first time this subject [of Western impact] has ever been considered combining the Pacific and Eastern Asia" and "The subject of

this volume almost automatically divides itself into two parts . . . presenting very different problems." The book is in fact clearly divided into two parts, and there is little integration between the two. To my mind lumping together two such different areas was a serious mistake, for they simply have nothing in common. The East Asia part is wholly derivative and only one third of the book anyway. It deserves a full volume written by a specialist. Dodge is an eminent authority on the Pacific. If only he could have had a full volume to expand on his present excellent, but necessarily rather compressed, coverage of this area.

M. N. PEARSON
University of New South Wales
Sydney
Australia

RIAD EL-RAYYES and DUNIA NAHAS. *Guerrillas for Palestine*. Pp. i, 155. New York: St. Martin's Press, 1976. $15.95.

This thin, polemic-free volume presents a fragmentary, badly organized, but seemingly accurate description of some fifteen Palestinian guerrilla organizations. It is incredibly candid regarding their acts of terrorism and their internal conflicts. It includes a partial description of their "political apparatus," and a useful but all too brief account of their relations with the Arab states and with China and the USSR. Finally, it devotes some eleven pages to brief biographical sketches of eight of their principal leaders.

A scholarly study of, or even a comprehensive report on, the Palestinian "resistance" movement would be a welcome addition to the knowledge that is essential for understanding and resolving one of the world's most serious conflicts. For reasons in addition to those already indicated, however, this monograph has very limited utility: First, the authors are not identified, although it appears that they are Palestinians. Second, there is no documentation and no bibliography. An introductory statement reveals only that the book, which was first published in London, "is based largely on contacts and interviews . . .

conducted by the Palestinian affairs specialists on the research staff of *An-Nahar Arab Report.*" Third, the authors assume that the reader is already thoroughly familiar with the history, the politics, and the continuing issues that are central to understanding the creation and the mission of *Guerrillas for Palestine.* In consequence, there is no summary of the evolution of the problem. Moreover, there is no indication of who the Palestinians are, how many and where they are, what their specific grievances are, or what has been done—apart from guerrilla activity—in their behalf.

In spite of its limitations, this work provides much useful information, although most of it is already familiar to careful readers of *The New York Times* and other informed sources. Here is an account of the loose confederation called the Palestine Liberation Organization, from its creation in 1964, as a means of restraining Palestinian nationalism in favor of Nasser's pan-Arab movement, to its capture by Yasir Arafat and its domination in and after 1968 by his relatively moderate Fateh, dedicated initially to "the return of all Palestinian Arabs . . . to live in a secular, democratic state . . . with all of the present inhabitants, irrespective of their religion or their cultural background . . ." (p. 20).

As all should know, the PLO has always been a fragmented confederation of semi-autonomous organizations. Terrorist activities of some of its components—particularly those organizations comprising the "rejection front"—have often embarrassed Fateh and obstructed its programs. Since Fateh itself is a guerrilla force, it is not surprising that from time to time its "defecting" members have organized such extremist groups as Black September, the perpetrator of the Munich massacre of Israeli athletes in 1972. Thus, the PLO is polarized internally, with some of its components— particularly the "rejection front"— insisting on campaigns of terror, assassination, and sabotage against Israel in order to liberate the whole of Palestine, in contrast to the Arafat group (Fateh) and the Syrian-controlled organization

(Sa'eqa) which are "prepared to negotiate a settlement which approves the establishment of a Palestine (such as the West Bank and the Gaza Strip) as a step towards the goal of a secular democratic republic throughout the whole region" (p. 25). This relatively moderate goal, of course, is itself clearly an ultimate threat to Israel, but elsewhere the authors indicate that the PLO, early in 1971, implicitly accepted the terms of UN Security Council Resolution 242, as have Syria and Egypt, which recognizes the right to exist of all states in the region (pp. 93–94, 98).

Among the Palestinians' continuing problems, according to the authors, is the Arab states' tendency to put their national interests above those of the Palestinians. Most of these regimes thus seek an overall settlement, and all signs indicate that the Palestinians' principal sources of support—the more powerful Arab states and even the USSR and China—are hostile to the "rejection front."

Since the date when this book was completed, the extremist components within the PLO have been decimated by Syrian forces operating in Lebanon. In consequence, the "moderate" factions of PLO are stronger than ever, while the principal actors in this tragic conflict proceed, as requested by the 1976 General Assembly, to reconvene the Geneva conference "not later than" March 31, 1977, in negotiations that, according to the Assembly, must include PLO representation. As movement of this kind becomes productive, whether on schedule or not, *Guerrillas for Palestine* will be a useful reference work regarding the roles and limitations of the PLO and the Arab states in the quest for peace.

H. PAUL CASTLEBERRY
Washington State University
Pullman

ABRAHAM F. LOWENTHAL, ed. *The Peruvian Experiment.* Pp. x, 479. Princeton, N.J.: Princeton University Press, 1976. $22.50.

The most recent decade of Peruvian history is an appealing period for social and political analysis. In 1968, at the time of the Velasco military takeover, the nation exhibited many of the characteristics of developing nations; Peru's large indigenous population had not yet been incorporated in the mainstream of the country's development; there was a very unequal distribution of wealth and income; the economy relied heavily on natural resources; and there was a high degree of dependence on more developed nations—especially the United States.

When Velasco took power in 1968, political scientists groped unsuccessfully for a category to describe the new government's orientation. Nationalization of the International Petroleum Company, agrarian reform programs, and efforts to institutionalize "social property" were not consistent with actions of traditional right wing Latin American military dictatorships. Neither, however, did the Velasco regime align itself with the leftist regimes of the hemisphere.

This book is one of the first comprehensive efforts to analyze the Velasco government and to compare it with the civilian regime that preceded it. The ten essays it comprises resulted from a 1973 seminar on continuity and change in contemporary Peru sponsored by the Center for Inter-American Relations in New York. Generally, the essays are easy to read and do not require a high level of technical expertise in any specific academic field. In discussing such diverse topics as land tenure, squatter settlements, income distribution, foreign investment, education and urbanization, the authors did not attempt to develop a coherent theme. Rather, the dimensions and significance of the military regime were explored from the authors' own perspectives. Nevertheless, several overall impressions emerge from the volume.

First, there is still no consensus regarding how to classify the military government. There is a gap between the government's achievements and its own revolutionary slogans. It is not clear that it really is a different kind of government. There is some support for the view that it is just another military regime operating pragmatically within the nation's political and social constraints.

The Velasco government gave considerable attention to improving income distribution. While there have been absolute gains in the standards of living in most sectors, it appears that inequality has actually been growing. Furthermore, the sectors needing most improvement may be benefiting least.

Increasingly, it is recognized that even with the best of intentions, it is difficult to distribute wealth effectively and equitably in a country where much of the population is not socially mobilized. Those among the lower income groups who are best organized tend to receive the most. For example, despite the publicity given to a major program such as agrarian reform, the total income transfer is estimated to be less than 2 percent. "Furthermore, even if it is fully carried out, the agrarian reform will benefit less than 40 percent of all farm families needing assistance and less than 10 percent of the Indian communities" (p. 204).

A great deal of effort will be required to achieve popular participation. It is not clear whether a continuation of present policies will result in greater tension and the need for more force to retain control. One author anticipates growing confrontation with the supposed beneficiaries of the regime because of unrealized objectives.

The Peruvian Experiment represents a valuable contribution to the analysis of Peru's recent experience. It should definitely be read by students of Peru and will also be useful to readers with a general interest in developing nations who want to better understand what may be a more novel approach to development by a military government.

FRED D. MILLER
Director, Department of Energy
State of Oregon
Salem

KITSIRI MALALGODA. *Buddhism in Sinhalese Society, 1750–1900: A Study of Religious Revival and Change.* Pp. xiii, 300. Berkeley: University of California Press, 1976. $16.50.

Kitsiri Malalgoda, of the Department of Sociology, University of Auckland, has contributed a valuable study which will be indispensable to any serious student of modern Sinhalese Buddhism. While various writers have addressed themselves to the relationship between religion and society in Ceylon since independence, this has been done without benefit of the kind of detailed historical analysis of the early modern period provided by the present book. Much of the previous writing on the British period has played the nationalist theme of the "betrayal of Buddhism," without greatly adding to our knowledge of the internal dynamics of Buddhism challenged by an aggressive Christianity. Dr. Malalgoda's study, on the other hand, in filling this gap presents scholarship of a high order: good documentation, sound generalizations, balanced judgments.

After a quick overview of the historical development of Buddhism in Ceylon and the impact of the Portuguese and Dutch, Malalgoda goes to his two major themes. Part One deals with schisms within the Sangha (monastic order) and the rise of new monastic fraternities. Under King Kirti Sri Rajasinha's remarkable reforms, monks were brought from Siam to reestablish the Theravada ordination, resulting in a steady increase in the number of duly ordained Sinhalese monks. As these were all recruited from the high Goyigama caste, low-caste protests resulted in the rise of the Amarapura and other fraternities. The author's detailed treatment of this caste-inspired segmentation of the Sangha emphasizes the shift of the effective center of Buddhism from Kandy to the low country.

Part Two is entitled "Protestant Buddhism," and deals with the response of resurgent Buddhism to the Christian missionaries' challenge. Among other things, the author stresses the point that a highly effective defense of Buddhism was being made by Sinhalese monks long before Colonel Henry Steel Olcott arrived on the scene in 1880. Olcott himself described his visit as "the beginning of the second and permanent stage of the Buddhist revival," and attributed the first to the monk Ven. Mohottivatte. The author suggests that

the monkhood's ancient tradition of keeping on good terms with the established political authority, whatever it might be, helps to explain the fact that the Buddhist revival never developed into an organized nationalist movement to drive the British out.

DONALD E. SMITH
University of Pennsylvania
Philadelphia

RICHARD H. MITCHELL. *Thought Control in Prewar Japan.* Pp. 226. Ithaca, N.Y.: Cornell University Press, 1976. $10.95.

The *system* of the control of "subversive" political thought of the variegated left and also later of the ultraright in Japan from around the turn of the century to 1941 is the subject of this slim but well documented study. Not only is the legislative history of the "notorious" Peace Preservation Law of 1925 and its subsequent revisions of 1929 and 1941 traced but also examined are the applications of the law, alternative administrative procedures (such as preventive detention), new techniques that would help induce "conversion" (*tenkō*), and the whole governmental structure that became involved. This included particularly the Justice and Home Ministries, the thought procurators and thought police. Thought control was spearheaded by Hiranuma Kiichirō (a Justice official who became Prime Minister in 1939), whose bureaucratic faction had made the system work across the grain of the independent and rival sections of the government. The author reviews the Morito (1920) and Kyoto Student Association (1925) cases, the mass arrests (March 15, 1928), and the public trials of Communists (1931–32). These were milestones lining the way to the "spiritual mobilization" of 1938–39 and the acceptance of a narrow, authoritarian value system and support for all-out war.

Professor Mitchell attempts to write an objective account. He states that the Communist "threat" was pitifully small and shows how the definition of "dangerous" and "unhealthy" thought widened to cover the mildest liberalism. Nevertheless, he describes the problems through the eyes of the bureaucrats and makes some of his value judgments from their point of view, such as regarding the "success" of the program, though in the end it helped bring defeat to Japan. Mitchell argues that Hiranuma was not a "fascist" but a "conservative" who ultimately opposed a more repressive system (p. 175).

While not discussing this, in Japan today there remains on the books the early postoccupation antisubversive law of 1952 ("Habōhō") that could, under changed circumstances, be applied in what Mitchell characterized as a "nonrational" manner. In the United States, too, not all the laws from the Joe McCarthy period have been expunged. Thus, the unique characteristics of Japanese antidemocratic thought control should not hide the more general dynamics that come into play when conservatism tries to stop change in its tracks even in a non-fascist polity, where there is no dictator and where the populace is well-educated and better-off financially than in the less developed nations. It is in this sense that his study holds intrinsic interest not only for those who specialize in Japanese politics, law, and history, but also for those interested in preserving civil liberties in modern, affluent societies.

GEORGE OAKLEY TOTTEN, III
University of Southern California
Los Angeles

JAMES C. SCOTT. *The Moral Economy of the Peasant: Rebellion and Subsistence in Southeast Asia.* Pp. ix, 246. New Haven, Conn.: Yale University Press, 1976. $15.00.

In many ways this is a gem of a book. To a high level of scholarship conceptualization, analysis, and an original and consistent approach, it adds clear and readable prose.

The core of the argument is the nature of the subsistence ethic, described analytically in the first chapter. The subsistence ethic stems from peasant preoccupation with minimal subsistence needs and protection against crisis periods resulting from crop failures and, in market economies, price fluctuations. Subsistence is considered by the peasant as a right and much of traditional peasant society is concerned with the security of this right. Minimal subsistence involves more than food, it involves performance of social obligations as these are defined in each society. From this ethic flow much of the moral value systems of each group and their perception of what is right and just, and from it flow not only the nature of economic decisions and acceptable alternatives but unrest, resistance, and rebellion as well.

Chapter 2 elaborates the moral dimensions as revealed in various social and economic arrangements. In traditional societies individual household security is provided by reciprocity (viewed more broadly than it is by Polanyi) and redistributive mechanisms, although there is no protection for collective disaster. Chapters 3, 4 and 5 apply these arguments to the development of colonial economies and peasant politics in Southeast Asia. Structural changes in the colonial economy and the effects of fiscal claims by the state upon the peasant are examined. Chapter 5 analyzes two major peasant rebellions in Burma and Vietnam in the light of the subsistence ethic and the search for security. Chapter 6 deals with the influence of the political economy of the subsistence ethic on peasant politics. This involves analysis of the peasant ideas of social justice and offers an operational definition of exploitation. Chapter 7 considers the why and when of peasant rebellions or their failure to occur.

The theoretical approach draws on Marxist ideas but frequently departs from them. However some concepts are adopted uncritically. The term "peasant" is loosely used, reflecting widespread confusion about the term. It is not always clear what is meant, and smallholders, tenant farmers, artisans, and laborers evidently are all included. I happen to think this is proper in rural settings, but some disagree strongly. Employment of the term "class" is very loose and there is no clear definition of what is meant; in some cases occupational or status groups seem to be so labeled. Techniques of exploiting the peasant frequently attributed to the colonial regimes, are elsewhere recognized as present in pre-colonial situations. What emerges is that the colonial states are much more efficient.

The clearest departure from Marxism is in attempts to deal with the concept of "exploitation" in Chapter 6. Several definitions are examined and a new operational definition is offered.

Despite these minor caveats, the book should be useful to a wide variety of readers.

RALPH L. BEALS
University of California
Los Angeles

DAVID R. STURTEVANT. *Popular Uprising in the Philippines, 1840–1940.* Pp. 317. Ithaca, N.Y.: Cornell University Press, 1976. $17.50.

This book deals with violent peasant movements in the Philippines over a century spanning the late Spanish and the whole of the U.S. colonial periods, plus the first years of the Philippines Commonwealth. It will be of value to anthropologists, historians, political scientists and sociologists interested in peasant movements in general and in Southeast Asia.

Professor Sturtevant has been writing about Philippine peasant movements since the early 1960s. In this work he has revised and drawn together parts of previously published papers and expanded them with new data to make a readable book. As well as the usual official documents, he has used newspaper files and the memoirs and private papers of Spanish, U.S. and Philippine officials. He has let us hear the voice of the rebels themselves by including contemporary interviews with captives and his personal interviews with former leaders.

Professor Sturtevant's thesis is that the basic conflict in the countryside came from a cultural rather than economic or political clash. Thus the uprisings are revitalization movements that point to the existence of serious tensions between what Robert Redfield saw as the little tradition of village folk and the great tradition of a rational urban centered culture. The only common theme he finds in movements before about 1935 is the messianic behavior of leaders and the millenarian religious behavior of members who believed in an imminent apocalypse that only the purified members of rigorously egalitarian fraternities would survive. In confrontations with the authorities they trusted in the miraculous power of amulets to turn away the bullets and bring victory.

The Sakdal movement in the 1930s marks a transition from supernaturalism and utopian "impossibilism" to secular movements that had more limited goals, more rational and coherent leadership, and perhaps more effect. This was the time when urban middle and upper class intellectuals took a hand in peasant organization.

The rich detail of exotic belief and practice and the religious form of the earlier peasant utopias described remind us that it is only in recent times that people with a wider viewpoint have turned pandemic peasant discontent with their lot into well-organized and sometimes successful wars of national liberation or class war.

BRIAN FEGAN
Macquarie University
New South Wales
Australia

HUGH TINKER. *Separate and Unequal: India and the Indians in the British Commonwealth, 1920–1950.* Pp. 460. Vancouver, Ca.: University of British Columbia Press, 1976. $18.50.

The coerced migration of populations is as old and recurring as human history. The subject in all its tragic dimensions demands systematic attention, but for any major international movement of populations in the modern world, its demographic, cultural and political implications are enormously complex. This is preeminently true for the worldwide diaspora of the peoples of India over the past two hundred years. No historian except Hugh Tinker would be capable of the synthesis which his new two-volume history of the subject achieves. Broadly experienced as both administrator and scholar in several parts of the Empire and Commonwealth, Tinker provides both an intimate understanding of politics and society in India and a balanced analysis of the diplomacy of the Empire.

In the first volume, *A New System of Slavery: The Export of Indian Labour Overseas, 1830–1920,* he traces the migration of Indian labor after the formal abolition of slavery in the British Empire, from homelands in several provinces of British India to plantations around the tropical world. His account is acutely aware not only of the imperial politics and international economics of the subject, but of the cultures of the castes in question, and even the soil and weather conditions which underlay the entire story.

Separate and Unequal continues this epic story for the years between World War I and the birth of the British Commonwealth, this time with relatively greater emphasis on the politics of empire and nationalism. From the Indians' perspective this entailed at least three foci of political initiative. From the time of Gandhi's work in Africa onward, the Indian National Congress persistently struggled to gain from London a policy guaranteeing full civil equality for Indians in all parts of the Empire. The Viceroy's government in New Delhi, responding to pressures from Congress, for the most part urged London to construct a single policy imposed consistently on all colonies and Dominions.

But the Colonial Office in London was responding to different sets of pressures; its sympathies were for the most part incompatible with India's sense of justice and consistency. The colonial elites maintained white supremacist policies, and even Dominions like Canada limited immigration of Indians after World War I. Together they fought for what they euphemistically described as a decentralized approach for the Empire, one

which would allow each colony or Dominion control over its own policies. British Africa especially, which was central to the interests of the overseas Indians, successfully defended the principle of local control even through the intricate negotiations which transformed the Empire into the Commonwealth in the 1940s. Tinker's final chapters trace the intricate diplomatic maneuvering which brought independent India into the Commonwealth after 1947, despite London's continued failure to resolve the demand for racial equality with the power of the white supremacists.

The author makes it evident that this diplomatic tightrope resolved the question to no one's permanent satisfaction. The issue, of course, is still with us, as negotiations over control of Southern Rhodesia continue into 1977. Hugh Tinker's analysis of its background as seen from London and New Delhi thus takes on contemporary urgency as well as great distinction for all historians interested in colonization, nationalism and multiracial politics.

RICHARD P. TUCKER
Oakland University
Rochester
Michigan

FRANKLIN B. WEINSTEIN. *Indonesian Foreign Policy and the Dilemma of Dependence—From Sukarno to Soeharto.* Pp. 384. Ithaca, N.Y.: Cornell University Press, 1976. $17.50.

This is an uncommonly interesting and valuable study, if for no other reason than that the author looks at the problem through the eyes and with the words of the Indonesian foreign policy elite. Overwhelmingly, the vast literature on the problems of the developing countries assays them from our Western perspective. Ideally, we should read as much written by them and give at least as much attention to what they think as we do to our own Western studies. This volume is a happy compromise since Dr. Weinstein can hardly divest himself of everything he is.

Clearly, there is an almost inevitable

and largely unresolvable ambivalence in Indonesian thinking. Its leaders see the world as hostile, whatever the ideological stripe of any given country, each being motivated by its own self-interest, which means at the expense of Indonesia. Hence, the urge for total independence in all areas of activity and the need for self-reliance. Many leaders admire the Peoples Republic of China, but they either cannot bring themselves to follow that path, or believe that Indonesians are incapable of the discipline it would require.

In contrast, there is a general conviction that Indonesian poverty and underdevelopment are so great that they can be solved only through massive foreign aid, and that means some degree of limitation on freedom of action—dependence. Indonesian leaders are fixed on the idea that development means industrialization and produce, produce, produce—an idea of course picked up while studying in Western universities, and primarily in American ones. Surely, in the Hereafter there must be some special form of punishment reserved for economists who for a generation now and still proselytize Western development models for the rest of the world, totally oblivious of the fact that the conditions which made Western development possible simply do not exist in most of the rest of the world and never will.

This study is a well informed and perceptive account of the struggle between these two main themes, as modified and influenced by other internal and external forces. The final impression is not exactly hopeful. I would even call it bleak.

Dr. Weinstein asserts that a principal purpose in his study is to find lessons for other developing countries. His conclusions are so few and so general that they are either cliches or not conclusions at all. Although he does not say so, I read him as implying that each country is a problem unique to itself. I would add that each one must make its own decision as to whether and to what extent to compromise its freedom of action, or whether to stand alone—and pay the price. The last sentence in the book

seems to me the most significant: "It may well be that the only way for them to develop is to seek their own more autonomous paths."

JOHN F. MELBY
University of Guelph
Ontario
Canada

EUROPE

JOSEPH P. LASH. *Roosevelt and Churchill, 1939–1941*. Pp. 528. New York: W. W. Norton, 1976. $12.95.

This book is an account of the highly unusual personal and political friendship between the President of the U.S.A. and the Prime Minister of the U.K. during the first two years of the Second World War. The relationship has been the subject of much comment in autobiographies (including, notably, Churchill's own) and biographies, so that the general picture has long been familiar. But Joseph Lash, a former newspaperman, adds much that is new, supported as he is by the recently opened Roosevelt-Churchill correspondence.

There was, of course, a tremendous difference in the positions of the two statesmen. Churchill headed a warring nation, to whose leadership he had been called in the time of its greatest peril. The power of the British executive gave him great scope and maneuverability in decision-making, and he was able to indulge his dash and flair for unconventional solutions. Roosevelt faced an isolationist opposition between 1939 and 1941, and his freedom in conducting foreign policy was much restricted by the constitutional powers of Congress. His strength with the American voters was qualified by the knowledge that the great majority of them did not want United States involvement.

Both men wished and worked for this outcome. Churchill for the most part understood the President's predicament and only in secret letters did he reveal how much he desired American intervention. He was certainly not above painting the British picture even blacker than it was in reality, in order to encourage American support. Roosevelt saw the defense of Britain as essential in terms of American strategic self-interest. (Much of his concern in 1940 was about what would happen to the British Navy if Britain surrendered.) Yet what emerges strikingly from these pages is how ideological was the President's commitment. More aware than most Americans of the nature of Nazism, and of the ir.divisibility of freedom, he felt that it was right that his country should be at war with Hitler. Thus those of us of the wartime generation who looked to him as the true leader of the world's democratic peoples were correct in our impression.

Roosevelt, the idealist, needed Roosevelt the Machiavellian when it came to getting the United States embroiled. Using his powers as Commander-in-Chief he instituted Atlantic patrols that assisted the hard-pressed British Navy, and he took over the occupation of Iceland from the British. At the same time he carefully consulted constitutional lawyers before introducing Lend-Lease and maintained a careful check on public and congressional opinion. The touch-and-go nature of the latter is exemplified by the passage in the House of Representatives in August 1941 by only one vote of the Bill to extend the selective draft even after the clause to allow the use of draftees outside the Western hemisphere had been abandoned. But only three weeks later when the destroyer *Greer* was attacked Roosevelt used the incident to broadcast to the nation a declaration that the Atlantic fleet would henceforward protect all Allied ships in the Western Atlantic, though German and Italian ships would enter such waters "at their own peril." Thus Roosevelt gradually edged public opinion toward an acceptance of belligerency, looking always for pretexts for greater intervention. Never, however, did he move without carrying American public opinion with him.

While the book caters to the male "coffee-table" interest, especially that section of it, very strong in Britain, which consists of World War II veterans; it is nevertheless more than an account of the

development of a political friendship. Doubtless diplomatic historians will analyze more thoroughly the correspondence and relate it more knowledgeably to the political circumstances of the time. Yet the author's treatment is not without erudition and, if his style sometimes stumbles into journalese, for the most part it sustains the reader through the fascinating story.

FRANK BEALEY
University of Aberdeen
Scotland

JACQUES LERUEZ. *Economic Planning and Politics in Britain.* Pp. xi, 324. New York: Barnes & Noble, 1975. No price.

FRANK STACEY. *British Government, 1966–1975: The Years of Reform.* Pp. ix, 243. New York: Oxford University Press, 1975. $17.00.

The economic misfortune which has befallen Great Britain has caused many social scientists to re-examine the classic model of British Government in terms of economic policy. Such a reexamination is central to two very different kinds of books which give insights into the operation of British Government, especially in new areas of endeavor. In *British Government, 1966–1975* Frank Stacey examines reform in the electoral system, Parliament, including attempts to change the House of Lords, the ministries and central planning, the Civil Service, local and regional government, the National Health Service and procedures for the redress of grievances. In a study of much greater depth entitled *Economic Planning and Politics in Britain* author Jacques Leruez traces planning and a significant amount of general economic policy in theory and practice from 1945 to 1972.

Neither of these books will be useful for people who do not have a sound knowledge of the British political system. In many respects the Stacey book can be considered a sequel to a longer book written by the same author entitled *The Government of Great Britain.* In the *British Government, 1966–1975* Stacey primarily focuses on institutional reform and the book is fundamentally descriptive. Little attention is paid to the enormous social change that has taken place in Great Britain in the post World War II era, change which must be considered as background to any study of reform.

Leruez is a French scholar who offers the benefits of a comparative perspective and his reference to French planning is an important element in his book. This is especially true in a brief but very thoughtful concluding chapter. This is a thorough work which displays significant insights into the economic and political forces which bear on planning as well as the operation of the structural elements involved in the making of economic policy. Particularly interesting is the comparison the author gives of the idealistic approach of the Labour Party to planning and the begrudging use of it by Conservative Governments. The discussion of the failure of the 1965 National Plan and the consequences of this failure provide vital material necessary to understand Britain's economic plight. In fact, Leruez argues persuasively that the enormity of the economic difficulty in which Britain finds itself can be traced to its approach to planning and the few real achievements of its planning efforts. This book is undoubtedly one of the most important comprehensive approaches to British economic policies written in recent years.

STEPHEN P. KOFF
Syracuse University
New York

RALPH B. LEVERING. *American Opinion and the Russian Alliance, 1939–1945.* Pp. xv, 262. Chapel Hill: The University of North Carolina Press, 1976. $17.95.

Soviet Russia has long been unknown and often distrusted by Americans and its image as a result has always had an unreal quality about it. And at no time were American fantasies about Russia greater than during World War II when attitudes fluctuated wildly from suspicions, to extreme hostility, to friendship and brotherhood in a crusade to save the free world, back to suspiciousness and ultimately to deep enmity and fear during the cold war period. Professor Levering has carefully plotted these oscillations of attitudes from 1939 to 1945 using the numerous public opinion polls of the period and a wide variety of publications and broadcasts. He uses these materials to document the changing views of the conservatives, liberals, the various hues of intellectuals and the popular press.

In his review and analysis Professor Levering found nothing new or startling. Popular and elite attitudes fluctuated primarily according to what Americans thought Russia was contributing to the war against fascism and their optimism about the postwar world. At the height of friendship for Russia in 1942–43 many Americans came to believe the United States and the Soviet Union had common postwar goals. This latter fiction was kept alive as long as possible by the government and particularly Roosevelt. But by 1944 suspicions of Soviet motivations steadily began to increase and soon after 1945 led to the cold war. Although the majority of American opinion shifted back and forth from the beginning to the end of the war there was a hard core of opinion makers and about one quarter of the population who remained distrustful of the Russians throughout. For the most part the spectrum of views of the elite and masses coincided and from this the author concludes that the opinions of the rank-and-file Americans on Russia were determined and guided by the elite opinion makers. He assumes that the level of knowledge about Russia was so low that people looked to the accepted opinion leaders rather than judging themselves the contributions being made by the Russians and their trustworthiness as allies.

For the most part this study is a straightforward chronology of American attitudes, but at times Professor Levering is very judgmental toward certain views which were expressed, calling some excellent and others ill-conceived. From historical hindsight it may be tempting to criticize certain views but it really does not belong to a detached analysis of changing attitudes. At the end of the volume the author is particularly critical of Roosevelt for not warning the American people about the different and contrary postwar objectives of Russia and the United States. In this case I think the author may have missed the point of Roosevelt's policy which was based on the belief that Churchill, Stalin, and he, Roosevelt, could personally reach compromises and settlements for the world and keep the peace under a benevolent three power hegemony. At least until after Yalta Roosevelt seemed to have believed that such a postwar arrangement would be possible. Furthermore, there is evidence that Stalin was also taken with this scheme as the best means to get what he wanted and to avoid conflict with the United States. Therefore, for Roosevelt to have warned the American people of the differences between Russia and the United States would have directly undermined any hope of settling issues at the summit. That Roosevelt may have underestimated the problems and overestimated his own ability is another question. In spite of the judgmental quality of some of the discussion, this volume makes a valuable contribution in summarizing and carefully documenting the fluctuations of American popular and elite attitudes toward the Soviet Union during World War II.

DAVID T. CATTELL
University of California
Los Angeles

JOHN PAXTON. *The Developing Common Market: The Structure of the E. E. C. in Theory and in Practice, 1957–1976.* Pp. 240. Boulder, Colo.: Westview Press, 1976. $25.00.

Since the late 1960s there has been increasing comment in the popular press on the declining health of the European Economic Community. These fading hopes for a united Europe have been engendered by both the narrowly nationalistic attitudes of member states and, increasingly, by perceived structural imperfections in the Community's institutions. Largely ignoring these pessimistic winds which have been blowing around the Community's headquarters in Brussels, is a new book by John Paxton of Great Britain, *The Developing Common Market: The Structure of the E. E. C. in Theory and in Practice, 1957–1976.*

Mr. Paxton's optimistic treatment of Common Market structure and practice is unique in several ways. First, his emphasis is on explanation and operation rather than discussion and evaluation. Possible criticisms of current practice are largely ignored in favor of precise descriptive analysis. Second, an attempt is made by the author to show the actual economic results of various provisions of the Rome Treaty and its resultant regulations. The use of charts to explain the practical operation of tariffs, social security rules and taxes is quite helpful in gauging the importance of certain procedures to the operation of the complete system. Of key importance to Mr. Paxton's approach is the political nature of the Community's origin and current functioning. Although the author's prediction that "on the horizon lies political union" belies current realities, there is an infectious quality to his optimism that carries the reader beyond the depressing noises made by other commentators.

The approach taken by Mr. Paxton is a largely episodic one, dealing first with a summary of post-war economic developments in Western Europe, and then proceeding through an examination of the Community's institutions and policies. Particular attention is given to matters of concern to business leaders. The chapters dealing with the rules of competition, the operation of the Value Added Tax (VAT) and the scope of common agricultural policies are the most detailed. The section dealing with the operation of community law within the member states is also well done and is important because it is often omitted or mishandled in books of this type.

Despite the brisk tone, brevity and general accuracy of Mr. Paxton's treatment, there are several criticisms that should be made of his work. First, too much effort is expended in discussing the details of prior provisional periods in the operation of the Community. Second, to provide a tie to ongoing developments in the Community's operation there should have been specific references to the case law that has built up over the past two decades. These references are of substantial import in the merger regulation area. Third, the author's insistence on explanation rather than evaluation is a bit more stringent than it needs to be.

Overall, Mr. Paxton has given us an excellent short treatment of the operation of the Common Market. The book's genesis most likely was an attempt to explain to the educated public in Great Britain the operation of the Economic Community to which they had only recently become attached. One hopes that the author will be willing in his next volume to offer a little more interpretive embroidery to this excellent beginning.

JAMES R. SILKENAT
Member of the New York Bar
New York City

JOHANNES STEINHOFF. *Wohin treibt die NATO? Probleme der Verteidigung Westeuropas.* Pp. 279. Hamburg, Germany: Hoffman and Campe, 1976. DM 28.

Where is NATO drifting to? This is not a new question and is asked frequently these days. Steinhoff, a retired German Air Force General, answers it by proposing specific recommendations to the problems associated with defense of Western Europe. Although others have tried a similar approach, this is not a rehash of old proposals. Steinhoff presents an independent assessment that is amplified by his work as Chairman of NATO's Military Committee. Readers will recall that this is the highest military authority in the Alliance.

In assessing the current NATO-Warsaw Pact military balance, he concludes, as most others, that the Soviet threat to Europe has matured and is now more serious than ever before. Rather than orienting its military strategy and diplomatic policy toward this specific threat, Steinhoff argues that NATO is drifting as though this situation did not exist.

Broad answers to tactical and strategic concerns are found in his discussion of five scenarios outlining possible attacks on NATO. No one will be too shocked that a scenario featuring a surprise, limited attack in the central sector offers the best possibility for Soviet success. It capitalizes on the defects of the Alliance's decision-making structures, the absence of coordinated tactical maneuvering, the maldeployment of NATO armies, the poor positioning of the Lines of Communication, and lack of integration of its air forces. Most importantly, it fits current Soviet capabilities and intentions.

By completing a detailed structural-functional analysis of the defense problems of each of the European countries comprising the Alliance and then evaluating problems associated with such specific areas as ground forces, tactical air forces, and tactical nuclear weapons, Steinhoff develops specific recommendations that could halt NATO's drift. Many of his suggestions on improving NATO armed forces could be accomplished within his concept of total standardization. Such military standardization goes beyond armaments and includes training and doctrine, logistics, communications, and tactics. It would have the additional advantage of lessening the dependence on nuclear weapons by vastly improving conventional force effectiveness within the NATO structure.

As an "Atlanticist," Steinhoff is critical of French attitudes. Yet, he does not waste time with invective and considers France a vital part of the NATO solution. He would welcome them back into the NATO forces structure for a price. The price is acceptance of Atlantic *interdependence*, which he believes each member nation must pay if NATO is to successfully prioritize requirements and accomplish these consonant with its resources.

Steinhoff displays a faith in NATO's efficacy and survival that many may consider remarkable, given the viability of his critique. He recognizes that only an Alliance can defend Western Europe and he wants NATO strengthened both militarily and politically to accomplish that. And he does not want the Germans to have the primary responsibility to accomplish this. To stop NATO's drifting, he advocates an Alliance with more integrated, totally standardized armed forces with a policy stressing Atlantic interdependence in defense, political, and economic matters.

JOHN D. ELLIOTT
The George Washington University
Washington, D.C.

TRAIAN STOIANOVICH. *French Historical Method: The Annales Paradigm.* Pp. 260. Ithaca, N.Y.: Cornell University Press, 1976. $12.50.

Professor Stoianovich has a thesis, albeit one that would be shared by few of the historians whose work he discusses. He believes that *Annales* historians have created a paradigm or "disciplinary matrix" for the world community of scholarship. This, he says, is the third paradigm in Western historiography. The first, perfected by Machiavelli and Guicardini, was that of exemplary history, which sought in the study of the past to find lessons for contemporary politics. The second was developmental history developed during the nineteenth century by the Germans and closely allied with the idea of linear progress. The third is functional history in which society is considered as a communications system.

This paradigm, according to Stoianovich, has been created by three generations of French historians. The first generation consisted of the founders, Marc Bloch and Lucien Febvre. The second is identified above all with Fernand Braudel. The third includes those working in the tradition of Braudel, of whom the best known in this country are probably Emmanuel Le Roy Ladurie and Pierre Goubert. In Stoianovich's view, the period 1946–72 was critical for the emergence and refinement of the paradigm. His book defines the paradigm, then reconstructs some of the debates that have taken place among *Annales* historians and between *Annales* historians and their Marxist and Struc-

turalist critics with respect to its usefulness and proper implementation. Stoianovich discusses in particular the question of global or total history, the study of cultural areas versus the study of modes of production favored by Marxists, the attention paid to marginal groups without written histories, the use of series and fascination with functions, and the relative rehabilitation of the event as a legitimate topic of historical research.

One can only admire Stoianovich's command of the literature of French historiography. His generous footnotes are sure to be ransacked eagerly by those anxious to bring themselves up-to-date on the writings of the French historians and their critics. But unfortunately, his book cannot be recommended without serious reservations. First, as Braudel points out politely in his introduction, Stoianovich does not provide an adequate account of the origins of the *Annales* School, nor does he delineate properly (as an *Annales* historian would be expected to) the social and institutional context within which French history has been written during the past half century. Second, in his zeal to demonstrate that French historiography possesses a paradigm or model, Stoianovich exaggerates to the point of distortion the unity of method of French historians. Indeed, his book might more appropriately have been entitled "French Historical Methods," for (again as Braudel comments) it was an openness to a multiplicity of approaches and a rejection of monistic models that characterized the *Annales* enterprise, as it was formulated by Marc Bloch and Lucien Febvre. Third, and most seriously, Stoianovich is too entangled in the coils of the vocabulary used by French historians and too beguiled by the glitter of their words to explain satisfactorily what their words mean or to explore the ambiguities implicit in such concepts as "structure," "conjuncture," and "eventmental history." The student who seeks an introduction to the topic is better advised to turn to George Iggers's clear, well-informed, and elegant essay in his recent book on *New Directions* in

European Historiography (Middletown, Connecticut, 1975), pages 43–79; while those desiring a critical assessment of the *Annales* achievement will not find it here.

ROBERT WOHL
University of California
Los Angeles

UNITED STATES

JACK S. BLOCKER, JR. *Retreat from Reform: The Prohibition Movement in the United States, 1890–1913*. Contributions in American History, No. 51. Pp. xii, 261. Westport, Conn.: Greenwood Press, 1976. $14.95.

In this carefully reasoned and arresting study, the author concentrates his attention on the tribulations and decline of the Prohibition party and the emergence and success of the Anti-Saloon League. He shows that in 1896 the Prohibition party became a single issue party, fighting off intruders with other reforms to peddle. Until then, party leaders considered supporting one or more of such varied reforms as free silver, antilynching, woman suffrage, tax reform, antimonopoly legislation, and better treatment of wage earners. In 1892 the party platform embraced several such reforms, but its disappointing showing in the election of that year precipitated a long drawn out intraparty debate over what stance to pursue henceforth. Party platform makers often found it difficult to please church leaders. Whenever they sought to endorse non-prohibition reforms, these leaders pulled away from the party. In some cases this was because of the conservatism of individual churchmen, and in others because of the hesitancy of organized religious groups to become identified with political issues.

Blocker asserts that, although the silver issue was an important cause of the 1896 split, other reform proposals and how to deal with the churches produced wounds too deep to make effective party action possible. This split in the Prohibition party added to the attractiveness of the already expanding Anti-Saloon League. Using the balance of power approach, the League eventually accomplished passage of the 18th Amendment.

In his attempt to find reasons for party failure, one might wonder why Blocker neglects to analyze the characters, personalities, and abilities of the leaders of the movement, and why he takes occasion, in a seemingly "tacked on" Introduction and Epilogue, to burden his narrative with intellectual musings and unresearched discussion of the movement following the period of his study. These digressions tend to weaken the impact of his well researched and thoughtful presentation of the 1890–1913 period. He refers to the Prohibition cause as a middle class movement, but waits until almost the final page to indicate what he considers to be the middle class; and all along he writes as though prohibition is not a reform. The title of the book, *Retreat from Reform*, means retreat from certain reforms but not from prohibition.

Blocker makes a friendly bow to Gabriel Kolko. He suggests that corporate interests may have been responsible for the enactment of the 18th Amendment, but concedes that such a conclusion must await "the kind of intensive analysis of the legislative process through which Kolko has discovered corporate influence behind other Progressive reforms." Such caution is commendable and, in this particular instance, might well be fortuitous. This reviewer and some other historians find Kolko unconvincing.

HORACE SAMUEL MERRILL
University of Maryland
College Park

JOHN W. DEAN. *Blind Ambition: The White House Years*. Pp. 415. New York: Simon and Schuster, 1976. $11.95.

In May 1970 John Dean was asked if he would be interested in working in the White House. It was a time of massive convulsions over the Indochina War, including the ill-fated American inva-

170b

study of American history and politics

UNITED STATES V. NIXON
The President before the Supreme Court
Edited by Leon Friedman, Hofstra Law School

Introductory Essay by Alan Westin, Columbia University

"The documents in this collection tell the story of one of the most important legal and constitutional events in our history: the Supreme Court decision in **United States v. Richard Nixon**. The title of the case itself illustrates the drama. It is usually the President who represents the people and embodies the power of the nation. But in this case the equation was reversed: It was the nation and the people against the President. And the great authority of the Presidency ultimately bowed to the courts and to the people represented by that uniquely pragmatic institution of our times, the Watergate Special Prosecution Force." —**from the Preface by Leon Friedman**

From Judge Sirica's first opinion on the subpoenaed Presidential tapes to the unanimous decision of the Court, **United States v. Nixon** presents the legal steps — the actual briefs, decisions, even the verbatim transcript of the unprecedented three-hour argument before the Supreme Court — which led to the first Presidential resignation in American history.

CONTENTS

Preface by Leon Friedman. The Case for America by Alan F. Westin. Judge Sirica's First Opinion on Presidential Tapes. Court of Appeals Decision in Nixon v. Sirica. Judge Sirica's Opinion in United States v. Nixon. The Petitions to the Supreme Court. Special Prosecutor's Main Brief in United States v. Nixon. Special Prosecutor's Main Supplemental Brief in United States v. Nixon. The President's Main Brief in United States v. Nixon. Special Prosecutor's Reply Brief in United States v. Nixon. The President's Reply Brief in United States v. Nixon. The ACLU Amicus Brief in United States v. Nixon. The Oral Argument in United States v. Nixon. The Supreme Court Decision in United States v. Nixon.

0-8352-0802-8, 1974, xxi + 620 pp., $15.00

PUBLIC OPINION
Changing Attitudes on Contemporary Political and Social Issues (A CBS News Reference Book)
Compiled by Robert Chandler

A guaranteed minimum income, the morality of abortion, and the use of police force at riots are among the nine issues that CBS news questioned thousands of Americans on in the late 1960s. Extensive introductions precede each survey, which place the responses in historical perspective and explain the polling procedure.

0-0352-0548-7, 1972, 195 pp., $12.95

All orders include shipping and handling. Prices are subject to change and slightly higher outside U.S. and its' possessions.
Outside Western Hemisphere: Bowker, Erasmus House, Epping, Essex England.

Invaluable source materials for the serious

PROGRESSIVISM AND MUCKRAKING

By Louis Filler, Antioch College

Here is a bibliographic essay that meets the needs of librarians, historians, educators, and students for an evaluative guide to the literature of a major 20th-century social movement. The book links some 1,160 relevant titles in essay form, and in so doing provides a broad panorama of a uniquely American experience.

CONTENTS

Foreword. Preface. A MEANING FOR MODERN TIMES. The Progressive Impulse. Progress and Progressivism. The Effect of Darwinism. Morality and Expediency. Women, Women as Progressives and Unprogressives. Ethnics, Including Southerners and Indians. Gentility. Christian Socialism and Associated Reforms. PROGRESSIVISM. Background and Bibliography. Works for Orientation. Theodore Roosevelt. Imperialism and Anti-Imperialism. The World Progressives Faced. Muckraking. Journalists. The Magazines. Muckrakers. The Literary Factor and Upton Sinclair. The Challenge of David Graham Phillips. Work that Needs to be Done. Progressive Issues. Settlement Houses and the Immigrants. Various Issues. Progressives. La Follette. Southern White and Negro Progressivism. Labor and Capitalism. Progressivism at Peak. Woodrow Wilson. The Youth Movement. PROGRESSIVISM: SECOND PHASE. Progressives and World War I. Prohibition, Woman Suffrage, and Progressivism, Forces Affecting Progressivism. The Twenties Arrive. Progressivism in Depression. Post-Depression Conditions. Progressives: 1948. The McCarthy Era and Adlai. Vestiges of Muckraking and Progressivism. New Frontiers. SEARCH FOR VALUES. The Anguish of Change. Nader. Watergate. BIBLIOGRAPHY/AUTHOR INDEX. SUBJECT/TITLE INDEX.

0-8352-0875-3, 1976, xiv + 200 pp., $15.95

CITIES

By Dwight W. Hoover, Ball State University

This volume is a critically annotated guide to more than 1000 books, games, journals, records, films, and filmstrips on all aspects of the American urban experience. A Producer/Distributor Directory is supplied for those who wish to purchase or rent nonprint materials. Each section is prefaced by a concise introduction.

CONTENTS

Foreword. Preface. I. THE CITY IN PRACTICE. Introduction. General Urban Problems. Blacks in the City. Ethnic Groups in the City. Housing in the City. Education in the City. Transportation and the Cities. Urbanization and Suburbanization. Crime and the Police. Civil Disorders. Urban Poverty. Urban Bosses. Urban Reform and the Provision of Services. II. THE CITY IN PERSPECTIVE. Introduction. Cities of the World. Urban Theory. Urban Images. Architecture and the City. Urban Planning. Urban Sociology. Urban Geography. Urban History. Urban Economics. Urban Government. Urban Biographies. JOURNALS ON URBAN THEMES. PRODUCER/DISTRIBUTOR DIRECTORY. AUTHOR INDEX. TITLE INDEX: Books and In-print Materials. Other Media.

0-8352-0790-0, 1976, x + 231 pp., $14.95

Order from:
R.R. Bowker, P.O. Box 1807 Ann Arbor, Michigan 48106

sion of Cambodia, nationwide campus insurrections, and the murder of unarmed students at Kent and Jackson State universities. For Dean, however, these were peripheral matters, if he noticed them at all. Opportunities for power, influence, cars, and women all beckoned the bright young lawyer, who promptly sank into booze-filled reveries about "what a big shot I would be as counsel to the President."

Dean's national prominence, as well as the popularity of this book, owes much to his role in planning and later exposing the Watergate coverup. Yet, *Blind Ambition*'s major value lies in its picture of life in the Nixon White House. We read about the subterranean retreat where national leaders will operate the government during a nuclear war, the Situation Room where Henry Kissinger brought his girlfriends to impress them, and the executive command post for monitoring public demonstrations (also used by government officials for a secret showing of *Tricia's Wedding*, a pornographic film featuring cavorting transvestites). More significantly, we learn about the day-to-day job of counsel to the President: ordering IRS investigations of Administration critics; superintending spying on political opponents; facilitating plans for wiretaps, mail intercepts, and burglaries; suppressing satirical films; and harassing individuals or organizations out of favor. The orders for these operations came from Dean's White House superiors, and we discover much about their activities as well.

The most striking aspect of this portrait is the commonality of motivation among those wielding high-level executive power. Issues of principle are rarely, if ever, discussed. Human emotions are subordinated to expediency. From the lowest to the highest, White House officials calculate, dream, and scheme how to expand their office space, their influence, and their jurisdiction. At the top of the heap sits the brooding, suspicious President, his personality and life blighted by the exigencies of ambition. It would be comforting to view the ruthless careerists of the Nixon era as aberrations, but their pathology is all too familiar. As

long as the scramble for wealth and power is accorded a place of honor in American life, we should prepare ourselves for a longer nightmare than Watergate.

LAWRENCE S. WITTNER
State University of New York
Albany

IRVING LOUIS HOROWITZ. *Ideology and Utopia in the United States, 1956–1976.* Pp. vii, 464. New York: Oxford University Press, 1977. $17.95. Paperbound, $5.95.

One of the most significant features of modern classical conservatism—that is, of 18th and 19th century conservatism—is that it emanated from the very soil of politics, Professor Irving Louis Horowitz contends. Modern conservatism was the product of political policymaking and of such statesmen as John Adams and Edmund Burke, who were directly involved in the making and breaking of nations; it began not as an ideological movement with a blueprint for utopia but, rather, as a reactionary movement seeking to preserve order amidst the social and political turbulence of the times.

Twentieth century conservatism is in sharp contrast to the conservatism of Burke and Adams, Professor Horowitz believes. The conservatism of Burke and Adams was a response to political involvement, while 20th century conservatism is a response to alienation from that involvement. Twentieth century conservatism, in other words, is marked by its recognition of the "nonprimacy" of politics: the recognition that there are areas of life which, quite simply, are beyond the competence of politics and of the state to cope with. Twentieth century conservatism, then, is a reaction, perhaps an antidote, to modern utopianism, that is, the belief that paradise can be recreated here on earth purely through human endeavor.

Sharply opposed to American conservatism is American radicalism, which is abrasive, moralistic, egoistic, impatient, and utopian and revolutionary in intent and in character. American radicalism, observes Professor Horowitz, emphasizes the primacy of the individual will over group interests, and seeks to mobilize the wills of individuals into one total will. American radicalism is strongly and self righteously moralistic, and totalistic: it attacks socialism as well as capitalism, industrialism as well as agrarianism. American radicalism seeks to impose on our society a new social, economic and political order; it wants a violent, sudden, revolutionary and mutational change of our society in order to attain the utopian aim of changing the nature of man.

Very interesting, indeed, is Professor Irving Horowitz's analysis of American radicalism. But it seems to me that, because of the limitations and restrictions of Professor Horowitz's philosophical perspective (he is a man of the Left: a scholar whose mentor is C. Wright Mills), he fails to take into account the view that American radicalism essentially is a pernicious substitute for religion: an attempt to achieve redemption not through faith in a Supreme Being but, rather, through an involvement, a total immersion, in messianic revolutionary politics.

HAVEN BRADFORD GOW
Arlington Heights
Illinois

ANTHONY JACKSON. *A Place Called Home: A History of Low-Cost Housing in Manhattan.* Pp. ix, 359. Cambridge, Mass.: The MIT Press, 1976. No price.

Anthony Jackson's *A Place Called Home: A History of Low-Cost Housing in Manhattan* is an account of the evolution of dwelling places for the poor in the heart of the nation's principal city. Jackson contends that developers build for that part of the population which can afford to pay and that while this portion included the majority of Manhattan's poorer population in the nineteenth century, in the twentieth century it no longer is the case. Ironically some of the factors which contributed to driving rentals beyond the reach of the poor were the result of requiring builders of new structures to comply with improved minimum building standards which in turn raised the cost of building.

In unfolding his story Jackson relates a thorough, if pedantic, history of the subject throughout the nineteenth century as he records the frustrations encountered in striving to provide adequate housing for all—a noble if elusive goal. The elusiveness is attributed in part to the prevalence of antiquated laws such as one which required buildings to be constructed within the framework of a 25×100 lot—a standard originally enacted for single home buildings but never intended for multiple dwellings.

Furthermore, the reader is introduced to the important figures and institutions of the era, such as Charles Chandler, Felix Adler, and *The Plumber and Sanitary Engineer*. As the twentieth century unfolded some important changes in the direction of improved housing seemed to be detected (for example, the requirement for inner courtyards in the construction of new buildings). Of greater importance than specific legislation of this type, however, was legislation directing a unitary administration for housing acts. Eschewing the continuance of numerous government agencies with overlapping and ambiguous jurisdiction, opponents of unitary administration such as Lawrence Veiller supported by Theodore Roosevelt, helped usher in a new era for low-cost housing. These and other progressive moves of a similar nature notwithstanding, the story of adequate twentieth century housing for the poor is largely a story of failure as even the more recent theoretical innovations proved unsuccessful according to Jackson. Thus the twentieth century's reliance on the filtering theory wherein an expansion of housing for upper income levels would eventually provide more housing for the poor, resulted instead in a shortage. The increased cost of home building shrank the number of units built for the middle class and consequently fewer units were available for the lower class.

In his analysis of low-cost housing Jackson makes a number of telling points such as: the public which accepts the principle of taxation for the purpose of providing access to equal educational opportunities for all, but rejects a parallel principle of equity when it comes to adequate housing for all—almost an admission that this is not an inherent right, whereas education is. "With housing as in education the responsibility of government is to satisfy the essential requirements of its electorate." Another of Jackson's points is the assertion that suburban housing receives covert subsidization while inner city dwellings fall into obsolescence. He calls also for an end to unrestricted development.

On the other hand, Jackson's admonition that the responsibility for adequate housing lies with government rather than with private industry is not overly reassuring given its track record. Jackson calls for a role in housing akin to that which it recognizes in providing sewerage or other services (which are not left to private enterprise). Unconvincing also is Jackson's facile comparison of American suburban housing with regulation Soviet apartments, a comparison which would warrant credibility only after a more extensive elucidation than the author provides.

Because of a certain aridity of writing style but even more because of the technical nature of the topic, A Place Called Home probably will not gain a wide reading. Nevertheless the book is a useful, informative and interpretive history of low-cost housing, which will undoubtedly serve as a reference work for students of the field. The fact that it concentrates on Manhattan while seemingly of narrow appeal is not in and of itself a limiting factor since it provides a recognizable case history with which to compare and evaluate adequate housing for the poor in other urban centers.

SALVATORE J. LaGUMINA
Nassau Community College
Garden City, N.Y.

JOHN W. C. JOHNSTONE, EDWARD J. SLAWSKI and WILLIAM W. BOWMAN. *The News People: A Sociological Portrait of American Journalists and Their Work.* Pp. ix, 257. Urbana: University of Illinois Press, 1976. $9.95.

In reviewing *The News People*, one is torn between two opposing evaluations depending upon one's level of analysis. At the descriptive level, the book makes a significant contribution to our understanding of American journalism. Employing a sampling technique which, despite certain problems of representativeness, is both innovative and probably the best possible for identifying the members of this decentralized population, the authors provide us with an unprecedented volume of demographic and other information on journalists employed by all types and sizes of news organizations. They discuss the basic characteristics of those engaged in the profession, their education and training, career aspirations, professional standards, and other job-related attitudes.

The authors delineate a field dominated by whites, males, and Anglo-Saxons in which two dimensions of conflict emerge. First, journalists are found to be divided over the question of advocative versus objective reporting, or as the authors cleverly put it, "whole truth" versus "nothing but the truth" journalism, with the former claiming strongest support among the more educated, younger, better paid, and urban news people, the latter among their opposites. Second, journalists are found to be torn between a preference for jobs in small organizations which provide for substantial professional autonomy and for those in certain larger organizations which provide for less autonomy but greater professional prestige. The book thus provides needed quantitative support for some rather widely held expectations.

At the analytical level, however, *The News People* is somewhat less satisfying. Too many opportunities are simply over-

looked. For example, the implications of
the authors' findings on the distribution
of party preferences and political philosophies among journalists, particularly
as they relate to the assertions of Efron
and others, remain wholly unexplored.
Similarly, where their respondents are
clearly critical of journalism education
in the United States, the authors struggle
with several alternative explanations of
this finding yet seem somehow to remain
unaware of the indictment itself. Given
the defensive tone of the preface, perhaps the best way to summarize the
point is to say that the authors are just
too timid. In their effort to be "deliberately sober and academic," Johnstone
and his colleagues have been overly concerned with taxonomy and have not
sufficiently exploited their data.

Although the book thus fails to live up
to its full potential, its strengths are such
that anyone interested in journalism or
journalists would find *The News People*
well worth the reading.

JAROL B. MANHEIM
Virginia Polytechnic Institute and
State University
Blacksburg

MORTON KELLER. *Affairs of State:
Public Life in Late Nineteenth Century
America.* Pp. xii, 631. Cambridge,
Mass.: Harvard University Press, 1977.
$17.50.

Affairs of State examines the character
of American public experience from the
Civil War to 1900. Viewing politics, law,
and government as components of a
"polity," Professor Keller has attempted
to analyze public life in the same way
other historians have tried to analyze the
economy or society. In doing this, he has
delineated two separate polities: The
Post-War Polity (1865–1880), which
dealt with the consequences of the Civil
War, and The Industrial Polity (1800–
1900), which confronted the challenge of
rapid industrialization.

Generally, this period is thought of as
politically barren, permeated by graft,
corruption, subservience to vested interests, and governmental lethargy. Instead, Professor Keller argues that the

late nineteenth century was a time of
intense conflict between old values and
the pressure of massive change: conflicts between dependence on government and hostility to the state, between
the desire for freedom and the need for
social order, between localism and
nationalism. The Civil War's legacy of an
active, expanded government and a broad
view of civil equality spread throughout
the entire country, both North and South
until the early 1870s when the typical
social values of nineteenth-century
America—racism, localism, and *laissez-
faire*—recaptured their dominance in
public policy.

The major development during this
period was the move away from the
politics of ideology, characteristic of the
decade prior to the Civil War and the
War itself, to the politics of political
organization which lasted to the turn of
the century. Ironically, the triumph of
political organization led to the increase
in civil service-protected government
positions—the party in power protected
its adherents by increasing the number
of protected posts before elections just
in case of defeat at the polls.

Based on printed sources and a vast
body of secondary literature, *Affairs of
State* is an impressive work of scholarship and analysis producing many useful insights. For example, state governments and the courts were a more potent
force in national life than is commonly
supposed today. In addition, the author
refutes the contention that all the
best nineteenth-century American minds
avoided politics for business. The political leaders of the late 1800s bridged
the gap between an agricultural and
an industrial society; they made things
work and should be viewed by the
moral standards of their time, not our
own. Political bribes and kickbacks were
an accommodation, a way of getting
things done.

Specialists will find much to admire
and dispute in this work. For example,
the interpretation of Reconstruction as
symptomatic of developments in post-
Civil War America rather than as a
unique southern experience is likely to
find opposition. General readers should

find *Affairs of State* an impressive, read-able analysis of public life in late nine-teenth-century America. The primary lesson to be learned from this work is that after 1900 the forms in which public concerns were expressed changed while their content and the social anxieties which produced them remained the same.

RANZ C. ESBENSHADE
University of New Hampshire
Durham

GABRIEL KOLKO. *Main Currents in Modern American History.* Pp. xi, 433. New York: Harper & Row, 1976. $9.95.

It is the thesis of this book that the past century of American history is dominated by the development of a mature industrial capitalism. During that time period, American capitalism sought political, economic and social solutions to the challenges it confronted. But because of the very nature of industrial capitalism, says Kolko, po-litical and economic solutions are fore-doomed to fail, and crisis must inevitably follow crisis, each progressively more serious and more insoluble than the last. America at the second century mark finds itself unstable: "a society dangerously adrift and now locked into an enduring, permanent crisis at home and in the world."

Industrial capitalism not only in-fluences domestic and foreign policy, it is all-pervasive and absolutely evil. Industrial capitalism is blamed for poverty, war, inflation, credit, and "Presidents and their mellifluous men who lied as a way of life." Since America is myopic to these realities (a conse-quence of "pervasive self-satisfied chau-vinism"), the country "marches into a future with its eyes turned toward the past, remaining astonishingly indulgent of its own tragedies and foibles, and as menacing to itself and the world as ever." Kolko views many of the events and all the crisis situations he discusses as "un-controllable" or "inevitable." This re-viewer was struck by the sense in which Kolko implies men have no control over their destinies. It is as if Industrial

Capitalism is the evil force controlling hapless, helpless men.

This book is not without its virtues. The author has done a great deal of original research as well as synthesizing much recent scholarship. His style is readable and enjoyable in places. But the work as a whole is flawed by an over concern with the present, particularly in the foreign policy discussions. In these areas the work reads like an apologia for the opponents to the Vietnam war. Per-haps the author gives himself away in his dedication: "To the Vietnamese Revolution and the heroic people who made it."

DONALD B. SCHEWE
Franklin D. Roosevelt Library
Hyde Park
New York

ERNEST R. MAY. *The Making of the Monroe Doctrine.* Pp. viii, 306. Cam-bridge, Mass.: Harvard University Press, 1975. $12.50.

On August 16, 1823, the British Foreign Secretary, George Canning, suggested to the American Minister in London that Britain and the United States should issue a joint statement of policy concerning the Spanish colonies in South America which had revolted from Spain. In the end, the United States did not agree to a joint statement; but the substance of Canning's proposal was included in President Monroe's message to Congress on December 2, 1823, and became known in later years as the Monroe Doctrine.

In exploring how all this came about, Professor May asked himself three ques-tions. (1) Could someone living in 1823, knowing what we know about the values and beliefs of Monroe, Adams, Calhoun, Crawford, Clay and Jackson, have guessed what position these men would have taken and how their debate would conclude? May's answer is "no." (2) Could the imaginary observer of 1823, knowing what the principals knew about the foreign pressures on the United States, have guessed what the adminis-tration's foreign policy would be? Again the answer is "no." There were no constraints in the foreign scene powerful enough to determine the policies of the American government. (3) Finally, would our imaginary observer of 1823, knowing that all the principals except the President himself were presidential candidates, and examining what they would see as their personal political stake in issues of foreign policy, have been able to predict how they would react to Canning's proposal? The answer this time is "yes." "The test of what was and what was not in the personal political interest of the various candidates would have yielded much more specific predictions . . . [and] most of these predictions would have been right on the nose" (p. 189).

May concludes that domestic policy may be a critical determinant of foreign policy and that in the case of the Monroe Doctrine it was the determinant because of the structure of American politics— the nature of the democratic electoral system compelled the actors to follow the course they did. "The Monroe Doctrine may be said to have epitomized the foreign policy of democracy" (p. 206). May suggests that political scientists should pay more attention to the relationship between foreign policy and governmental structure.

Finally, May claims that his procedure of situating himself at some moment before the event, asking what weighting of causal factors would have produced the best forecast of what actually happened, and explaining the event accordingly, is an important new method of historical investigation. But May tells us in his Preface that he had already intuited, from reading the Adams papers, what his conclusion would be. His new method turns out to be a splendid expository device rather than a new tool of discovery.

This is an elegant work, beautifully written, learned, convincing, and a pleasure to read.

RICHARD SCHLATTER

Rutgers University
New Brunswick, N.J.

GEORGE H. THOMPSON. *Arkansas and Reconstruction: The Influence of Geography, Economics, and Personality.* Pp. xii, 296. Port Washington, N.Y.: Kennikat Press, 1976. $15.00.

This book is a welcomed addition to the scarce literature on Arkansas during Reconstruction. It is the first monograph on the subject since the 1920s. Although it is not a comprehensive study of Arkansas under Republican administrations it does add significantly to an understanding of a complex period in Arkansas history. Thompson's central theme is that Reconstruction is best understood as a continuum, not an interregnum, studied through a careful interpretation of geographic, economic, and "personality of leadership" influences rather than a recitation of party politics.

The author divides his work into three principal parts and a conclusion. Part I discusses the three sections of the state —delta, northwest, and southwest—instead of the usual two of lowlands and highlands, and lays the foundation for the part they play in the state's political, economic, and social development. It also deals with the concept of patriotism in a border state as it relates to secession and post-war amnesty.

Part II concerns what Thompson calls "De Jure v. De Facto Government." He argues that Arkansans such as David Walker and Augustus H. Garland viewed Republican controlled government as *de facto* to be ignored or endured by refusing to take the oath required for participation or take the oath and try to eliminate Republican ascendancy through the electoral process. It is here the author lays stress upon the personality of leadership as exemplified by Walker, ante-bellum Whig and Unionist president of the secession convention, who refused to take the oath; and Garland, ante-bellum Whig and Confederate legislator, who took the oath. Thompson gives an excellent account of the contest between Joseph Brooks and Elisha Baxter, both Republicans, for the governorship, 1872–1874, which led to the end of Republican rule, and the establishment in the eyes of Democratic-Conservatives of a *de jure* government in 1874.

Part III deals with the most pernicious economic problem in nineteenth-century Arkansas—the use of state credit to promote economic development. Thompson correctly contends that the pledging of state bonds in 1836 for banks and in 1868 for railroads and levees ruined the credit of the state and retarded economic growth. First, by the failure for years to pay the interest on the bank bonds and secondly, the repudiation in 1884 by constitutional amendment of the railroad-aid, levee, and some bank bonds.

Arkansas and Reconstruction is based on thorough research in the sources, especially hitherto unexploited manuscript collections. It is well-illustrated, detailed, amply documented, and objective. The minute discussion of the promoter's frustrations in building the Little Rock and Fort Smith railroad adds little to the basic premise of the work and the publisher may be faulted for placing the footnotes at the end of the book.

GARLAND E. BAYLISS
Texas A & M University
College Station

SOCIOLOGY

FRANK F. FURSTENBERG, JR. *Unplanned Parenthood: The Social Consequences of Teenage Childbearing.* Pp. vii, 293. New York: The Free Press, 1976. $13.95.

This book is an outgrowth of research which began quite simply as an effort to evaluate a comprehensive hospital service program for teenage mothers. From this modest start, the study was transformed into a comprehensive five-year investigation of all of the consequences of early childbearing. Viewing maternity as one of the unscheduled events of adolescence, the author utilizes a life-course adaptation approach to early parenthood. This perspective "age locates" individuals in both the social structure and in a specific developmental, historical context as well.

The model utilized offers a gripping picture of adolescent unplanned parenthood, viewing it as an outcome of a particular sequence of events in the moral lives of young women. Furstenberg's concentration is on explanations which relate directly to the most provocative social issue: why do some girls engage in a particular sexual activity while others do not?

When all is said and done, we are left with an "accidental" theory of adolescent parenthood. Although this conclusion is described in the foreword as running contrary to the popular assumption that out-of-wedlock births are the consequence of some special kind of motivation, it does seem to me to be consonant with judgments reached through treatment experiences with adolescent patients.

More surprising, however, is the tempering of the notion that an unplanned child leads inevitably to a life of deprivation for all concerned. Furstenberg's case histories strike at the heart of this shibboleth and, despite the fact that cohort group was from black, low income families, their subsequent lives seemed to defy a simple accounting scheme.

Some young women were indeed destroyed by this ill-timed event; others were able to repair the disorder by rearranging their lives and resuming their education. Marriage (or no) did not appear to be a highly predictive variable, while worst of all was the group whose lives were clearly damaged by early pregnancy and whose future prospects were clearly delimited by social, emotional, and economic deprivation.

Furstenberg makes effective use of a controlled group of young women who did not become pregnant in adolescence and also has paid close attention to the infant's developmental experience as one of the important measures in arriving at an assay of the mother's life prospects. While sociology books are not my metier,

I was consistently interested in this book and strongly moved by the author's evocative conclusion:

. . . the assistance we are prepared to offer [unwed mothers] is woefully inadequate and often temporary as well. Is it possible that we owe the vicious cycle of poverty not to the poor themselves but to the vicious cycle of social inaction?

MORTON LEVITT
University of California
Davis

ANTHONY GIDDENS. *New Rules of the Sociological Method: A Positive Critique of Interpretive Sociologies*. Pp. 192. New York: Basic Books, 1976. $10.95.

The hope of early sociologists such as St. Simon and Comte was that sociology could free society from blind adherence to tradition and in its place substitute a more enlightened way of life. By turning from religion and studying society in as value-free way as possible, sociologists have often tried to develop predictive powers very much along the lines of the physical sciences.

In the *New Rules of the Sociological Method* Anthony Giddens argues that scientific sociology has been a failure not because its methods are less than perfect but because there exists a transformative relationship between the human and the physical world. Giddens believes that sociology, rather than freeing humans from irrational traditions, has succeeded in overturning tradition as a guide to action only to put in its place falsely-labeled natural principles which are neither natural, logical nor eternal. Giddens concludes, "But that knowledge discloses that men are in the thrall of 'external' societal causes which bring about mechanically events that they suppose to be under their rational control; the subject initiating the investigation rediscovers himself as an object" (p. 153).

For Giddens the transformative relationship between subject and object is the key to evolving new rules for the study of society. After telling the reader that Schutz, Winch, Weber, Durkheim, Godamer, Apel and Habermas, among others, have also failed to successfully solve the epistomological and ontological problems of modern society, the author makes his most telling attack on Parsons. Giddens calls Parsons a reductionist because he places the purpose of society at the individual level and thus neglects to explain that power—not individual needs—is the basis of society and its reproduction. I especially recommend Giddens' discussion of Parsons to all sociologists. Parsons may have succeeded in giving Durkheim a psychology, but Giddens may yet give Parsons a viable theory of social power and social action.

While I am impressed with this book and highly recommend it, it is likely that the new rules for sociology will arouse heated debate by empiricists and others who may reply that while empirical evidence is not as good as hoped for in predicting behavior, speculation about ontology and construction of secular eschatologies may be even less successful at prediction. It also will be of interest to see if Giddens succeeds in making functionalism acceptable to Marxists. Because this book is so well written, I recommend it for all those who wish to brush up on some of the current issues of sociological theory construction.

GEORGE H. CONKLIN
Sweet Briar College
Virginia

STEPHEN GUDEMAN. *Relationships, Residence and the Individual: A Rural Panamanian Community*. Pp. xiii, 274. Minneapolis: University of Minnesota Press, 1976. $18.75.

This book is essentially a community study of a small group of subsistence farmers living along the Inter-American Highway in central Panama. In a number of ways the community resembles communities in other parts of Latin America, and the author of the book, an anthropologist, is well aware that the patterns of behavior he has observed are local versions of a widespread social system. Gudeman maintains that "few satisfactory analyses, explanations or models of these systems have emerged. Much of the reportage has remained at the ethnographic level" (p. 10). His treatment of his community is clearly meant to rectify this situation.

The group that Gudeman studied was very loosely structured. The basic unit was the household, composed usually of a nuclear family. There was very little cooperation except among the closest kin (parents and children, and siblings), hardly any ceremonial life or community activity, a great stress on individualism, and pronounced suspicion of outsiders. The major instances of interaction among members of different households were agricultural labor, which was sometimes exchanged but more often purchased, and the system of *compadrazgo* (godparenthood).

In attempting to make sense of these patterns of behavior, Gudeman operates almost entirely at the cultural level (culture is defined as involving beliefs, ideologies and values). He begins with the religious conceptions of the people, then deals with the notions of respect and shame and how these influence the behavior of individuals. The household is discussed in terms of values relating to the division of labor, conjugal relationships, and raising children. The forms of conjugal unions and their instability are explained in terms of individuals choosing certain values over others. And finally, the *compadrazgo* system is described by giving the basic rules which define how godparents are chosen, what their responsibilities are, and the kind of interaction expected of *compadres*.

Since anthropologists are not entirely agreed on the best way to explain social systems, opinions are likely to vary as to whether Gudeman has succeeded in providing a satisfactory "analysis, explanation or model" of his Panamanian community. To this reviewer, it seems clear that Gudeman has produced only another ethnographic (descriptive) account. What makes this description superior to many others is the detail, the obvious care with which the author sought to determine the basic values of his informants, and his success in showing how the values are systematically interrelated. The discussion of *compadrazgo*, in particular, is one of the best in the literature. But description, however detailed, is still description. Gudeman has failed to provide us with either explanation or model.

SETH LEACOCK
University of Connecticut
Storrs

TED ROBERT GURR. *Rogues, Rebels, and Reformers: A Political History of Urban Crime and Conflict.* Pp. 192. Beverly Hills, Calif.: Sage, 1976. $10.00.

What do urban planners and criminologists do when they see middle class flight from the city and those left to fend for themselves bolted behind closed doors? They look longingly to societies where cities are *relatively* clean, orderly, economically supportive and the streets are safe from crime. Professor Gurr and associates of Northwestern University take this a step further. For the purpose of analysis of crime, they ask what are the best and worst cities? Can one by studying cross-culturally and across a 150 year period of various eras isolate correlates of crime? What did the best cities do in terms of criminal justice systems, public policy, treatment of civil disorder, and cultural variations of crime to create safe and just cities?

The criterion of the researchers was that Stockholm, London (until its recent economic downturn), and Sydney were the "best" examples and Calcutta, the "worst."

Through a maze of descriptive statistics, charts, journalistic accounts, hueristic models, and a review of theories from left to right, the authors conclude that criminality and urbanization are here to stay and strongly correlated. They also contend that cities are divided by their internal heterogeneity of special interest groups that cancel each other in terms of criminal justice application. Gurr also indicates that reactionary and liberal reforms are less likely to work. Thus, some level of public disorder is in the cards and they describe this in a quasi-path model.

To the authors' credit, they have covered huge hurdles and tried to make

THE ANNALS OF THE AMERICAN ACADEMY

sense of large masses of data. The reader discovers that the three Western cities are not all that crime-free, have had in certain instances turbulent pasts, and have a growing crime rate today. One also finds that Calcutta is indeed in a class by itself. Periodic "order" occurs when the elite and mass converge on ideology and etiology of crime. However, "peace" extracts its costs and periodic reforms appear to be short-lived. In simple terms, the bigger and more complex society evolves, the more unlikely consensus is to emerge. This conclusion was made by Durkheim (and others) numerous years ago, but the French sociologist was hidden away in a short footnote.

On the other hand, an entire section is devoted to defending criminal statistics. The authors' major defense is that private studies support higher incidences of crime but of relative proportion to public crime data. Critics will not rest with this, and the authors lamely conclude that they may be in error, but at least one knows their procedure.

This is not a cheap shot though, for the book has its overwhelming merits in describing the complexity of the problem. And it is not a book to dash the hopes of reformers. For Gurr and his fellow researchers see the problem as tolerable, but not easily legislated out of existence. Crime and public disorder should be thought of as a "given" in contemporary urban life.

The book is heavy going for undergrads, but is a must for researchers and graduate students. For Gurr, the underlying theme is to establish the delicate balance of power between the thief and the policeman and who will break down your door. Some cures, he notes, are worse than the illness.

JOEL C. SNELL

Dana College
Blair
Nebraska

MICHAEL B. KATZ. *The People of Hamilton, Canada West: Family and Class in a Mid-Nineteenth-Century City.* Pp. xiii, 381. Cambridge, Mass.: Harvard University Press, 1975. $17.50.

A mixture, in the author's words, of "hard data and rash speculation," Michael Katz's book is the first major product of the "new" social history in Canada. It joins the recent, considerable volume of publications dealing with the reinterpretation of the demographic and social history of urban and rural areas in Europe, Great Britain, and the United States. Katz began work on Hamilton in 1967 and, after tantalizing his readership with several journal articles and interim project reports, has now produced this long-awaited monograph. The book presents in detail the results of his data analysis for the decade 1851 to 1861 with occasional forays into the 1870s, but in many ways it represents a progress report on his continuing research into the social and demographic effects of industrialization on Hamilton from 1850 to 1900.

The "stratified, transient, and anxious world of the nineteenth century city" is Katz's canvas, and his case study of Hamilton is based on a careful, even loving, reconstitution of the personal histories of individuals using the manuscript census records of 1851 and 1861, the assessment rolls for 1852 and 1861, city directories, newspapers, and so forth. These sources contain data on personal characteristics, including age, marital status, birthplace, religion, ethnicity, literacy, school attendance, occupation, property ownership, and permit the study of changes in residential patterns, social and economic mobility, wealth, family composition, and transiency over the decade.

According to Katz, nineteenth-century urban history is characterized by high levels of transiency and inequality. "Persisters" (only 31 percent of males enumerated in the 1851 census appear in the 1861 census [p. 122]) are persons who can be linked from an earlier data source to a later one, and "transients" are those who disappear. (Linkage techniques are discussed briefly in Appendix 3, pp. 349–52.) Clearly, the rate of transiency is upward-biased because of deaths, errors and ambiguities in enumeration, and coding errors. Most of the results are not very surprising. Transiency appears to have been affected by age and family status: transiency is highest for males in the 16–25 year old age group and for those 61 and over, and is lower for married males than for singles. Home ownership also seems to be an important determinant of persistence: tenants are more likely to be transients.

With regard to inequality, Katz considers property ownership and income as possible measures but concludes that a wealth concept which is a "construct of different items and does not correspond exactly to either total income or assessed property . . . is . . . the best available indicator of economic rank" (p. 25). Later, this concept is defined as "the sum of an individual's assessed worth based on all his property holdings throughout the city" (p. 53). Since these two statements do not agree, a more complete definition of the concept could profitably have been included in the book, even if relegated to an Appendix. In any case, the results show that persons with economic ranking in the 90–100th percentiles owned 60 percent of assessed wealth in Hamilton in 1851 and 63 percent in 1861, whereas persons in the 0–59th percentiles held 13 percent and 10 percent respectively (p. 54).

Changes in occupational structure are analyzed using Katz's classification of occupations (Appendix 2, pp. 343–8), and show varying rates of mobility from one occupation to another, with much persistence in the skilled, building trades and little in transitional employment as teamsters, porters, and servants. Incidentally, his analysis of occupational mobility must yet come to grips with the way in which occupation, in the nineteenth century, tended to be regarded more as a characteristic of an individual (like birthplace) than as an activity in which he was engaged currently.

Why did mobility occur? Katz argues it was partly a function of personal characteristics—intelligence, energy, perseverance, and education, among them—but, given his data sources, turns to look, in particular, at the influence of age and ethnic (religious) differences. Both occupational mobility and changes

in economic ranking appear to be related to age: the variation is clearest in the latter case, where economic rank increases for the young (under 30) and decreases for the elderly (over 60). "Men who did not succeed early by and large did not succeed at all" (p. 162). According to Katz, ethnicity had an even greater impact on a man's prospects of economic advancement. The Irish had the lowest rate of upward economic mobility and were most likely to remain poor compared with the Scots, English, or Canadian-born. "Laboring as well as poverty formed a way of life for the Irish and a temporary state for other groups" (p. 165).

The second major theme involves changes in the family and the household. The simple family household comprised of married couple (or widowed person) and children was predominant and the classic extended family was rare. However, Katz found that boarders and servants were normally resident in about 30 percent of households in 1851 and about 20 percent in 1861, and that some 15 percent of households had at least one resident relative (pp. 220–2). Boarders were predominantly male, and relatives and servants predominantly female. Mean household size declined over the decade from 5.8 persons in 1851 to 5.3 persons in 1861 (p. 224), reflecting the decrease in the numbers of boarders and servants. Household size appears to have varied with wealth: a large household comprised of children, relatives, boarders, and servants was likely to be associated with high economic ranking. Size was also influenced, as expected, by the age of the household's head.

Katz emphasizes the role played by boarding and by entering service in the socialization of young men and women. Consider, for example, the situation of young men. Katz's figures show that a young man tended to leave home at 16 or 17, find work and live as a boarder with a "surrogate" family until marriage, usually between the ages of 25 and 30. This period of about 10 years he considers an age of "semi-autonomy," a transitional step between childhood/dependence and adulthood/independence. Young men were expected to establish themselves financially before beginning a family, as young married couples almost always established their own households away from their parents. The length of this period of semi-autonomy fell by 1861 and again by 1871, possibly as a result of economic conditions but also because of shifting behavioral patterns as young men and women began to remain longer at home. The rate and length of school attendance increased during this period as well. This is an interesting argument which Katz intends to refine as data for the late nineteenth century become available, but his use of data for one decade, especially a decade ending in a severe depression, makes the selection of the appropriate causal mechanism appear to be as yet problematic.

This is a book with shortcomings. One major problem of indeterminate effect is the questionable reliability of the primary data sources. Nineteenth-century censuses were flawed by under-enumeration and enumerator error, and it is impossible to assess the consequences of such errors for Katz's empirical findings. Secondly, I have some methodological concerns about Katz's reliance on cross-classification tables and whether some of his inferences can be substantiated. In his discussion of transiency, for example, Katz writes: "Clearly, the life cycle, reflected in age and household status, exerted an independent influence on persistence. The same cannot be said for ethnicity which . . . exerted no independent influence whatsoever. . . . Undoubtedly their wealth, rather than any independent cultural factor, most often accounted for the small ethnic differential in the tendency to remain within the city" (pp. 125–7). The problem here is that the unique and separable effects of the many social and economic factors cannot be disentangled one from the other unless a different technique, such as regression analysis, is employed.

These reservations aside, Michael Katz has written an important book and so-cial historians eagerly await his next installment on the Hamilton project.

PETER GEORGE
McMaster University
Hamilton, Ontario, Canada

CHARLES E. LEWIS, RASHI FEIN and DAVID MECHANIC. *A Right to Health: The Problems of Access to Primary Medical Care.* Pp. v, 367. New York: John Wiley & Sons, 1976. $17.95.

DAVID MECHANIC, ed. *The Growth of Bureaucratic Medicine: An Inquiry into the Dynamics of Patient Behavior and the Organization of Medical Care.* Pp. vii, 345. New York: John Wiley & Sons, 1976. $14.95.

It is widely held that the introduction of a new element into any system changes the entire system. The three essays in *A Right to Health: The Problem of Access to Primary Medical Care* demonstrate that government interventions into a "non-system," namely the American health care scene, have tended to produce little significant change. The authors argue that past and current piecemeal responses to medical care problems are ineffective not necessarily because they are piecemeal *per se*, but because these limited (and often extremely costly) efforts are not backed by sound and coherent policies.

This theme has been repeated many times by many different authors but not always with the clarity and sound documentation found in this book. The clarity of the presentation is due in part to the definitions and conceptual model set forth in the first section by David Mechanic. In Part II, Charles Lewis, employing Mechanic's classification of barriers to health care, analyzes eleven different programs which were designed to affect either the supply of or the demand for health care services. Lewis's concise and well documented discussion of these various projects indicates that most have been costly, have failed to have the desired impact, and, in some instances, have been politically unfeasible. Rashi Fein, in the final section, considers the policies which have led to these interventions and goes on to argue for fundamental changes in the financing and delivery of health care. Fein does not necessarily minimize the value of a piecemeal approach, but he insists that any type of intervention should be based on a coherent health policy.

Individuals who agree with more radical criticisms of the American health care system will find this volume rather tame. It remains an excellent discussion backed up by good factual information.

The Growth of Bureaucratic Medicine is also concerned with trends in modern medical care and the author, at times, deals with issues similar to the ones raised in the earlier book. However, the basic orientation is quite different. Here, Mechanic indicates that he is primarily concerned with the nature of the complex organizations that are now becoming such an important part of the delivery of health care. The basic theme of the book is that while organizational coherence is a necessity in the highly technical field of modern medicine, the application of the traditional bureaucratic model to health care "would be inappropriate for the effective and humane performance of medicine" (p. 1). This basic theme is then presented and developed in a series of essays written either by Mechanic himself or by some of his colleagues. Part I looks at the growth of bureaucratic medicine in a comparative perspective. Parts II and III consist mainly of empirical studies focusing, first, on different delivery programs and, second, on patient perspectives on illness and how these perspectives relate to the organization of services. In Part IV, the author looks at broader issues concerning policy, evaluation, and the role of the social scientist in medicine.

The growing complexity of medical practice is an extremely important trend and Mechanic clearly understands the process and its implications. The main shortcoming of the book is that it ap-

pears to consist of essays strung together by transitional phrases and paragraphs. While many of the chapters are excellent, the book itself does not represent the kind of in-depth, step-by-step analysis of increasing bureaucratization that seems to be needed. This reviewer also found that while the empirical papers presented in Parts II and III were of some interest, they hardly reflected the level of theoretical sophistication that Mechanic quite rightly called for in Chapter Four.

CHARLES S. BOURGEOIS
McGill University
Montreal
Canada

GRAEME NEWMAN. *Comparative Deviance: Perception and Law in Six Cultures.* Pp. xii, 332. New York: Elsevier, 1976. $12.95.

With encouragement by the United Nations Secretariat and a grant from the Ford Foundation, Graeme Newman has undertaken an ambitious cross-cultural study of public attitudes toward deviant behavior. The author is interested in assessing the evidence for three issues: the respective theoretical positions of absolutism and of relativism in deviant behavior; comparisons of public perceptions and substantive law in each country; and the validity of the concept of subcultures of deviant behavior.

This book reviews the literature and theoretical background of these topics, describes the methodologies used in the present investigation, and presents both the empirical results and the author's theoretical conclusions. From about 200 to 500 respondents provided the samples from each of the countries: India, Indonesia, Iran, Italy (Sardinia), United States (New York City and State), and Yugoslavia. Subjects were interviewed to obtain responses to six components of their perceptions (intensity of reaction, knowledge of the law, definition of the act, recommendations for societal reaction, should act be prohibited by law, and perception of how official agencies deal with violations), with respect to ten short descriptions of crimes or deviant behavior (robbery, incest, appropriation of public funds, homosexuality, abortion, taking drugs, factory pollution, individual pollution, not helping, and public protest).

Although the results indicate that the magnitude of response to deviance varies widely among countries, the rank order of responses to different types of deviant behavior are very similar; and so are the qualitative categories into which respondents of each country classify different types of deviance. The author accepts this evidence as supporting the notion of absolutism (or universalism) of moral norms. There are considerable gaps between public preferences and minimal sanctions prescribed by law. With the exception of Sardinia, the evidence is ambiguous regarding subcultural differentiation of rural-urban areas.

There are some interesting empirical results reported. The author not only utilizes sophisticated statistical techniques for analysis of his data, but he shows an awareness of many of the methodological and theoretical problems of comparative analysis. In the opinion of the present reviewer, however, the research report can be faulted on a number of serious counts, about which only brief mention of a few can be indicated here.

(1) The presentation of raw data, empirical analysis, and conceptual conclusions is difficult to follow (inconsistent use of concepts, incomplete information for meaningful reading, poor indexing).

(2) A plethora of empirical findings are often irrelevant and undigested, exacerbated by ex post facto explanations of unexpected findings.

(3) Resolution of the issue of absolutism versus relativism of cultural norms is in no way aided by the limited empirical data of this study nor by the inadequate theoretical conceptualization of the problem. Ignored is the fact that all of these countries have had extensive contact with European culture.

(4) It is incorrect and misleading to identify "consensus" theory with absolutism of morals; and "conflict" theory with relativism. The proportion of a population which agrees on the definition of a norm is, in itself, almost irrelevant to "consenses" or "conflict" theories.

(5) Some stated implications of the findings for consensus, Marxian, and labelling theories grossly oversimplify and misjudge the nature of these theories.

(6) The data of this study can in no way serve as a basis for judging the case for the "evolution" of morals.

(7) Absence of correlations of sex, age, education, and religion with deviance perceptions is *not* evidence that "sociological" factors are unimportant (these factors are only crude indicators; there are other "sociological" factors).

(8) The gaps found between legal sanctions and public perceptions are essentially meaningless because of the nonrepresentative samples used; and, in any case, that these gaps "should" be narrowed is a value judgment. Policy decisions depend, in addition, on other considerations.

ARTHUR LEWIS WOOD
University of Connecticut
Storrs

DAVID T. STANLEY. *Prisoners Among Us: The Problem of Parole.* Pp. xvii, 205. Washington, D.C.: The Brookings Institution, 1976. $9.95. Paperbound, $3.95.

For correctional institution staff members or parole officers David Stanley's *Prisoners Among Us* is a good summary statement of the whole field of parole and its problems. This work is not written, like Jessica Mitford's *Kind and Usual Punishment*, to influence a larger audience of intelligent laymen, nor is it, in the reviewer's opinion, designed for academic criminologists. The author, at the time of the study a senior fellow in the Brookings Governmental Studies program, presents a mix of results from published studies along with interviews and statistics which he himself collected in six jurisdictions. A description of his research design and any consideration of the representativeness of his interviews with officials and others is very fragmentary and incomplete. He does mention visits to four halfway houses and indicates that he or an assistant talked to 36 parolees who happened to be in offices on days when officials were being interviewed. The reader will encounter a text which shifts from general statements about the parole systems in the United States to summaries of studies conducted in a variety of jurisdictions and then to observations about the state and federal parole systems visited by the author.

The book tries to do too much in 191 pages of text, ranging from a consideration of theories of punishment to supervision on parole, and dealing with complicated issues such as decision-making by parole boards in a rather brief fashion, even though the literature in such a field is now quite extensive. Although individual chapters may be good summaries of the "state of the art" and its evaluation, a knowledgeable practitioner or academic will hardly be surprised at the author's major conclusions such as, for example, that decisions by parole boards have little accuracy, that parole hearings tend to be cursory, and that supervisory strategies are unreliable and real parole surveillance is impossible.

The author concludes his work by proposing a series of recommendations including release without parole combined with a modified system of sentencing discretion. Rehabilitation does not work; sentences should be appropriate punishment for crime. A brief selected bibliography is included at the end of the book.

Although the ideas in this work are quite unexceptional and do not seem to add to our knowledge in the field, the author does bring together a large amount of material for the relatively uninitiated. Chapter III, on the parole board hearing itself, presents one of the best descriptions I have seen of the actual questioning and atmosphere during a board hearing, along with a statement of the pros and cons of such hearings.

NORMAN JOHNSTON
Beaver College
Glenside
Pennsylvania

JOHN WESTERGAARD and HENRIETTA RESLER. *Class in a Capitalist Society: A Study of Contemporary Britain.* Pp. xv, 432. New York: Basic Books, 1976. $15.00.

The authors of this important volume on social inequality are not Americans, which in itself might be taken as a significant qualification. John Westergaard is a specialist on class structure and urban development and is Professor of Sociology at the University of Sheffield in Great Britain. Henrietta Resler teaches in the Department of Sociology at the University of New South Wales, Sydney, Australia. Using British society as a case study, they have produced a singularly lucid, incisive and searching analysis of the structural sources and consequences of inequality in modern capitalist society. Their perspective is Marxist and their structural and comparative orientation provide an important supplement to the "parochial" studies of social stratification done by American sociologists.

Eschewing data derived from the subjective views of interested respondents, the authors rely mainly on official statistics and government reports for documentation of existing class inequalities in contemporary Great Britain. The book is divided into five parts: "Themes and Issues," "Inequalities of Condition and Security," "Inequality of Power," "Inequalities of Opportunity," and "Acquiescence and Dissent: Responses to Inequality."

While there is no bibliography as such, the excellent footnoting and ample documentation serve the same purpose. Included are discussions of the functionalist versus the Marxist approach to stratification, the various meanings of equality and inequality, the relation be-

186

tween color (race) and class, the nature of power and its relation to inequality and the various forms of adaption and response by social groups to the conditions of social inequality.

In emphasizing the "concentration of power and property in a very small section of the population" as the basis of social inequality, the authors go far in overcoming the tendency of the commonly used language of class to conceal its most central feature. They make a major contribution in illuminating some of the complex issues in this difficult and critical area of investigation. The volume is highly recommended for all social scientists and is must reading for specialists in social stratification.

SEYMOUR LEVENTMAN
Boston College
Chestnut Hill
Massachusetts

JOZEF WILCZYNSKI. *The Multinationals and East-West Relations: Towards Transideological Collaboration.* Pp. vi, 235. Boulder, Colo: Westview Press, 1976. $27.50.

Anyone interested in the economic development of Eastern Europe or in the evolution of East-West trade relations is familiar with the numerous publications of Jozef Wilczynski on these and related subjects. Wilczynski's most recent book, *The Multinationals and East-West Relations*, although in a field that has been inundated with new monographs, provides a very useful description of the economic ties that have developed during the past decade between the major multinational corporations of the West and the socialist governments—primarily those of Europe.

One of the most beneficial contributions, especially for the person uninitiated into the intricacies of East-West economic relations, consists of the numerous tables that summarize such information as that concerning the major industrial multinationals that are involved in commercial dealings with the socialist states; the major contracts, licenses, and cooperation agreements between individual Western multina-

tionals and their socialist partners; and the credits extended to socialist states by Western banks.

In general, *The Multinationals and East-West Relations* is a straightforward descriptive account of both the development of East-West commercial relations and the benefits which both sides expect to gain from their "transideological collaboration." Wilczynski covers the topics that have now become *de rigueur* in books in East-West commercial relations— trade, licenses, industrial cooperation including joint ventures, and finance. One of the more interesting sections concerns the development of socialist "multinationals" and the activities of socialist enterprises in the West. The discussion of socialist exports of licenses and of specialized manufactured products, including entire manufacturing plants, is especially valuable.

Wilczynski views the expansion of East-West commercial ties largely in optimistic terms, with expanding economic ties serving to reduce the hostility of socialist and Western industrial states. However, one wonders that the author does no more than mention the arguments of those who have maintained that expanding commercial contact serves primarily to strengthen the Soviets and their allies militarily. The assumptions about the benefits from continued East-West collaboration run directly contrary to those of critics of East-West trade like Antony Sutton.

ROGER E. KANET
University of Illinois
Urbana-Champaign

ROBERT WUTHNOW. *The Consciousness Reformation.* Pp. x, 309. Berkeley: University of California Press, 1976. $12.50.

Addressing those who hope to improve society and those who seek to understand the changes occurring in our lives today, Wuthnow's *The Consciousness Reformation* explores the experimentation going on from the late 1960s to the present, in politics, family styles, dress, leisure, education, and religion, which constitutes, the counterculture.

What changes are actually taking place? How many people are experimenting? What kind of people in terms of age, race, sex, attitudes are experimenting? Why is experimentation going on and to such a marked degree? What is the attitude of those not actively part of the counterculture toward the changes observed? Most importantly, how much impact are these changes having, or may they be expected to have, on the traditional culture that at present remains dominant?

To answer these questions, Wuthnow brings into service a very impressive skill in the devising, administering, and evaluating of test questions and responses presented to a sampling of 1000 individuals in the Bay Area of San Francisco. While aware that this area exhibits a greater degree of change than other sections of the country, particularly as the study emphasizes the under 30 group, Wuthnow theorizes that the Bay Area is very probably an advance agent of change and therefore represents a trend, not a unique sector of the country. Defining consciousness as *"the ongoing process of constructing reality out of symbols and experience"* [italics the author's], Wuthnow considers differing ways Americans make selections that determine their relationship as individuals to some meaningful pattern of existence. His study involves four meaning systems: theistic, rugged individualism, social science, mysticism. Through the use of national polls as well as his questionnaire, plus an excellent chapter giving a historical and philosophical perspective on religion and individualism in America, Wuthnow notes the previous reliance on these systems. He further traces their decline and the rise of faith in social science and in mysticism. Though the vast majority still hold traditional values, and the actual percentage of experimenters is 5 percent or less in most areas of activity, the experiments are still of major importance. Increasingly, those who are not actually experimenting at present, are accepting the idea of others doing so, or are considering participation themselves. For instance, census figures in 1960 re-

vealed 17,000 persons reported living with a partner of the opposite sex to whom they were not married. The 1971 figure was 143,000. This is a large increase but still represents a small percentage of the total population. However, a recent poll shows 25 percent of the population approves of living together out of wedlock, and 15 percent express interest in trying it themselves.

There is a high correlation between those whose system of values has shifted to social science and/or mysticism and a willingness to change or to accept change. This seems to indicate a society that will be more and more varied, and one which must learn to interact cooperatively in new ways.

Sociologists, philosophers, political scientists, and those interested in religion will find much of value in this painstaking and well documented study. All of us should find some degree of optimism in Professor Wuthnow's faith that in diversity and the interaction of differing systems, a new and dynamic society will hopefully emerge.

DOROTHY RUDY
Montclair State College
Upper Montclair, N.J.

ECONOMICS

JAGDISH N. BHAGWATI and T. N. SRINIVASAN. *Foreign Trade Regimes and Economic Development: India*. Pp. xii, 261. New York: National Bureau of Economic Research, 1975. $15.00.

The National Bureau of Economic Research has sponsored a comprehensive program of study into the relationships between foreign trade policies and economic development. This series, which uses a common analytical framework, consists of ten country case studies (by individual authors) and two summary volumes (by the general editors, Jagdish Bhagwati and Anne Kreuger). The volume under review is Number 6 in this series.

Bhagwati and Srinivasan analyze India's experience with foreign trade controls and, more explicitly, the impact—both external and internal—of the 1966 devaluation of the rupee and the associated changes in the type and magnitude of the intervention in foreign trade. Although major attention is devoted to examining the period from 1966 to (approximately) 1972, the study includes in a comprehensive fashion an overview of the trade regimes, and the implications thereof, that prevailed from 1950–1966.

The first four chapters—largely summarized from the relevant portions of J. Bhagwati and P. Desai, *India: Planning for Industrialization* (London: Oxford University Press, 1970)—establish the background of Indian economic development since 1950 and of the increasing recourse to trade controls since 1956. The impact of such controls, generally the *ad hoc* response to the latest foreign exchange crisis, is briefly (pp. 41–51) but masterfully developed. There is little that is new here, but it is so well done that it is very welcome.

Major attention attaches to evaluating the 1966 devaluation and associated policy changes. Since policy changes do not take place under controlled conditions it is particularly important to avoid *post hoc ergo propter hoc* type of reasoning. Bhagwati and Srinivasan argue that all too much of the discussion of the measures, particularly that undertaken soon after the devaluation, was of this type. They provide, instead, a simple yet largely persuasive method of accounting for the impact of stochastic events, such as harvest failures or other policy changes (which were not directly related to devaluation or trade policies); attention is also directed to lags in the adjustment process. Particularly welcome is the substantial attempt (Chapters 12–16) to go beyond traditional static allocational efficiency issues to consider the impact of trade policies on investment, innovation, and savings and thus on the pattern and pace of growth.

A brief review cannot hope to do justice to this important and stimulating work. Complex arguments are presented with clarity; at the same time no attempt is made to gloss over inherent complexities and areas of disagreement, so that the

work is remarkably stimulating and provocative. It is highly recommended: it is required reading for students of the Indian economy but it is also of significant interest to those concerned with general problems of trade policies and development strategies.

J. K. S. GHANDHI
University of Pennsylvania
Philadelphia

CLAUDIA DALE GOLDIN. *Urban Slavery in the American South, 1820–1860: A Quantitative History.* Pp. vii, 168. Chicago, Ill.: The University of Chicago Press, 1976. $12.95.

Although slaves in cities composed no more than 10 percent of the American South's slave population, the sharp decline in their numbers during the 1850s has led some historians to conclude that slavery could not flourish in an urban environment, and that slavery as an institution was in decline. Analyzing censuses for the 10 largest Southern cities, Professor Goldin finds that the numbers of urban slaves both increased and decreased between 1820 and 1860. She convincingly explains these fluctuations with economic variables.

The traditional literature offers theories which Goldin summarizes as either "push," that is, demand for urban slaves declined due to their unruliness, or "pull," demand for slaves increased faster in the countryside than in the cities because of the greater suitability of slave labor to large-scale agriculture. After three interesting chapters characterizing the urban slave population as disproportionately female, roughly one-fifth skilled, and relatively freer through self-hire and living-out arrangements, Goldin presents her modified "pull" hypothesis and proof.

She constructs equations using changes in slave and free populations, slave prices and wage rates, costs specific to holding slaves, income per capita and value added, in order to determine price elasticities of demand. Solving the equations proves that elasticities in the cities were 17 times greater than those in rural areas. In other words, given a certain rise in slave prices or hire rates, or a fall in wages, an urban slave user would be much more disposed to sell or stop hiring slaves than a rural slave user.

Goldin explains this greater disposition to shift back and forth between slave and free labor as the result of the presence in cities of groups of native or immigrant free workers who could substitute for slaves. In rural areas, "for reasons which are not yet entirely clear, free labor could not be mobilized for large-scale gang labor on farms at a wage rate competitive with the shadow price on slaves" (p. 105). She does not quantify mortality changes, however, which could have been important also.

Goldin concludes that slavery was not incompatible with the cities nor in decline in the 1850s, and that demand depended upon the growth of the urban market and the cost of free labor relative to slave labor, and not upon control costs, which did not increase significantly. Her study, originally a dissertation under Robert W. Fogel, is tightly argued and clearly written. It deserves reading by those who prefer more exact specifications of historical processes to impressionistic evidence and vague lists of causal factors.

PETER L. EISENBERG
Universidade Estadual de Campinas
São Paulo
Brazil

MARKOS J. MAMALAKIS. *The Growth and Structure of the Chilean Economy: From Independence to Allende.* Pp. vii, 390. New Haven, Conn.: Yale University Press, 1976. $20.00.

Chile is one of the most interesting and controversial of the developing countries because it has had a varied political and economic experience which has inspired a number of generalizations about the development process: the secular deterioration in the terms of trade of primary producers, the structuralist causes of inflation, the regressive role of *latifundio* in distribution and development, and the implications of international *dependencia*. Mamalakis has been immersed in studies of the Chilean experience for well over a decade. This long-awaited book summarizes his analysis of the Chilean experiences.

The scope of the book is large. It covers the more than a century and a half from independence in 1818 to the fall of Allende in 1973. Part 1, about one fourth of the book, is devoted to the pre-Great Depression years. Part 2, over half of the book, discusses the 1930–1973 period. Part 3, about a fifth of the book, explores two aspects of capital accumulation (that is, the role of CORFO, the Development Corporation, and the reasons for negative estimates of personal savings in the national accounts) and summarizes the study.

Mamalakis argues that to understand the development process in general and the Chilean experience in particular, one must take a broader view than do either Western or Marxian economists and consider the processes of production, distribution, and capital formation and the interactions among them. He also emphasizes the pluralistic nature of the Chilean experience and the importance of sectoral, as opposed to class, conflicts.

In regard to production, he attributes the increasing agricultural import desubstitution to the disincentives created by policies designed to transfer surplus from that sector due to a "latifundio psychosis" in which the nonagricultural population had excessive preoccupation with the incorrect notion that Chile was a *latifundio* based society. Mining, first through nitrates and then through copper, provided exports and large rents which could have been transformed into the human and capital basis for sustained growth, but largely were used in subsidizing consumer imports and in Chilean and foreign capital flight (induced substantially by internal economic instability). Industry, through import substitution and other preferential policy treatment, grew to include a wide variety of consumer and intermediate products, but failed to become a dynamic leading sector. Services became the largest and, except for mining, the most productive sector by performing relatively well the time-, quantity-, and location transformation functions to complement commodity production and the quality maintenance function associated with education and housing. However, the incentives caused this sector to perform some functions, such as quality improvement and financial intermediation poorly and others, such as transportation, at high social costs.

In regard to distribution, the secular shift in recent decades of the period covered was toward greater national, as opposed to foreign, control and a greater share for laborers. Rents were transferred from mining and, to a lesser extent, agriculture to industry and the urban services. However, great disparities remained among and within factors and sectors. Also certain functions—most importantly, food production, quality improvement, and financial intermediation—were discouraged by redistribution policies, with high social costs in terms of development.

In regard to capital formation, finally, Chile has been plagued by gaps between actual and potential (primarily mineral) resource surpluses, between actual and potential supplies of producer durables and between actual and desirable financial intermediation and surplus/reinvestment ratios. The conversion of potentialities into realities was limited by leakages to consumption and to abroad, by fluctuations generated internally and in international markets, and by distorted incentives due to inflation, protection and redistribution policies.

This book has some very strong points: (1) The analysis is based on careful consideration of Chilean data, with some new combinations of series to provide insights in regard to savings, distribution, and the foreign position. (2) The overall perspective is broad, both in a cross section and in a time series sense. (3) Services, with their large production and employment shares, are considered in some detail. (4) Mamalakis raises important questions about many of the conclusions of other analyses of the Chilean experience: the Ramirez-Véliz conclusion that industry was stifled prior to 1930 by free trade; the Fetter-Ramirez claim that inflation was due to

policies designed to benefit heavily indebted landlords; the extent to which rents from mineral exports went to Chilean capital flight abroad; the widespread belief in the importance of the *latifundio* in controlling Chilean society. (5) He also shows extensive familiarity with studies of the Chilean economy published by the late 1960s. (6) Moreover, he makes some insightful observations on the longer run implications of the Allende years.

The book also has some major shortcomings: (1) An introductory historical perspective or listing of important dates is not provided, so a reader who is not already familiar with Chilean history will be confused. (2) The Mamalakis scheme of production-distribution-capital accumulation is not a theory with testable hypotheses, but is only descriptive. (3) The book ignores most of the important studies of the Chilean economy which have become available in the past decade. (4) In some curious ways, such as in regard to the operations of the Development Corporation, the book also ignores much recent experience even though it acknowledges that such experience was quite significant. (5) There is almost no attempt to apply the modern empirical tools of economics to test hypotheses.

The book would be a much more substantial contribution if it did not suffer from these major inadequacies. Nevertheless, it is a significant addition to the literature on the Chilean experience with numerous insights and provocative observations for the serious student of that important experience.

JERE R. BEHRMAN
University of Pennsylvania
Philadelphia

RALPH NADER, MARK GREEN and JOEL SELIGMAN. *Taming the Giant Corporation.* Pp. 296. New York: W. W. Norton & Co., 1976. $10.50.

ARTHUR SELWYN MILLER. *The Modern Corporate State: Private Governments and the American Constitution.* Pp. xi, 264. Westport, Conn.: Greenwood Press, 1976. $15.00.

These provocative books are part of the debate about "what the American economy is *really* like," and "where do we go from here?" Answers to these questions range from the view that the market system is alive and well—or that we should *post haste* return to such a system—to the Marxist judgment that America is controlled by a corporate octopus and that socialism is the cure.

The ambiguities and complexities of reality help explain the difficulty of *really* ascertaining what the economy is like—thus opening to varying interpretations and to the genuine possibility that nearly everyone, including Miller and Nader *et al.*, is at least partially correct in his analysis.

Miller describes the corporate state, American style, leaving to others, such as Nader and his colleagues, the task of prescribing what is done about it. The Nader-Green book is basically prescription and that of Miller description. His description is, in short, a reasonably documented, scholarly portrayal of Galbraith's new industrial state. We have evolved into a coalition of big government, big business, unions, and universities who coordinate the affairs of the nation in a kind of interest-group, latter-day feudalism. In his conception many of the blue chips in the game belong to the blue chip corporations. But Miller's model is much more complex than a Marxist image, or that of Nader-Green, for the federal government with its executive branch and administrative apparatus is viewed as a dominant player as well.

He documents in a rather balanced way the transformation of the American system from an individualistic, market-based, limited and representative government scheme to one of interest-group power and "functional federalism," wherein the "new governments" of large corporations and labor unions together with the executive branch seek to direct the course of events. American society is one which trades freedom for materialism and an elitism within large organizations and society at large. As you would expect from a student of constitutional law, significant attention is directed to

constitutional implications of the shift from individualism to corporativism.

Miller's book is a rather rich analysis, well-written (but occasionally repetitious), portraying a corporativist system that must be frightening to liberals and conservatives alike. Part of the perplexity of his analysis is that some of the elements of the "new order" were introduced for good reasons that elicit the support of many. His book points up the fundamental necessity for a constant vigilance and wisdom to maintain a free and just society.

Nader and his associates, undoubtedly writing for a different audience, have a simpler picture of what is wrong in America. As the title indicates, essentially all problems can be assigned to the machinations of big business. However, much of the book concentrates on prescriptions for reform. These are spelled out in detail, some aimed at reorganizing the power balances of the corporation, as with vigorous federal chartering and independent, full-time directors. These directors would represent constituencies, but along with responsibility for general policies, become experts in assigned functional areas. Interlocking directorates are completely outlawed; stockholders get new power, and referendums are provided when local communities are affected by corporate activity.

A sharp increase in disclosure is part of the Nader-Green package, on every conceivable item of social and employee cost and with full financial facts concerning product-line and conglomerate divisions. A bill of rights for corporate constituencies would be devised, based on the contention that corporations are indeed governmental structures as well as economic enterprises. Finally, antitrust laws would be significantly expanded and rigorously enforced, increasing the policing powers of competition.

The Nader-Green book is a capstone for earlier volumes. For those who are interested, it gives a current picture of the Nader position and his policy proposals. For example, it is obvious from this book that Nader is not a traditional socialist, but an advocate of strong regulation and strong competition.

Both of these books are worth reading, although Miller's is the more sophisticated and complex.

HAROLD L. JOHNSON
Emory University
Atlanta
Georgia

NATHAN ROSENBERG. *Perspectives on Technology.* Pp. x, 353. New York: Cambridge University Press, 1976. $24.95. Paperbound, $6.95.

Economic historians have long been fascinated with the subject of technology, and it has only recently been replaced by an interest in social and urban history. All of the noteworthy new economic historians have worked in this field— Paul David researched the mechanics of reaping, Peter Temin explored iron and steel, and Douglass North investigated ocean shipping, to mention a few. But Nathan Rosenberg, in his many articles and other publications, has surveyed this entire field. His volume *Perspectives on Technology* contains fifteen of his articles, and for those requiring some background it can be read in conjunction with his book *Technology and American Economic Growth*, which covers both theory and applications on a textbook level.

What accounts for this general interest by economic historians in the subject of technology? The most important questions in economic history have concerned growth, and Denison, Kendrick, and Solow, among others, have shown that economic growth can be explained only to a small degree by the increase in factors as conventionally measured. A large part of economic growth therefore remains unexplained and has been termed the "residual." This so-called "measure of our ignorance" must then be due to technological change of some sort. And so the study of the history of an economy becomes the study of the history of technological change. Rosenberg adds two further reasons to study the history of technology. Technological change is far more complicated, notes

Rosenberg, than economic theory has led us to believe. Although it is convenient for economists to conceptualize technological advance as a shift of the production function and not merely a movement along an existing one—that is, not merely a substitution of factors within a given technological context—it is far harder to distinguish between the two in practice. Shocking as it is to economic theorists, the very definition of technological change is ambiguous in most real world applications. Furthermore, adds Rosenberg, it is not technological change itself that leads to growth, it is its eventual utilization. Diffusion and adaptation become more important than the forces generating inventions. By studying history we can understand the determinants of a technological menu and an economy's utilization of an existing technology. There are few historians of science or economists of technology more able to demonstrate these lessons from history than Nathan Rosenberg.

His fifteen previously published articles have been arranged in four sections: (1) a discussion of the history of American technological advance in the machine tool industry and in woodworking, with a very suggestive piece on Anglo-American wage differences in 1820; (2) a section of how technologies change, with an article on the problems of implementing current economic theory; (3) a part on the diffusion and adaptation of technology, which is probably Rosenberg's strongest chapter and his greatest contribution to the whole topic; and (4) a somewhat contemporary, although retrospective, section on natural resources and the environment, which is weaker than the rest of the book.

Rosenberg excels at demonstrating the problems raised by the economic concept of production functions, why diffusion and adaptation are the most important aspects of technological change, and how the neglected factors on the supply side have operated to generate technological change. Rosenberg will disappoint many readers by not following these examples with some concrete addition to theory and with a simple measurement of their relative impor- tance. But these areas are not Rosen- berg's strengths and are best left to the Griliches and Jorgensons of economics. This collection of papers is nonetheless an important addition to the history of science in an economic framework. It both serves as a caution and provides a series of suggestions to the economist formulating and testing theories of growth. It is also a well written and engaging series of articles by someone who has now solidly established him- self as the dean in the economic realm of the history of technology.

CLAUDIA GOLDIN
Princeton University
Princeton, N.J.

LEONARD SILK and DAVID VOGEL. *Ethics and Profits: The Crisis of Confidence in American Business.* Pp. 250. New York: Simon & Schuster, 1976. $8.95.

Every American institution of late has come under extensive criticism and the public seems to have less faith in many of these institutions including American business. Recently, American corpora- tions were under investigation for alleged bribery, kickbacks, and illegal campaign contributions.

Many of the economic problems re- sulting from the oil crisis, inflation, re- cession, unemployment, and high in- terest rates, have shaken the confidence of the American public and increased their doubt about the role of corporations in maintaining the economic health of the nation.

The Conference Board had conducted a series of meetings during September 1974 and 1975 and invited some 360 top executives of major American corpora- tions. The authors were invited to attend the meetings and the book is the com- pilation of the authors' impressions, ob- servations and analysis of the discussion that took place during these meetings. The discussions were very candid, honest as well as soul searching. Many of the executives who participated have remained anonymous. The object of the book has been to present what the authors

hope is an accurate and fair portrait of the thinking of American business leaders on a wide variety of issues which are covered in eight chapters ranging from crisis of confidence, national economic planning, corporate autonomy and political freedom plus many others. I think the authors have succeeded in their venture.

Another major issue facing the cor- porations today is the extent to which they consider themselves threatened by increased governmental control of busi- ness. They believe such control is detrimental, unnecessary and inefficient. The authors pinpoint that the "dominant attitude of corporate executives towards government officials, whether elected or appointed, is one of hostility, distrust, and not infrequently, contempt."

What should be the role of Federal Government in terms of managing the health of the economy through economic planning? The authors point out the skepticism and fear among many of the executives about the introduction of economic planning in the U.S.A. It is gratifying to note that the growing num- ber of business leaders believe that to solve the crucial national problems the U.S. Government should engage in some form of economic planning. As the authors point out, "industries would still be free to make their own decisions, but they would do so on the basis of more complete information about long term trends as affected by government policies."

Business executives feel that the press, television, electorate and the elite are hostile and do not try to appreciate what they are doing. It may be true that better economic education about the American economic system is needed. At the same time, the corporations have to become more responsive as well as responsible to meet the changing needs of the society.

The book provides an excellent ac- count of the thinking of American corporate leaders on a variety of issues that form the American society and outline the steps that some businessmen are taking, not only to confront their moral dilemma but also to search for a new system that will preserve the fabrics of American capitalistic society and maintain the virtues of the American system with economic and political liberty.

The authors have presented the material with clarity and in a style and language that can be understood by the general public. The book will contribute to a better informed public debate about the role of the corporation in America's economic system.

ABDUL Q. J. SHAIKH
North Adams State College
Massachusetts

OTHER BOOKS

AARON, HENRY J., ed. *Inflation and the Income Tax*. Pp. 340. Washington, D.C.: The Brookings Institution, 1976, $12.95. Paperbound, $5.95.

ABERNATHY, M. GLENN. *Civil Liberties Under the Constitution*. 3rd ed. Pp. vii, 656. New York: Harper & Row, 1977. $11.50. Paperbound.

ADELMAN, MORRIS A., et al. *No Time to Confuse: A Critique of the Ford Foundation Energy Policy Project*. Pp. v, 156. San Francisco, Calif.: ICS, 1975. $12.50. Paperbound, $2.95.

ALTSHULER, ALAN A. and NORMAN C. THOMAS. *The Politics of the Federal Bureaucracy*. 2nd ed. Pp. ix, 379. New York: Harper & Row, 1977. $10.95. Paperbound.

ANDERSON, BERNARD E. *The Opportunities Industrialization Centers: A Decade of Community-Based Manpower Services*. Pp. iii, 156. Philadelphia: University of Pennsylvania Press, 1976. $7.95. Paperbound.

AUERBACH, JEROLD S. *Unequal Justice*. Pp. viii, 395. New York: Oxford University Press, 1977. $13.95. Paperbound, $3.95.

BALDWIN, K. D. S. *Demography for Agricultural Planners*. Pp. i, 185. New York: UNIPUB, 1975. $7.00. Paperbound.

BARAN, HENRYK, ed. *Semiotics and Structuralism: Readings from the Soviet Union*. Pp. vii, 369. White Plains, N.Y.: IASP, 1976. $15.00.

BARDACH, EUGENE, et al. *The California Coastal Plan: A Critique*. Pp. v, 199. San Francisco, Calif.: ICS, 1976. $12.50. Paperbound, $3.95.

BARTH, HANS. *Truth and Ideology*. Pp. 218. Berkeley: University of California Press, 1977. $12.75.

BEDAU, HUGO ADAM and CHESTER M. PIERCE, eds. *Capital Punishment in the United States*. Pp. x, 567. New York: AMS Press, 1976. $25.00.

BELL, GEOFFREY. *The Protestants of Ulster*. Pp. 159. New York: Urizen Books, 1976. $4.95. Paperbound.

BELOTTI, ELENA GIANINI. *What are Little Girls Made Of? The Roots of Feminine Stereotypes*. Pp. 158. New York: Schocken Books, 1977. $7.95.

BENT, ALAN E. and RALPH A. ROSSUM, eds. *Urban Administration: Management, Politics and Change*. Pp. 385. Port Washington, N.Y.: Kennikat Press, 1976. $18.50. Paperbound, $8.95.

BERGER, PETER L. and RICHARD JOHN NEUHAUS. *To Empower People: The Role of Mediating Structures in Public Policy*. Pp. 45. Washington, D.C.: American Enterprise Institute for Public Policy Research, 1977. $2.50. Paperbound.

BERKOWITZ, MORTON, P. G. BOCK and VINCENT J. FUCCILLO. *The Politics of American Foreign Policy: The Social Context of Decisions*. Pp. v, 310. Englewood Cliffs, N.J.: Prentice-Hall, 1976. $6.95. Paperbound.

BERRY, BRIAN J. L., ed. *Urbanization and Counterurbanization*. Pp. 336. Beverly Hills, Calif.: Sage, 1976. $17.50. Paperbound, $7.50.

BOBO, BENJAMIN F. et al. *No Land is an Island: Individual Rights and Government Control of Land Use*. Pp. v, 221. San Francisco, Calif.: ICS, 1975. $12.50. Paperbound, $3.95.

BOGGS, CARL. *Gramsci's Marxism*. Pp. 145. New York: Urizen Books, 1976. $2.95. Paperbound.

BRAIN, ROBERT. *Friends and Lovers*. Pp. 287. New York: Basic Books, 1976. $10.95.

BRAISTED, WILLIAM R. *Meiroku Zasshi: Journal of the Japanese Enlightenment*. Pp. vii, 532. Cambridge, Mass.: Harvard University Press, 1976. $20.00.

BRAND, CHARLES M. *Deeds of John and Manuel Comnenus*. Pp. xi, 274. New York: Columbia University Press, 1976. $20.00.

BRANDON, ROBERT M., JONATHAN ROWE and THOMAS H. STANTON. *Tax Politics: How They Make You Pay and What You Can Do About It*. Pp. v, 297. New York: Pantheon Books, 1976. $6.95. Paperbound.

BRIGGS, B. BRUCE et al. *The Politics of Planning: A Review and Critique of Centralized Economic Planning*. Pp. v, 367. San Francisco, Calif.: ICS, 1976. $12.50. Paperbound, $4.95.

BRODY, BARUCH. *Abortion and the Sanctity of Human Life: A Philosophical View*. Pp.

162. Cambridge, Mass.: MIT Press, 1975. $4.95. Paperbound.

BROWN, RAY, ed. *Children and Television*. Pp. 368. Beverly Hills, Calif.: Sage, 1976. $17.50. Paperbound, $7.50.

BURNS, E. BRADFORD. *Latin America: A Concise Interpretive History*. 2nd ed. Pp. v, 307. Englewood Cliffs, N.J.: Prentice-Hall, 1977. $7.95. Paperbound.

CALHOUN, LAWRENCE G., JAMES W. SELBY and H. ELIZABETH KING. *Dealing With Crisis: A Guide to Critical Life Problems*. Pp. ix, 275. Englewood Cliffs, N.J.: Prentice-Hall, 1977. $9.95. Paperbound, $4.95.

CALLINICOS, ALEX. *Althusser's Marxism*. Pp. 133. New York: Urizen Books, 1976. $2.95.

CANFIELD, ROBERT LEROY. *Faction and Conversion in a Plural Society: Religious Alignments in the Hindu Kush*. Pp. iii, 142. Ann Arbor: University of Michigan Press, 1973. $3.00. Paperbound.

CARMICHAEL, JOEL. *Arabs Today*. Pp. 240. New York: Doubleday, 1977. $2.95. Paperbound.

CASSIERS, JUAN. *The Hazards of Peace: A European View of Detente*. Pp. 94. Cambridge, Mass.: Harvard University Press, 1977. $6.95. Paperbound, $3.50.

CENSER, JACK RICHARD. *Prelude to Power: The Parisian Radical Press, 1789–1791*. Pp. xi, 186. Baltimore, Md.: Johns Hopkins University Press, 1976. $12.50.

CHEN, PI-CHAO. *Population and Health Policy in the People's Republic of China*. Occasional Monograph Series, no. 9. Pp. v, 157. Peaks Island, Maine: NEO Press, 1976. $8.00. Paperbound.

CHITNIS, ANAND. *The Scottish Enlightenment*. Pp. 279. Totowa, N.J.: Rowman & Littlefield, 1976. $17.50.

CIPOLLA, CARLO M., ed. *The Emergence of Industrial Societies*, Vol. IV: *The Fontana Economic History of Europe*. Pp. 375. New York: Barnes & Noble, 1977. $16.50.

CLARK, DON. *Loving Someone Gay*. Pp. vii, 192. Millbrae, Calif.: Celestial Arts, 1977. $4.95. Paperbound.

CLECAK, PETER. *Crooked Paths: Reflections on Socialism, Conservatism, and the Welfare State*. Pp. ix, 206. New York: Harper & Row, 1977. $10.95.

CLOWERS, MYLES L. and LORIN LETENDRE. *Understanding American Politics Through Fiction*. 2nd ed. Pp. vii, 251. New York: McGraw-Hill, 1976. $4.95. Paperbound.

CLYNES, MANFRED. *Sentics: The Touch of Emotions*. Pp. 288. New York: Doubleday, 1977. $7.95.

Congressional Quarterly's Guide to Congress. 2nd ed. Pp. vii, 675. Washington, D.C.: Congressional Quarterly, 1976. $49.50.

CONSTANTINO, RENATO. *A History of the Philippines*. Pp. iii, 459. New York: Monthly Review Press, 1976. $21.50.

COOMBS, CHARLES A. *The Arena of International Finance*. Pp. vii, 243. New York: John Wiley & Sons, 1976. $12.95.

CRANE, PHILIP M. *The Sum of Good Government*. Pp. 214. Ottawa, Ill.: Green Hill, 1976. $1.95. Paperbound.

CRUNDEN, ROBERT M., ed. *The Superfluous Men: Conservative Critics of American Culture, 1900–1945*. Pp. viii, 289. Austin: University of Texas Press, 1977. $14.95.

DE FELICE, RENZO. *Fascism: An Informal Introduction to its Theory and Practice*. Pp. 128. New Brunswick, N.J.: Transaction Books, 1976. $5.95.

DE OLIVEIRA-MARQUES, A. H. *History of Portugal*. 2nd ed. Pp. 310. New York: Columbia University Press, 1976. $9.95. Paperbound.

DE VILLIERS, ANDRÉ, ed. *English Speaking South Africa Today*. Pp. iv, 387. New York: Oxford University Press, 1976. $17.50.

DINNERSTEIN, LEONARD and FREDERIC COPLE JAHER, eds. *Uncertain Americans*. Pp. vii, 325. New York: Oxford University Press, 1976. $4.00. Paperbound.

DOLIVE, LINDA L. *Electoral Politics at the Local Level in the German Federal Republic*. Pp. 110. Gainesville: University Presses of Florida, 1976. $4.00. Paperbound.

DOUGHERTY, JAMES E. and DIANE K. PFALTZGRAFF. *Eurocommunism and the Atlantic Alliance*. Pp. 66. Cambridge, Mass.: Institute For Foreign Policy Analysis, 1977. $3.00. Paperbound.

DOUGLAS, JACK et al. *Public Employee Unions: A Study of the Crisis in Public Sector Labor Relations*. Pp. vii, 248. San Francisco, Calif.: ICS, 1976. $12.50. Paperbound, $3.95.

DRILON, J. D., JR. et al. *Southeast Asian Agribusiness*. Pp. i, 326. New York: UNIPUB, 1976. $26.25.

DURAND, JOHN D. *The Labor Force in Economic Development: A Comparison of International Census Data, 1946–1966*. Pp. v, 259. Princeton, N.J.: Princeton University Press, 1976. $15.00.

ECKBO, PAUL L. *The Future of World Oil*. Pp. 160. Cambridge, Mass.: Ballinger, 1976. $15.00.

EGAN, E. W., L. F. WISE and C. B. HINTZ, eds. *Kings, Rulers and Statesmen*. Pp. 512. New York: Sterling, 1976. $20.00.

ELKINS, STANLEY M. *Slavery: A Problem in American Institutional and Intellectual Life*. 3rd ed. Pp. v, 320. Chicago, Ill.:

University of Chicago Press, 1976. $12.50. Paperbound, $3.95.

ELVERMAN, ROBERT. *A Reliable Source.* Pp. 184. Hicksville, N.Y.: Exposition Press, 1977. $7.00.

EVANS, RICHARD J. *The Feminist Movement in Germany, 1894–1933.* Pp. 324. Beverly Hills, Calif.: Sage, 1976. $13.50. Paperbound, $7.50.

FELDSTEIN, MARTIN S. et al. *New Directions in Public Health Care: An Evaluation of Proposals for National Health Insurance.* Pp. v, 277. San Francisco, Calif.: ICS, 1976. $12.50. Paperbound, $3.95.

FLEXNER, STUART BERG. *I Hear America Talking: An Illustrated Treasury of American Words and Phrases.* Pp. viii, 505. New York: Van Nostrand Reinhold, 1976. $18.95.

FLINK, JAMES J. *The Car Culture.* Pp. ix, 260. Cambridge, Mass.: MIT Press, 1975. $4.95. Paperbound.

FLYNN, CHARLES P. *Insult and Society: Patterns of Comparative Interaction.* Pp. 131. Port Washington, N.Y.: Kennikat Press, 1977. $9.95.

FLYNN, JAMES J. *Winning the Presidency.* Pp. ix, 141. Brooklyn, N.Y.: Theo. Gaus Sons, 1976. $5.95.

Foreign Relations of the United States 1949: National Security Affairs, Foreign Economic Policy. Vol. I. Pp. iii, 836. Washington, D.C.: U.S. Government Printing Office, 1976. $11.00.

Foreign Relations of the United States: The United Nations, the Western Hemisphere 1950. Vol. II. Pp. iii, 1088. Washington, D.C.: U.S. Government Printing Office, 1976. $13.00.

Foreign Relations of the United States 1948: The Near East, South Asia, and Africa. Vol. V, Pp. vii, 1730. Washington, D.C.: U.S. Government Printing Office, 1976. No price.

FOX, RICHARD G. *Urban Anthropology: Cities in Their Cultural Settings.* Pp. vii, 176. Englewood Cliffs, N.J.: Prentice-Hall, 1977. No price.

FRANK, LEWIS ALLEN. *Soviet Nuclear Planning: A Point of View on SALT.* Pp. 63. Washington, D.C.: American Enterprise Institute for Public Policy Research, 1977. $3.00. Paperbound.

GARCIA, F. CHRIS and PAUL L. HAIN, eds. *New Mexico Government.* Pp. vii, 280. Albuquerque: University of New Mexico Press, 1977. $6.50. Paperbound.

Gatt Activities in 1975. Pp. 70. New York: UNIPUB, 1976. $5.00. Paperbound.

GEISS, IMANUEL. *German Foreign Policy, 1871–1914.* Pp. vii, 259. Boston, Mass.: Routledge & Kegan Paul, 1976. $4.95. Paperbound.

GENDRON, BERNARD. *Technology and the Human Condition.* Pp. v, 263. New York: St. Martin's Press, 1976. $12.95. Paperbound, $4.95.

GILLESPIE, JOHN V. and DINA A. ZINNES, eds. *Mathematical Systems in International Relations Research.* Pp. v, 430. New York: Praeger, 1977. No price.

GLASER, BARNEY G. *Experts Versus Laymen: A Study of the Patsy and the Subcontractor.* Pp. vii, 172. New Brunswick, N.J.: Transaction Books, 1976. $12.95.

GOLDMAN, RALPH M. *Contemporary Perspectives on Politics.* Pp. v, 454. New Brunswick, N.J.: Transaction Books, 1976. $14.95.

GOODIN, ROBERT E. *The Politics of Rational Man.* Pp. vi, 210. New York: John Wiley & Sons, 1976. $14.95.

GREW, RAYMOND and NICHOLAS H. STENECK, eds. *Society and History: Essays by Sylvia L. Thrupp.* Pp. 363. Ann Arbor: University of Michigan Press, 1977. $18.50.

GRIGORENKO, PETER G. *The Grigorenko Papers.* Pp. 187. Boulder, Colo.: Westview Press, 1976. $12.50.

GUTKIND, PETER C. W. and IMMANUEL WALLERSTEIN, eds. *The Political Economy of Contemporary Africa.* Pp. 320. Beverly Hills, Calif.: Sage, 1976. $17.50. Paperbound, $7.50.

HALL, EDWARD T. *Beyond Culture.* Pp. 320. New York: Anchor Press, 1977. $2.95. Paperbound.

HARMAN, CHRIS. *Bureaucracy and Revolution in Eastern Europe.* Pp. 296. New York: Urizen Books, 1976. $11.50. Paperbound, $4.95.

HARRINGTON, ALAN. *The Immortalist.* Pp. 313. Millbrae, Calif.: Celestial Arts, 1977. $5.95. Paperbound.

HASAN, PARVEZ. *Korea: Problems and Issues in a Rapidly Growing Economy.* A World Bank Country Economic Report. Pp. v, 277. Baltimore, Md.: Johns Hopkins University Press, 1976. $15.00.

HAYEK, F. A. *Law, Legislation and Liberty.* Vol. II: *The Mirage of Social Justice.* Pp. vii, 195. Chicago, Ill.: University of Chicago Press, 1977. $10.00.

HEINTZ, KATHERINE MCMILLAN. *Retirement Communities for Adults Only.* Pp: vii, 239. New Brunswick, N.J.: Rutgers University Press, 1976. $15.00.

HELLMANN, DONALD C., ed. *Southern Asia: The Politics of Poverty and Peace.* Vol. XIII. Pp. v, 297. Lexington, Mass.: Lexington Books, 1976. No price.

HILDEBRAND, GEORGE C. and GARETH PORTER. *Cambodia: Starvation and Revolution.* Pp. 124. New York: Monthly Review Press, 1976. $6.95.

HILL, B. W. *The Growth of Parliamentary Parties, 1689–1742.* Pp. 265. Hamden, Conn.: Archon Books, 1976. No price.

HILL, LARRY B. *The Model Ombudsman: Institutionalizing New Zealand's Democratic Experiment.* Pp. vii, 411. Princeton, N.J.: Princeton University Press, 1977. $18.50.

HOROWITZ, IRVING LOUIS. *Genocide: State Power and Mass Murder.* Pp. 80. New Brunswick, N.J.: Transaction Books, 1976. $5.95.

HOWE, IRVING, ed. *The Basic Writings of Trotsky.* Pp. 427. New York: Schocken Books, 1976. $6.95. Paperbound.

HSUEH, CHUN-TU, ed. *Dimensions of China's Foreign Relations.* Pp. vi, 293. New York: Praeger, 1977. No price.

HUANG, AL CHUNG LIANG and SICHI KO. *Living Tao: Still Visions and Dancing Brushes.* Millbrae, Calif.: Celestial Arts, 1976. No price.

JOHNSTON, DOUGLAS M., ed. *Marine Policy and the Coastal Community.* Pp. 338. New York: St. Martin's Press, 1976. $18.95.

JONES, GRACE. *The Political Structure.* 2nd ed. Pp. vii, 125. New York: Longman, 1976. $4.75. Paperbound.

JONSEN, ALBERT R. and MICHAEL J. GARLAND, eds. *Ethics of Newborn Intensive Care.* Pp. 193. Berkeley: University of California Press, 1976. $4.00. Paperbound.

KAPLAN, MORTON A. *Alienation and Identification.* Pp. v, 206. New York: The Free Press, 1976. $10.95.

KAPLAN, MORTON A. *Justice, Human Nature, and Political Obligation.* Pp. vii, 283. New York: The Free Press, 1976. $12.95.

KING, FRANK P., ed. *Oceania and Beyond: Essays on the Pacific Since 1945.* Pp. xxx, 265. Westport, Conn.: Greenwood Press, 1977. $22.50.

KITCHEN, HELEN, ed. *Africa: From Mystery to Maze.* Pp. v, 412. Lexington, Mass.: Lexington Books, 1976. No price.

KOSS, STEPHEN. *Asquith.* Pp. viii, 310. New York: St. Martin's Press, 1976. $12.95.

KRAMNICK, ISAAC, ed. *William Godwin: Enquiry Concerning Political Justice.* Pp. 825. New York: Penguin Books, 1976. $6.95. Paperbound.

KYLE, JOHN F. *The Balance of Payments in a Monetary Economy.* Pp. ix, 192. Princeton, N.J.: Princeton University Press, 1976. $12.50.

KYNASTON, DAVID. *King Labour: The British Working Class, 1850–1914.* Pp. 184. Totowa, N.J.: Rowman & Littlefield, 1977. $12.00.

LANDY, MARC KARNIS. *The Politics of Environmental Reform: Controlling Kentucky Strip Mining.* Pp. iii, 399. Baltimore, Md.:

Johns Hopkins University Press, 1976. $8.95. Paperbound.

LAQUEUR, WALTER, ed. *Facism: A Reader's Guide. Analyses, Interpretations, Bibliography.* Pp. 488. Berkeley: University of California Press, 1977. $20.00.

Latin America, Spain, and Portugal: An Annotated Bibliography of Paperback Books. Pp. iii, 323. Washington, D.C.: U.S. Government Printing Office, 1976. $3.00. Paperbound.

LEDER, ARNOLD. *Catalysts of Change: Marxist versus Muslim in a Turkish Community.* Pp. viii, 56. Austin: University of Texas Press, 1976. $3.95. Paperbound.

LEE, PATRICK C. and ROBERT SUSSMAN STEWART, eds. *Sex Differences: Cultural and Developmental Dimensions.* Pp. 478. New York: Urizen Books, 1976. $17.50. Paperbound, $5.95.

LEGUM, COLIN. *Africa Contemporary Record: Annual Survey and Documents, 1975–76.* Vol. 8. Pp. x, 1153. New York: Holmes & Meier, 1976. $50.00.

LEONTIEF, WASSILY. *Essays in Economics.* Vol. I. Pp. vii, 252. New York: IASP, 1977. $12.50.

LEVI, WERNER. *Law and Politics in the International Society.* Pp. 192. Beverly Hills, Calif.: Sage, 1976. $11.00. Paperbound, $6.00.

LEVINE, ANDREW. *The Politics of Autonomy: A Kantian Reading of Rousseau's Social Contract.* Pp. vii, 211. Cambridge: University of Massachusetts Press, 1976. No price.

LEVINE, HERBERT M. and DOLORES B. OWEN. *An American Guide to British Social Science Resources.* Pp. v, 281. Metuchen, N.J.: Scarecrow Press, 1976. $11.00.

LIFSHITZ, MIKHAIL. *The Philosophy of Art of Karl Marx.* Pp. 118. New York: Urizen Books, 1973. $5.95. Paperbound, $2.95.

LINDEN, GLENN M. *Politics or Principle: Congressional Voting on the Civil War Amendments and Pro-Negro Measures, 1838–69.* Pp. 106. Seattle: University of Washington Press, 1976. $12.50.

LOWENTHAL, ABRAHAM F., ed. *Armies and Politics in Latin America.* Pp. 356. New York: Holmes & Meier, 1976. $22.00. Paperbound, $9.00.

MACCOBY, MICHAEL. *The Gamesman: The New Corporate Leaders.* Pp. 285. New York: Simon & Schuster, 1977. $8.95.

MACHLUP, FRITZ. *International Payments, Debts, and Gold: Collected Essays.* 2nd ed. Pp. iii, 514. New York City: New York University Press, 1976. $15.00. Paperbound, $7.50.

MALLOY, JAMES M., ed. *Authoritarianism and Corporatism in Latin America.* Pp. ix, 549. Pittsburgh, Pa.: University of Pittsburgh Press, 1977. $19.95. Paperbound, $5.95.

MANNING, D. J. *Liberalism*. Pp. 174. New York: St. Martin's Press, 1976. $10.95. Paperbound, $4.95.

MARTIN, LAURENCE, ed. *The Management of Defence*. Pp. viii, 137. New York: St. Martin's Press, 1976. $15.95.

MAXWELL, JAMES A. and J. RICHARD ARONSON. *Financing State and Local Governments*. 3rd ed. Washington, D.C.: The Brookings Institution, 1977. $10.95. Paperbound, $4.95.

McCONNELL, GRANT. *The Modern Presidency*. 2nd ed. Pp. v, 131. New York: St. Martin's Press, 1976. $7.95.

MEYER, MILTON W. *Japan: A Concise History*. Pp. ix, 265. Totowa, N.J.: Littlefield, Adams, 1976. $4.50. Paperbound.

MICHAEL, KATANKA, ed. *Writers and Rebels*. From the Fabian Biographical Series. Pp. 238. Totowa, N.J.: Rowman & Littlefield, 1976. $15.00.

MORLAN, ROBERT L. *Capitol, Courthouse, and City Hall: Readings in American State and Local Politics and Government*. 5th ed. Pp. 347. Boston, Mass.: Houghton Mifflin, 1977. No price. Paperbound.

MORLEY, JAMES WILLIAM, ed. *Deterrent Diplomacy: Japan, Germany, and the USSR, 1935–1940*. Pp. viii, 63. New York: Columbia University Press, 1976. $17.50.

Moving Towards Change: Some Thoughts on the New International Economic Order. Pp. 137. New York: UNIPUB, 1976. $4.00. Paperbound.

OLMSTEAD, ALAN L. *New York City Mutual Savings Bank, 1819–1861*. Pp. xiii, 236. Chapel Hill: University of North Carolina Press, 1976. $15.95.

ORNAUER, H., A. SICINSKY and J. GALTUNG, eds. *Images of the World in the Year 2,000: A Comparative Ten Nation Study*. Pp. vi, 729. Atlantic Highlands, N.J.: Humanities Press, 1976. $45.00.

O'SULLIVAN, N. K. *Conservatism*. Pp. 173. New York: St. Martin's Press, 1976. $10.95. Paperbound, $4.50.

PACKENHAM, ROBERT A. *Liberal America and the Third World: Political Development Ideas in Foreign Aid and Social Science*. Pp. xi, 395. Princeton, N.J.: Princeton University Press, 1973. $4.95. Paperbound.

PAMMETT, JON H. and MICHAEL S. WHITTINGTON, eds. *Foundations of Political Culture: Political Socialization in Canada*. Pp. ix, 318. Toronto, Ontario: Macmillan, 1976. $15.95. Paperbound, $9.95.

PASTOR, PETER. *Hungary Between Wilson and Lenin*. Pp. v, 191. New York: Columbia University Press, 1976. $13.00.

PEARCE, FRANK. *Crimes of the Powerful: Marxism, Crime and Deviance*. Pp. 172. New York: Urizen Books, 1976. $4.95.

PEASE, MINA, ed. *The Consolidated Index to the I.L. Legislative Series, 1919–1970*. Pp. vii, 264. New York: UNIFO, 1975. $35.00.

PELIKAN, JIRI. *Socialist Opposition in Eastern Europe: The Czechoslovak Example*. Pp. 221. New York: St. Martin's Press, 1976. $12.95.

PHILLIPS, D. C. *Holistic Thought in Social Science*. Pp. 149. Stanford, Calif.: Stanford University Press, 1976. $8.50.

POSNER, RICHARD A. *The Robinson-Patman Act: Federal Regulation of Price Differences*. Pp. 53. Washington, D.C.: American Enterprise Institute for Public Policy Research, 1976. $3.00. Paperbound.

POTTER, DAVID M. *Freedom and Its Limitations in American Life*. Edited by Don E. Fehrenbacher. Pp. vii, 89. Stanford, Calif.: Stanford University Press, 1976. $6.50.

PRANGER, ROBERT J., ed. *Detente and Defense: A Reader*. Pp. 445. Washington, D.C.: American Enterprise Institute for Public Policy Research, 1976. $4.50. Paperbound.

PRITCHETT, C. HERMAN. *The American Constitution*. Pp. xv, 616. New York: McGraw-Hill, 1976. $12.50.

RANDALL, JOHN HERMAN, JR. *The Making of the Modern Mind*. Fiftieth Anniversary Edition. Pp. viii, 696. New York: Columbia University Press, 1976. $20.00. Paperbound, $7.00.

REIN, MARTIN. *Social Science and Public Policy*. Pp. 268. New York: Penguin Books, 1976. $2.95. Paperbound.

REISMAN, W. MICHAEL and BURNS H. WESTON, eds. *Toward World Order and Human Dignity*. Pp. v, 603. New York: The Free Press, 1976. $20.00.

RIDKER, RONALD G., ed. *Population and Development: The Search for Selective Interventions*. Pp. vii, 467. Baltimore, Md.: Johns Hopkins University Press, 1977. $22.50.

RIVERA, ANGEL QUINTERO. *Workers' Struggle in Puerto Rico: A Documentary History*. Pp. 236. New York: Monthly Review Press, 1976. $11.95.

ROGERS, GEORGE C., JR. and DAVID R. CHESNUTT, eds. *The Papers of Henry Laurens*. Vol. V. Columbia: University of South Carolina Press, 1976. $27.50.

ROSENHEIM, MARGARET K., ed. *Pursuing Justice for the Child*. Pp. v, 361. Chicago, Ill.: University of Chicago Press, 1976. $12.95.

RUSSELL, DIANA E. H. and NICOLE VAN DE

VEN, eds. *Crimes Against Women.* Pp. iv, 298. Millbrae, Calif.: Les Femmes, 1977. $5.95. Paperbound.

SACHS, IGNACY. *The Discovery of the Third World.* Pp. 287. Cambridge, Mass.: MIT Press, 1976. No price.

SACKS, PAUL MARTIN. *The Donegal Mafia: An Irish Political Machine.* Pp. vii, 241. New Haven, Conn.: Yale University Press, 1976. $15.00.

SANSOM, ROBERT L. *The New American Dream Machine.* Pp. 264. New York: Anchor Press, 1976. $8.95.

SCHNELL, RUDOLPH LESLIE. *National Activist Student Organizations in American Higher Education, 1905–1944.* Pp. 258. Ann Arbor: University of Michigan Press, 1976. $3.00. Paperbound.

SCHULTZ, HELEN E. *Economic Calculation Under Inflation.* Pp. 340. Indianapolis, Ind.: Liberty Press, 1976. $8.95.

SCOTT, JAMES BROWN, ed. *Index to the Conferences of 1899 and 1907—Proceedings of the Hague Peace Conferences Series.* Pp. 288. New York: UNIFO, 1975. $25.00.

SEALEY, RAPHAEL. *A History of the Greek City States, 700–338 B.C.* Pp. 537. Berkeley: University of California Press, 1977. $15.00. Paperbound, $7.85.

SHERWIN, MARTIN J. *A World Destroyed.* Pp. 327. New York: Random House, 1977. $3.95. Paperbound.

SIK, OTA. *The Third Way.* Pp. 431. White Plains, N.Y.: IASP, 1976. $25.00.

SKARD, SIGMUND. *The United States in Norwegian History.* American Studies, no. 26. Pp. xii, 217. Westport, Conn.: Greenwood Press, 1977. $12.95.

SOLZHENITSYN, ALEKSANDER. *Detente: Prospects for Democracy and Dictatorship.* Pp. 112. New Brunswick, N.J.: Transaction Books, 1976. $5.95.

SPERBER, MICHAEL A. and LISSY F. JARVIK, eds. *Psychiatry and Genetics: Psychosocial, Ethical, and Legal Considerations.* Pp. vi, 204. New York: Basic Books, 1977. $10.95.

SPRIANO, PAOLO. *The Occupation of the Factories: Italy 1920.* Pp. 212. New York: Urizen Books, 1975. $4.95. Paperbound.

STANFORD, W. B. *Ireland and the Classical Tradition.* Pp. iv, 261. Totowa, N.J.: Rowman & Littlefield, 1976. $16.50.

STEINBRUNER, JOHN D. The *Cybernetic Theory of Decision: New Dimensions of Political Analysis.* Pp. xii, 366. Princeton, N.J.: Princeton University Press, 1974. $4.95. Paperbound.

STERNLIEB, GEORGE, ELIZABETH ROISTACHER and JAMES W. HUGHES. *Tax Subsidies and Housing Investment.* Pp. vi, 78.

New Brunswick, N.J.: Rutgers University Press, 1976. No Price.

STOHL, MICHAEL. *War and Domestic Political Violence: The American Capacity for Repression and Reaction.* Pp. 160. Beverly Hills, Calif.: Sage, 1976. $11.00. Paperbound, $6.00.

SUSSKIND, LAWRENCE, ed. *The Land Use Controversy in Massachusetts: Case Studies and Policy Options.* Pp. 148. Cambridge, Mass.: MIT Press, 1975. No price.

SYRETT, HAROLD C., ed. *The Papers of Alexander Hamilton, November 1799–June 1800.* Vol. XXIV. Pp. vi, 708. New York: Columbia University Press, 1976. $20.00.

TANNENBAUM, EDWARD R. *1900: The Generation Before the Great War.* Pp. 480. New York: Doubleday, 1977. $10.00.

THOMAS, JOHN ORAM. *The Giant-Killers: The Danish Resistance, 1940–1945.* Pp. 320. New York: Taplinger, 1976. $10.95.

THURSZ, DANIEL and JOSEPH L. VIGILANTE, eds. *Meeting Human Needs 2: Additional Perspectives from Thirteen Countries.* Pp. 288. Beverly Hills, Calif.: Sage, 1976. $17.50. Paperbound, $7.50.

UDOVITCH, A. L., ed. *The Middle East: Oil, Conflict and Hope.* Pp. v, 557. Lexington, Mass.: Lexington Books, 1976. No price.

The Use of Socio-Economic Indicators in Development Planning. Pp. 282. New York: UNESCO, 1976. $13.20. Paperbound.

VAJDA, MIHALY. *Fascism as a Mass Movement.* Pp. 132. New York: St. Martin's Press, 1976. $10.95.

VON BEYME, KLAUS, ed. *German Political Studies: Theory and Practice in the Two Germanies.* Pp. 234. Beverly Hills, Calif.: Sage, 1976. $17.50.

VREE, DALE. *On Synthesizing Marxism and Christianity.* Pp. vii, 206. New York: John Wiley & Sons, 1976. No price.

WATTENBERG, BEN J., ed. *The Statistical History of the United States: From Colonial Times to the Present.* Pp. v, 1235. New York: Basic Books, 1976. $24.00.

WHETTEN, LAWRENCE L., ed. *The Future of Soviet Military Power.* Pp. 208. New York: Crane, Russak & Co., 1976. $14.50.

WHITE, BURTON L. *The First Three Years of Life.* Pp. xi, 285. Englewood Cliffs, N.J.: Prentice-Hall, 1976. $5.95. Paperbound.

WILLIAMS, GWYN A. *Proletarian Order: Antonio Gramsci, Factory Councils and the Origins of Communism in Italy, 1911– 1921.* Pp. 368. New York: Urizen Books, 1975. $15.00. Paperbound, $5.95.

WILLMUTH, SIDNEY. *Mass Society, Social Organization, and Democracy.* Pp. 104. New York: Philosophical Library, 1976. $9.50.

200 THE ANNALS OF THE AMERICAN ACADEMY

WORKS, JOHN A., JR. *Pilgrims in a Strange Land: Hausa Communities in Chad.* Pp. viii, 280. New York: Columbia University Press, 1976. $15.00.

World Armaments and Disarmament: SIPRI Yearbook 1976. Pp. vii, 493. Cambridge, Mass.: MIT Press, 1976. $25.00.

World List of Social Science Periodicals. 4th ed. Pp. 382. New York: UNIPUB, 1976. $24.00. Paperbound.

World Tables 1976: The World Bank. Pp. v, 552. Baltimore, Md.: Johns Hopkins University Press, 1976. $22.50. Paperbound, $8.95.

WREH, TUAN. *The Love of Liberty: The Rule of President William V. S. Tubman in Liberia.* Pp. 140. New York: Universe Books, 1976. $12.00.

WRONG, DENNIS H. *Skeptical Sociology.* Pp. vi, 322. New York: Columbia University Press, 1976. $18.70.

YARBOROUGH, WILLIAM P. *Trial in Africa: The Failure of U.S. Policy.* Pp. v, 86. Washington, D.C.: The Heritage Foundation, 1976. $3.00. Paperbound.

YOUNG, JOHN PARKE. *An American Alternative: Steps Toward a More Workable Economy.* Pp. vii, 169. Los Angeles, Calif.: Crescent Publications, 1976. $8.95.

INDEX

Action Group, 30, 33, 34, 36
African Liberation Committee (ALC), 59
Afro-Asian People's Solidarity Organization, 97
Agriculture in Africa, 13–25
  large-scale farming, 16–17
  smallholder farming, 17–22
All-African People's Conference (AAPC), 56
Amin, Idi, 68
Angola, 62, 89
Arusha Declaration of 1967, 100–1
Atlanta Center for Disease Control, 6
Atlantic Charter, 55
Attlee, Clement, 55
Azania, see South Africa

Bailey, David, 49
Bálè, 32
Balewa, Abubaker Tafawa, 57
Banda, Hastings, 59
Bandung Conference of 1955, 97, 102
Bantustans, 116
BARNES, SANDRA T., Political Transition in Urban Africa, 26–41
Berger, P. L., 76
BINAISA, GODFREY, The Organization of African Unity and Decolonization: Present and Future Trends, 52–69
Bismarck, Otto von, 53
Black Consciousness, 65
Boserup, Esther, 10
Brazzaville bloc, see Union of African and Malagasy States
Buthelezi, Gathsha, 117
Byrd Amendment, 69, 111

Cairo Regional Centre for Social and Criminological Research, 48
Caldwell, John C., 4, 5, 6–7, 8
Carter, Jimmy, 117
CHALLENGE OF CULTURAL TRANSITION IN SUB-SAHARAN AFRICA, THE, Victor C. Uchendu, 70–9
Chen Yi, 97, 105
Chiao Kuan-hua, 106
Chinese-African interaction, 97–8
Chinese Model in Africa, 98–102
Chou En-lai, 97, 105
Churchill, Winston, 55
Colonial Africa, 53–4
  and restraints on African economies, 83–6
  and smallholder farming policy, 13–15
Committee of Eleven, see African Liberation Committee
Common Market, 82
Conference of Berlin, 53, 54
Conference of Independent African States, 55

CRIME IN DEVELOPING AFRICA, Lamin Sesay, 42–51
Crime trends in Africa, 46–7
Cultural transition in Africa, 71–9

Decolonization in Africa, 53–69, 81–3, 112
Demography of Africa, see Population trends in Africa
DuBois, W. E. B., 54

Economic nationalism in Africa, 89–90
Egypt, see United Arab Republic
Ethiopia, 2, 25

Fallers, Lloyd, 74, 77
FLN, 62, 67
FROM EUROPEAN COLONIES TO THE THIRD WORLD—THE DEVELOPING STATES OF AFRICA, Ruth S. Morgenthau, 80–95

Garvey, Marcus, 54
General Agreement on Tariffs and Trade (GATT), 93, 94–5
Ghana, 22–3, 86
Great Proletarian Cultural Revolution, 98, 103, 106, 107

Human rights in Africa, 111–12

Jen-min Jih-pao, 107

Kennedy, John F., 57
Kenya, 14, 44–5
Kenya Development Plan, 1964–70, 44
Kenya Development Plan, 1970–74, 45
Kenya Tea Development Authority, 19
Kenyatta, Jomo, 55
KRISHNA, K. G. V., Smallholder Agriculture in Africa—Constraints and Potential, 12–25

Lagos, Nigeria, 28, 29, 31
Lagos City council, 31, 34
Lagos State House of Obas and Chiefs, 33
Leopold, King, 53
Lerner, Daniel, 73
Levine, Donald N., 73
Libya, 89
Lomé Convention, 82–3, 92, 93

Marriott, McKim, 74, 75
Mazrui, Ali, 72, 75–6
MORGENTHAU, RUTH S., From European Colonies to the Third World—The Developing States of Africa, 80–95

201

Illusions of Choice
The F-111 and the Problem of Weapons Acquisition Reform
ROBERT F. COULAM
"This study makes an important theoretical contribution to our understanding of how bureaucracies make decisions. It also provides much
illumination about an important historical episode and about the significant policy question of how, if at all, the weapons procurement process
can be improved. It will be indispensable to understanding how national
security policy is made in the United States."—*Morton Halperin*
Illus. ● $21.50

The Economics of Population Growth
JULIAN L. SIMON
Comparison with stationary and very fast rates of population growth
shows moderate population growth to have long-run positive effects on
the standard of living. This is Julian Simon's contention, and he provides
support for its validity in both more- and less-developed countries.
Cloth, $30.00 ● Limited Paperback Edition, $12.50

The Silent Revolution
Changing Values and Political Styles among Western Publics
RONALD INGLEHART
This book contends that beneath the frenzied activism of the 60s and the
seeming quiescence of the 70s, a "silent revolution" has been occurring
that is gradually but fundamentally changing political life throughout the
Western world. "This highly original work will be an important basis for
discussion for years to come."—*G. Bingham Powell, Jr., University of
Rochester* Cloth, $30.00 ● Limited Paperback, $9.95

NOW IN PAPERBACK
KENYA
The Politics of Participation and Control
HENRY BIENEN ● *Written under the auspices of the Center of
International Studies, Princeton University and the Center for
International Affairs, Harvard University* ● Paper, $3.95 ● Cloth, $11.00

**MULTINATIONAL CORPORATIONS AND THE
POLITICS OF DEPENDENCE**
Copper in Chile
THEODORE H. MORAN ● *Written under the auspices of the Center
for International Affairs, Harvard University* ● Paper, $4.95 ● Cloth,
$14.00

ISLAM IN MODERN HISTORY
WILFRED CANTWELL SMITH ● Paper, $3.45 ● Cloth, $14.00

PEASANTS, POLITICS, AND REVOLUTION
**Pressures toward Political and Social Change
in the Third World**
JOEL S. MIGDAL ● Paper, $4.95 ● Cloth, $16.50

COMMUNISM IN ITALY AND FRANCE
Edited by DONALD L.M. BLACKMER and SIDNEY TARROW
Limited Paperback Edition, $9.75 ● Cloth, $25.00

Write for our new Political Science Catalogue.
Princeton University Press
Princeton, New Jersey 08540

Origin and Purpose. The Academy was organized December 14, 1889, to promote the progress of political and social science, especially through publications and meetings. The Academy does not take sides in controverted questions, but seeks to gather and present reliable information to assist the public in forming an intelligent and accurate judgment.

Meetings. The Academy holds an annual meeting in the spring extending over two days.

Publications. THE ANNALS is the bimonthly publication of The Academy. Each issue contains articles on some prominent social or political problem, written at the invitation of the editors. Also, monographs are published from time to time, numbers of which are distributed to pertinent professional organizations. These volumes constitute important reference works on the topics with which they deal, and they are extensively cited by authorities throughout the United States and abroad. The papers presented at the meetings of The Academy are included in THE ANNALS.

Membership. Each member of The Academy receives THE ANNALS and may attend the meetings of The Academy. Annual dues for individuals are $15.00 (for clothbound copies $20.00 per year). A life membership is $500. All payments are to be made in United States dollars.

Libraries and other institutions may receive THE ANNALS paperbound at a cost of $15.00 per year, or clothbound at $20.00 per year. Add $1.50 to above rates for membership outside U.S.A.

Single copies of THE ANNALS may be obtained by nonmembers of The Academy for $4.00 ($5.00 clothbound) and by members for $3.50 ($4.50 clothbound). A discount of 5 percent is allowed on orders for 10 to 24 copies of any one issue, and of 10 percent on orders for 25 or more copies. These discounts apply only when orders are placed directly with The Academy and not through agencies. The price to all bookstores and to all dealers is $4.00 per copy less 20 percent, with no quantity discount. Monographs may be purchased for $4.00, with proportionate discounts. Orders for 5 books or less must be prepaid (add $1.00 for postage and handling). Orders for 6 books or more must be invoiced.

All correspondence concerning The Academy or THE ANNALS should be addressed to the Academy offices, 3937 Chestnut Street. Philadelphia, Pa. 19104.